A FAMILIAR STRANGENESS

STUART BURROWS

A Familiar Strangeness

American Fiction and the Language of Photography, 1839–1945

The University of Georgia Press | Athens and London

Parts of chapter 2 originally appeared as "Stereotyping Henry James" and "The Golden Fruit: Innocence and Imperialism in *The Golden Bowl*" in the *Henry James Review*. Chapter 4 originally appeared, in a different form, as "'You heard her, you ain't blind': Seeing What's Said in *Their Eyes Were Watching God*" in *Novel: A Forum on Fiction* 34, no. 3 (2001): 434–52. Copyright *Novel* Corp. © 2001. Reprinted with permission.

Paperback edition, 2010

Athens, Georgia 30602
www.ugapress.org

Set in Sabon by Bookcomp, Inc.

Printed digitally in the United States of America

The Library of Congress has cataloged the hardcover edition of this book as follows:
Burrows, Stuart, 1967–
A familiar strangeness : American fiction and the language of photography, 1839–1945 / Stuart Burrows.
xii, 287 p. ; 24 cm.
Includes bibliographical references (p. 257–275) and index.
ISBN-13: 978-0-8203-3174-4 (alk. paper)
ISBN-10: 0-8203-3174-0 (alk. paper)
1. American fiction—19th century—History and criticism.
2. Literature and photography—United States.
3. Modernism (Literature)
4. American fiction—20th century—History and criticism.
5. Realism in literature.
6. Visual perception in literature. I. Title.
PS374.P43 B87 2008
810.9—22 2008010958

Paperback ISBN-13: 978-0-8203-3521-6
ISBN-10: 0-8203-3521-5

British Library Cataloging-in-Publication Data available

It'll never be known how this has to be told, in the first person or the second, using the third person plural or continually inventing modes that will serve for nothing. If one might say: I will see the moon rose, or: we hurt me at the back of the eyes, and especially: you the blond woman was the clouds that race before my your his our yours their faces. What the hell.
JULIO CORTÁZAR, "Blow-Up"

Contents

Acknowledgments

THANKS FIRST to the University of Georgia Press for supporting a book about photography that not only doesn't include images but doesn't even refer to any. Nancy Grayson and Jon Davies at the press have been a pleasure to work with from first to last; heartfelt thanks to them, to copy editor Marlene Allen, and to my two anonymous readers.

I first thought of writing about the relationship between photography and literature during Michael Jennings's wonderfully entertaining and eye-opening graduate seminar on the subject. My choice of topic led me naturally to Eduardo Cadava, who taught me that it was possible to think about the relation between literature and the visual arts as first and foremost a metaphorical one. Eduardo's influence is evident throughout this book; indeed, it wouldn't exist without him. The influence of my other advisor, Michael Wood, should also be obvious. No student interested in modern literature leaves Princeton without having been touched by Michael's extraordinary gifts as a reader and teacher; his commitment to analyzing the text on its own terms was the most important lesson I learned in graduate school. I was lucky enough to teach for or be taught by a number of wonderful faculty in the Princeton English Department, including Maria DiBattista, Diana Fuss, Mark Hansen, Jonathan Lamb, Doug Mao, Lee Mitchell, and Susan Wolfson. And Elaine Showalter's extraordinary willingness to share not only her experience and expertise but also her car and even her house enabled me to survive years of genteel poverty.

My graduate training began at Northeastern University, in conversations and classes with Rich Heyman, Marina Leslie, Mary Loeffelholz, and Kurt Rahmlow; Mary was kind enough to invite me back to Northeastern to give an early version of my Hurston chapter as a talk. The transition from Boston to New Jersey was made much easier by the friendship of Sally Bachner and Amada Sandoval. Evenings spent at Firestone Library were salvaged by the company of Elissa Bell, Paul Bou-Habib, Eric Trudel, Tim Watson, and Gillian White. Peter Barberie's impressive knowledge of photography made me realize how little I knew about the medium, while Dan Novak did his best to help me make up the deficit. I never thought I would miss Princeton, but so it has proved; the intellectual companionship and sheer good humor of Gage McWeeny and Barry McCrea are two of the principal reasons why.

I've spent much of the past six years on the West Coast, where my peripatetic existence has been brightened by the friendship of Mat Coleman, Tom Holden, Pria Jaikumar, Lionel Popkin, and Mary Thomas. This book owes much to conversations about Roland Barthes with Kenny Berger and about ekphrasis with Alex Purves. The influence of Mark Seltzer's thinking on this book is obvious; I only wish a fraction of his wit was here too. Thanks to the organizers of the Southern California Americanist Group, Paul Gilmore and Greg Jackson, for allowing me to present a version of my Hawthorne chapter, and to Mark Goble for organizing a panel on Richard Wright for the Modernist Studies Association conference, where I was lucky enough to meet Sara Blair. I've had the pleasure of presenting papers on various aspects of this book with Mark Eaton and Peter Lurie; thanks to both of them for being such good company in and out of session.

I'm particularly grateful to the outstanding staff of the Brown English Department, who have helped make the past seven years such enjoyable ones: Jane Donnelly, Lorraine Mazza, Suzie Nacar, Marilyn Netter, and Ellen Viola. Thanks to my graduate students for their support and input; a few of you are named in the notes, but all of you have made an impact upon me both personally and professionally. A Bronson fellowship gave me the time I needed to complete the book, while the Robert Gayle Noyes Assistant Professorship helped cover research expenses. Deak Nabers and Gavin Jones offered help and expertise with the perils of the publishing world, while John Plotz's intellectual acumen allowed me to rethink what the book was actually trying to accomplish. From the beginning of my time at Brown I've enjoyed the support and friendship of colleagues who've heard more than they ever wanted to hear about photography: Elliott Colla, Tamar Katz, Arlene Keizer, Jacques Khalip, Daniel Kim, Rolland Murray, Zachary Sng, and Esther Whitfield. Jim Egan has been a wonderful colleague and steadfast friend. Phil Gould first put me in contact with Georgia; I owe him for that and for much more. Kevin McLaughlin has been the ideal chair: patient, supportive, diligent, and kind. Life in Boston is made much more pleasant by the friendship and good cheer of Ravit Reichman and Swen Voekel, while Providence is unthinkable without the presence of Thangam Ravindranathan and Tim Bewes, whose intellectual curiosity and sense of humor are rare gifts. The same can certainly be said of Nancy Armstrong and Len Tennenhouse; indeed, I'm pretty sure I wouldn't still be at Brown myself were it not for their extraordinary help, encouragement, and know-how.

Thanks to my mum and stepdad for keeping me connected to home, and to my dad for instilling in me the love of reading. Finally, thank you to Michelle Clayton, who patiently suffers the irony of sharing her life with a man who rarely takes photographs and doesn't like being in them yet who has spent the last eleven years writing a book studying their influence. I once told you, ripping off Henry James, that I see nothing but you; the truth is, however, that I see all kinds of things only because of you: film, art, Latin America. Still, the line bears repeating, this time in the language I've been promising to learn ever since we met, and now finally have the time to: no veo nada sin ti.

A FAMILIAR STRANGENESS

With the daguerreotype everyone will be able to have their portrait taken—formerly it was only the prominent; and at the same time everything is being done to make us all look exactly the same—so that we shall only need one portrait.
KIERKEGAARD, *Journals*

INTRODUCTION

"Likeness Men"
Fiction and Photography

TWO GROUPS of young men—three Americans and three Mexicans—confront each other late one evening in an alley in Mexico City. One of the Americans has insulted one of the Mexicans. The only sober member of the American group, the New York Kid, stares at the aggrieved man:

> The Kid saw this face as if he and it were alone in space—a yellow mask, smiling in eager cruelty, in satisfaction, and, above all, lit with sinister decision. As for the features, they were reminiscent of an unplaced, a forgotten type, which really resembled with precision those of a man who had shaved him three times in Boston in 1888. But the expression burned his mind as sealing-wax burns the palm.[1]

Why, at the moment he believes he is about to die, should the hero of Stephen Crane's 1898 story "The Five White Mice" be reminded by the insulted Mexican "of a man who had shaved him three times" years before? Is the connection between the two men as simple as the fact that one carries a knife and the other wields a razor or that both men have stared intently into the New York Kid's face? Such parallels fail to account for how the features of a face described as a "yellow mask" can resemble "with precision" the face of someone else—someone almost certainly of a different ethnicity (Italian, most likely). The answer to this enigma has to do not just with the reproducibility of racial stereotypes but with what this book identifies as the crisis of identity in the photographic age.[2] Tellingly, despite the fact that the Mexican's features are striking enough to remind Crane's hero of his former barber, neither man's features are described. If we follow the passage closely, we see that the Mexican's features are compared to a "forgotten type," a type that is then said to resemble the barber. Yet, mysteriously, this type remains "unplaced" and forgotten even at the moment the comparison to the barber seems to place and remember it. What is being dramatized here, I believe, is not only the erasure of identity that is the result of seeing the world in terms of national, racial, and social types, but a fundamental revolution in how the modern subject sees the world.

The confusion of identity and temporality produced by the unlikely resemblance between Mexican and Bostonian is reflected in the puzzling inversion of the Kid's impressions. The narrator suggests that the Mexican's "expression burned [the Kid's] mind as sealing-wax burns the palm," an image that recalls Crane's Henry Fleming in *The Red Badge of Courage* taking "a mechanical but firm impression" of the battle around him. As critics have often pointed out, Fleming's impression can be thought of as photographic both because of its mechanical nature and because, like a photographic print, it is developed later—Crane's narrator comments that it was only *after* the battle that "everything was pictured and explained" to the soldier.[3] In "The Five White Mice," conversely, the Mexican's face makes an impression on the New York Kid's mind because it reminds Crane's protagonist of an earlier experience. Logically, then, it would seem more accurate to say that the barber's face, not the Mexican's, makes the impression. This about-face, as it were, is reflected in the fact that the Kid's mind is compared not *to* sealing wax but to skin burned *by* sealing wax, transforming the wax from being the receiver to the producer of impressions.

The reversal of the Kid's impressions, like the improbable resemblance he perceives between the Mexican and the barber, is crucial to the argument of this book. It will not come as news, of course, that Crane, in keeping with his fellow realists, repeatedly speaks of experience as leaving an impression on the mind "like a film."[4] That realist novelists specifically saw consciousness in photographic terms can be proved by any number of examples, most notably William Dean Howells referring to his "mental kodak" in his aptly named travelogue *London Films*, or the hero of Jack London's *Martin Eden* finding "every detail" of the world around him "registering itself on his brain."[5] American realism's persistent comparison of consciousness to the camera is often held up as evidence for what critics have described as this fiction's adoption of the "camera eye," by which they mean an attention to detail and concern with verisimilitude supposedly imitative of photography.[6] Realism's fondness for characterizing consciousness in photographic terms thus becomes the license for critics to characterize composition in exactly the same manner; if Crane's characters see the world photographically, so this logic runs, then Crane himself must.

Yet what allows us to call "The Five White Mice" photographic is neither its attention to detail nor the verisimilitude of the New York Kid's experiences; rather, it is the fact that these experiences—the Kid's sense of the reproducibility of identity and of the reversibility of impressions—are only imaginable in an era dominated by mass-produced photographic images. The New York Kid's consciousness is not so much like a camera, it is a product *of* the camera. What makes Crane's hero's experience photographic, in other words, is not the impression it makes upon him—as we have seen, it is the forgotten barber, paradoxically, who might be said to have impressed himself upon the New York Kid's consciousness—but the fact that photographic reproduction has shaped the Kid's consciousness to the extent that he sees two very different things—Boston barber and Mexican teenager—as the same. This explains why Crane goes on to depict these images as "perfectly stereopticon, flashing in and away from [the Kid's] thought with an inconceivable rapidity, until, after all, they were simply one quick, dismal impression" (768). A stereopticon is a projector with two lenses that can be used to dissolve two separate images into one composite one. The device was highly popular in the late nineteenth century and, as we shall see, does repeated duty in American fiction as a metaphor for modern consciousness. The "perfectly stereopticon" views that pass before the New York Kid's eyes are thus not doubles of one another so much as one composite image produced by two very different yet strangely indistinguishable subjects. And this indistinguishability is what makes Crane's narrative photographic, for it is the direct result of the ceaseless photographic reproduction of modern life.

"The Five White Mice," a story that appeared in the middle of the broad period covered in this study, is in this sense emblematic of what I think of as photographic fiction.[7] For what the ceaseless photographic reproduction of modern life does is render equivalent everything and everyone, producing a world inhabited by people possessing the "uniformity of facial expression" Walter Benjamin describes, paradoxically, as the identifying characteristic of the characters in Edgar Allan Poe's 1840 short story "The Man of the Crowd."[8] This uniformity can be detected on the "yellow mask" of Crane's Mexican youth and on the forgettable face of the Boston barber, who look like each other not because they have features in common, but because—like Herman Melville's white whale—they have no features at all.

"The Five White Mice" is typically read not against the work of Poe and Melville, of course, but against that of other writers from the 1890s such as Theodore Dreiser and Frank Norris. The genre to which these works belong, American naturalism or, more broadly, American realism, is believed to be the product of what Mark Seltzer characterizes as the "imperative of making everything, including interior states, visible, legible, and governable."[9] Seltzer's Foucauldian model is often appealed to by those critics who read American realist fiction as a kind of analogue to photography.[10] This book argues, conversely, that the American novel's engagement with the camera—whether in the form of photographic metaphors, the use of photographic terminology, or ekphrasis—actually points to a *crisis* of vision within American fiction. This crisis has typically been called modernism.[11] Yet modernism's notion of a radical break between the fiction of the late nineteenth century and that of the early twentieth overlooks the essential continuity of American fiction's engagement with the camera. In what follows I contend that realism's "compulsory and compulsive visibility" is actually the sign of a loss of faith in fiction's ability to represent the world—a loss that leads directly to "modernism's skepticism toward the continuity between seeing and knowing."[12] It is not so much that Paul Valéry was wrong to claim, in his speech on the centenary of photography in 1939, that "with the advent of photography . . . realism asserted itself in our literature," but that he was more right than he knew, in the sense that it is only in the age of photography that fiction begins to believe not that it can represent the world as it is, but that how the world *is* is more and more a matter of how it is represented. If this is realism—and I think it is—then it is a realism that should be thought of as in sympathy with modernism rather than as a counterpoint to it.[13]

Photographic fiction contends that the more visible the photographed subject becomes, the less it proves possible to distinguish what this subject looks like. This fiction does indeed depict a world in which, to borrow from Amy Kaplan's definition of American realism, "everyone is either a performer or a spectator, an inspector or a specimen"; it is just that photographic fiction responds to the threat of being overwhelmed by sheer detail by reducing things and people to the status of the typical or the representative—categories that are themselves products of photography.[14] Kaplan argues that realism's preoccupation with the visible represents a response to "the growing sense of unreality at the heart of middle-class life," an unreality partly the result of the spread of mass culture through print, advertising, and photography. The realist novel's "weightiness of descriptive detail often appears," she suggests, "in inverse proportion to a sense of insubstantiality, as though description could pin down the objects of an unfamiliar world to make it real."[15] I argue, conversely, that the detailed descriptions that characterize American realism are motivated less by a sense of the insubstantiality of things than by a sense of their *indistinguishability*. The problem for realism is not that the world is unfamiliar, it is that the world is all too familiar. Another way of accounting for the repeated descriptions of objects to be found in the fiction with which Kaplan is concerned, after all, is simply the difficulty of depicting mass-produced commodities "so similar that they could not be distinguished even by their owners."[16]

Consider, for example, the repeated descriptions of the photograph commemorating McTeague and Trina's wedding in Norris's *McTeague*—a loaded example, of course, yet also a peculiarly appropriate one. Here is the first of three almost identical descriptions of this image: "[The photograph] represented Trina, her veil thrown back, sitting very straight in a rep armchair, her elbows well in at her sides, holding her bouquet of cut flowers directly before her. The dentist stood at her side, one hand on her shoulder, the other thrust into the breast of his 'Prince Albert,' his chin in the air, his eyes to one side, his left foot forward in the attitude of a statue of a Secretary of State."[17] The photograph in *McTeague* is there not to assure the reader of the "reality" of the McTeagues, as Kaplan's reading would have it, but to assure the McTeagues of the reality of their married life. The photograph is not, in other words, an example of what Roland Barthes identifies as the motivation behind the realist novel's descriptions of trivial household objects, descriptions that signify nothing more than "*we are the real*," what he calls the "reality effect."[18] Rather, the image testifies that the wedding ceremony, which the couple experiences as "inadequate . . . disappointing" (95), has actually certified them as man and wife. As Pierre Bourdieu archly observes, "[T]here is no wedding without photographs," by which he means not just that every wedding is photographed, but that without the photographer there can be no wedding, since it is the photograph that confirms that a marriage has taken place.[19] The photograph assures the McTeagues that they were married and that on the day they were married they looked the way people look when they get married: "Trina sitting very erect in a rep armchair, holding her wedding bouquet straight before her, McTeague standing at her side . . . in the attitude of a statue of a Secretary of State."

The repetitiveness with which Norris describes the life of the McTeagues is matched by the repetitiveness of this life itself. This repetition has been brilliantly diagnosed either as a matter of repetition-compulsion (by Jennifer Fleissner in *Women, Compulsion, Modernity*) or as a matter of habit (by Bill Brown in *A Sense of Things*). As I see it, however, the repetitiveness of the life led by the McTeagues is a social rather than an individual affair in that it is a product of the existence of an abstract standard of behavior against which the McTeagues, like the rest of the inhabitants of Polk Street, measure themselves: "They could never be sure of themselves. At an unguarded moment they might be taken for 'toughs,' so they generally erred in the other direction, and were absurdly formal" (54). The McTeagues wish to prove—as much to themselves as to others—that they are *typical*, that they are just like everyone else. Their desire is mimicked by the "admirable" wallpaper covering their rented apartment (owned, appropriately enough, by a photographer), which shows "hundreds and hundreds of tiny Japanese mandarins, all identically alike, helping hundreds of almond-eyed ladies into hundreds of impossible junks, while hundreds of bamboo palms overshadowed the pair, and hundreds of long-legged storks trailed contemptuously away from the scene" (91). The things *in* the photographer's apartment resemble the scene outside the apartment, which the dentist observes every day from his window: "The little life of Polk Street, the life of small traders, drug clerks, grocers, stationers, plumbers, dentists, doctors, spirit-mediums, and the like, ran on monotonously in its accustomed grooves" (113).

Each day is the same, just as each person is the same—conforming to type with monotonous regularity. Norris's insight lies not, however, simply in seeing people as reproducible types, but in seeing that this is how people see themselves. McTeague quickly adapts to married life because in many ways living with Trina is simply a matter of learning a script: "[H]e began to observe the broader, larger interests of life, interests that affected him not as an individual, but as a member of a class, a profession, or a political party. He read the papers, he subscribed to a dental magazine. . . . He commenced to have opinions, convictions" (109). The things that supposedly make McTeague who he is (his convictions) are thus the very things that make him like everyone else.

States of Resemblance

Ever since Alexis de Tocqueville observed that "[i]n democracies . . . all men are alike," commentators have complained that the indistinguishability of the mass-produced commodity extends in America to the people to whom these objects belong.[20] As Charles Dickens's Martin Chuzzlewit says of the Americans he meets on his ill-fated trip through a very de Tocquevillean United States, "[They] did the same things; said the same things; judged all subjects by, and reduced all subjects to, the same standard."[21] In the photographic era this belief takes curiously literal form, in that de Tocqueville's uniformity of behavior is repeatedly depicted by modern fiction as a uniformity of feature. Indeed if the genre I identify as photographic fiction is any guide, not only are all Americans alike, they all *look* alike. The most emphatic of these depictions—albeit one suggested by film rather than photography—is supplied not by a novel but by Theodor Adorno and Max Horkheimer's 1945 essay "The Culture Industry." Readers have tended to ignore the fact that Adorno and Horkheimer see the culture industry's ability to impose a deadening homogeneity on its consumers as extending to bodies as well as to minds. The mass media's "constant reproduction of the same thing," the essay warns, finds its ultimate expression in the reproducible faces of the cinema-going public, so that "the natural faces of Texas girls already resemble those of the established models by which they would be typecast in Hollywood."[22] This "insatiable uniformity" is the result of Hollywood's insistence on "excluding any faces which do not conform" to preexisting models. The audience's desire to transform themselves into a mirror image of the actors they see on screen and in the illustrated magazines thus actually changes their faces, creating a society in which the homogenizing effect of the culture industry's endlessly repetitive narratives is readable on "the synthetically manufactured physiognomies of today."[23]

Adorno and Horkheimer thus intended their essay's rallying cry, "[c]ulture today is infecting everything with sameness," to be taken literally. As we shall see, the culture industry's unlikely conflation of literal and metaphorical provides the template for photographic fiction's depiction of a world infected with sameness, from the blank, affectless faces of the modern American subject to the repetitive, circular form of modern American history. The novels I examine depict American similarity not as a matter of shared features but as a shared absence of feature, since a world in which everyone and everything looks the same is also a world in which no one and nothing looks like anyone or anything at all. These faces—like the masklike countenances of Crane's Mexican youth and Boston barber—transform the metaphor of American homogeneity into literal fact; in turn, the literal fact of these "unrealistic" featureless faces can only be read metaphorically. Such a move is characteristic of the densely figurative writers who are the subject of this study, writers whose work is so challenging precisely because it repeatedly confuses the distinction between the literal and the figurative.

In confusing literal and metaphorical this fiction is ultimately following the logic of Americanness itself, which defines American identity in both metaphorical *and* literal terms. Take, for example, the following account of American identity in an article published in *Putnam's Monthly Magazine* in 1853: "The very foreigners are hardly landed, before they are melted up and turned out of the American mould, very passable specimens of Yankees. The fat Englishman is melted down and reduced into working shape; the light Frenchman acquires substance; the heavy German is lightened up; the wild Irishman is made tractable; the slumbering Spaniard opens his eyes and stirs his stumps."[24] The piece—which bears the somewhat bathetic title, "Are We a Good-Looking People?"—observes that Americans are necessarily "composite" in appearance, since they are "a race made up of every variety of people." Frederick Jackson Turner was to make use of very similar imagery thirty years later in his celebrated speech at the Chicago Exposition of 1893, "The Significance of the Frontier in American History." "In the crucible of the frontier," Turner declared, "immigrants were Americanized, liberated, and fused into a mixed race," producing what he characterized as a "composite nationality."[25] The frontier was thus not only an idea but a bodily process, fusing very different people into recognizably American types.

According to Franz Boas, the peculiarly physical nature of the process of Americanization had a basis in literal fact. His 1911 study *Changes in Bodily Form of Descendants of Immigrants* noted that "after living in the United States, children of immigrants physically more resembled one another (and other native-born immigrants) than their European progenitors." This was the result of the fact, Boas argued, that Americans enjoyed a significantly higher standard of living. Michael Elliott suggests that Boas's findings reassured Americans that mass immigration "would not change the literal face of the nation"—for the simple reason that the United States would change the literal face of its newest citizens.[26] Yet the fear that mass immigration *was* changing the American face was in fact expressed by a number of commentators in the late nineteenth century, most notably Joseph Simms, whose highly popular *Physiognomy Illustrated* warned that the American physiognomy was becoming "less marked," resulting in a situation in which Americans were becoming "nearly as indistinguishable as sheep."[27] What Simms sees as degeneration, however, the author of "Are We a Good-Looking People?" sees as consistency. The essay celebrates Americans for being "very evenly measured," suggesting that they "would range without picking or choosing, in a level platoon, that would delight the eye of a military martinet."[28]

Descriptions such as these lead Seltzer to contend that we should think in terms not so much of "the typical American as . . . the idea of the American *as* the typical—of Americans as typical, general, and reproducible." It is not that the author of "Are We a Good-Looking People?" believes that the typical American is of a certain height; rather, he or she believes that Americans are *all* of a certain height and thus all typical of one another. The reason Americans were so closely associated with the idea of typicality, according to Seltzer, is because American identity was understood from the middle of the nineteenth century on as "an artifact and a product, something mass-produced and reproduced."[29] Thinking of American identity in this way transforms the entire notion of typicality. The force behind this transformation, according to Frederick Douglass, was the "mass-produced and reproduced" photograph.[30] In his 1861 speech "Pictures and Progress," Douglass contends that all of society is beginning to look more and more the same, since the photographed subjects cannot help but model themselves after their own photographic reproduction: "Once fairly in the book and the man may be considered a fixed fact, public property. His position is defined, and his whole *persona* must now conform to, and never contradict the immortal likeness."[31] Douglass's model reverses the hierarchy of original and copy, so that rather than the image copying the subject, the subject now copies the image. And in conforming to his photographic likeness, the American subject conforms in another sense, turning himself into a reproducible copy of every other photographed subject.[32] Typical of every other American in that he perfectly reproduces his photographic image, the U.S. citizen ultimately ends up looking like everyone else.

The Photography Effect

In keeping with Douglass's sense of American identity as endlessly reproducible, American fiction is populated by a series of what we might call marvelous twins, characters whose relationship to one another is better understood according to a model of serial production rather than by the mimetic model of original and copy: Colonel and Judge Pyncheon in Nathaniel Hawthorne's *The House of the Seven Gables*; Pierre and his extended family in Herman Melville's *Pierre*; Nanda and Lady Julia in Henry James's *The Awkward Age*; the two Ralph Pendrels in James's *The Sense of the Past*; Clyde and Gilbert Griffith in Dreiser's *An American Tragedy*; Sutpen and his children in William Faulkner's *Absalom, Absalom!*; Monroe Stahr's two loves, Kathleen and Minna, in F. Scott Fitzgerald's *The Love of the Last Tycoon*. These subjects are neither doubles in the Gothic sense of Poe's prephotographic "William Wilson" nor identical copies; they are instead characters whose disturbingly close resemblance to one another is both highly particular—since it marks them as members of a certain family—and typical—in the sense that it marks them as American. What makes these characters distinctive, in other words, is that they are without a face of their own.

According to Roland Barthes, the theme of the double is most prevalent *before* the invention of the camera, "as if we repressed the profound madness of Photography."[33] My study, however, argues that the disappearance of the theme of the double represents not the repression of photography's "profound madness" but its culmination: it makes little sense imagining modern society as haunted by doubles, after all, in a world in which everyone doubles everyone else. This notion of modern identity as a matter of mass homogenization is memorably outlined in the following self-description uttered by a character in Norris's 1903 novel *The Pit*: "The individual—I, Laura Jadwin—counts for nothing. It is the type to which I belong that's important, the mould, the form, the sort of composite photograph of hundreds of thousands of Laura Jadwins. . . . what I am, the little things that distinguish me from everybody else, those pass away very quickly, are very ephemeral. But the type Laura Jadwin, that always remains."[34] In a move that almost deliberately echoes Turner's account of composite nationality, Norris imagines his heroine viewing herself in terms of the process of composite photography developed by British scientist Francis Galton in the late nineteenth century. Galton's dream was to produce visual proof of the existence of recognizable national, social, and racial types. This entailed overcoming the fact that, as he outlines in his 1883 *Inquiries into Human Faculty and its Development*, "[t]he general expression of a face is a multitude of small details."[35] Galton's solution was to meld together a series of photographs, each one underexposed in inverse proportion to the total number of images in the sample. If a composite were made from twelve people, for example, each image would receive one-twelfth of the required total exposure.

Galton believed that his procedure gave visual form to classes of people—"real generalizations," in his paradoxical formulation. Seltzer, in keeping with a number of recent critics, offers Galton's "standard, and standardizing, schema" as a model for modern photographic identity, in which *every* subject is seen as representative of every other subject.[36] Yet the very notion of a model of identity based on composite photography would seem to go against the defining feature of the medium itself, which, as Barthes puts it in *Camera Lucida*, depicts "the absolute Particular, the sovereign Contingency."[37] Allan Sekula, however, suggests that it was precisely what he calls the "messy contingency" of the photograph—together with the extraordinary proliferation of photographic images in the decades following the invention of the camera—that "transform[ed] the circumstantial and idiosyncratic into the typical and emblematic."[38] This transformation would not have been possible without what Sekula identifies as "the enormous prestige and popularity of a general physiognomic paradigm in the 1840s and 1850s."[39] In insisting that outer appearance corresponds to inner character, physiognomy trained people to see the world in terms of social, national, and racial types. Many early photographers were in fact also physiognomists, and the practice remained linked to portrait photography until the early decades of the twentieth century.[40] Indeed daguerreotypist J. F. Ryder went so far as to claim that photography proved the validity of physiognomy, since, as he saw it, "[t]he camera could read and prove character in a man's face on sight. To his eye a rogue was a rogue; the honest man, when found, was recognized and properly estimated."[41] In turn, many physiognomists borrowed their terminology from photography. In *Physiognomy Illustrated*, for example, Simms argued that

> Each of these feelings and emotions has itself reproduced and photographed in some lineaments of the exterior; and each of these pictures has its distinctive characteristic, as accurately defined and distinct, as its prototype of the interior. In proportion as any particular emotion, or set of emotions, holds sway in the human breast, so in proportion does its photograph, picture or Physiognomical equivalent, become more conspicuous and less evanescent; and it is the promise of the Science of Physiognomy so to formulate this unerring reproduction of the pencil of nature herself, as to enable its student to read the messages from the interior with unfaltering accuracy.[42]

In Simms's physiognomic model the face is to the subject's feelings as the photographic copy is to the original. The conceit transforms identity into a kind of ceaseless and unconscious process of photographic development, in which the subject's every emotion is pictured for all to see. Photography shows us what we already know, so physiognomy has it, since this knowledge is written on people's faces. Photographs of faces are thus, in a sense, tautological, since faces are *already* a kind of photograph.

This book will pay particular attention to the tautological nature of the quasi-literal, quasi-metaphorical relationship between photography and physiognomy. As Alan Trachtenberg observes, the physiognomic "method" possessed a peculiar resonance in America since, in the relative absence of the signs of rank and class that distinguished people in Europe, "[w]hat else is left but the face?"[43] Yet, as we shall see, the faces depicted in American fiction operate not as a means of distinguishing one American from another, but as means of establishing the subject's Americanness *per se*—their shared absence of expression operating as ironic proof of a shared national experience. Laura Jadwin's identification of herself as a reproducible type in *The Pit* is the very thing that marks her as distinctly American, since to be American is to be like everyone else. The indistinguishability of the American subject is reflected in both the masklike faces of American fiction and the blankness of the country itself, repeatedly represented in the American novel as failing to retain any trace of the past. The camera's role in this process of erasure is obviously paradoxical, since photography is itself the principal mode by which modern history is recorded. As American fiction sees it, however, it is precisely the ceaseless photographic reproduction of the past that is responsible for history's effacement. The camera, in deeming history to be that which can be photographed, can be seen as having reproduced the past into a series of reproducible images.

These processes whereby the American subject comes to understand her- or himself in terms of a reproducible type and American history comes to seem repeatable, can be understood in terms of what Jonathan Crary calls the "photography effect." The "new cultural economy of value and exchange" produced by modern capitalism, Crary suggests, "uproots and makes mobile that which is grounded, clears away or obliterates that which impedes circulation, makes exchangeable what is singular."[44] Crary notes that this modernization of vision was in fact well under way by 1820, two decades before the invention of photography. Photographs are thus simply one part of a vast representational rupture in which signs circulate and proliferate severed from a referent: "The very absence of referentiality is the ground on which new instrumental technologies will construct for an observer a new 'real' world. . . . vision is redefined as a capacity for being affected by sensations that have no necessary link to a referent."[45]

Crary's insistence that this representational revolution undoes what he calls the "conceptual similarity" between eye and camera—"[b]eginning in the nineteenth century, the relationship between eye and optical apparatus becomes one of metonymy: both were now continuous instruments on the same place of operation"—overlooks, perhaps deliberately, the fact that such analogies became ever more popular with the invention of photography.[46] But his model provides a compelling account of the move from a mimetic representational economy—in which there are originals and copies—to a simulacral one, in which there are only copies. As Seltzer notes, the simulacra's "*logic of equivalence*" is "the 'classic' logic of the market and of market culture." It is the logic of American democracy, which in promising the same rights to all its subjects produces "a world of undifferentiable subjects, a world in which everyone is 'marvelously twinned.'"[47] And it is the logic of photographic fiction. At least, it almost is. For what interests the writers in this study is not photography's supposed freedom from reference, but the fact that the photograph is wedded insolubly *to* its referent. "If we examine a work of ordinary art, by means of a powerful microscope, all traces of resemblance to nature will disappear," Poe declared in his 1840 essay "The Daguerreotype." "But the closest scrutiny of the photogenic drawing discloses only a more absolute truth, a more perfect identity of aspect with the thing represented."[48] To share a "more perfect identity" with something is not to double or reproduce that thing so much as it is to become it, so that, rather than freeing representation from reference, photography, in Poe's account, is imagined as having made referent and representation indistinguishable.

This, as I see it, is the actual photography effect: the abolition of the gap between copy and original rather than the liberation of the copy from the original. As his historical narrative suggests, Crary's simulacral economy has nothing essentially to do with photography. In what follows I argue that American fiction identified the camera less with the simulacral than with the referential. This is why, despite the fact that American realism has often been understood as depending upon the types, clichés, and taxonomies associated with the physiognomic paradigm, it can actually be seen as disabling it. In his dismissal of physiognomy in *Phenomenology of Mind* Georg Hegel observes that "how the face looks is an act rather than a sign; it is *of* and *for* itself, rather than a representation of something separate from it, such as 'character' or emotion." Here is how Alasdair MacIntyre summarizes Hegel's argument: "[W]e do not treat the facial expression simply as a sign of something else, the outer sign of something inner, any more than we treat the movement of the hand in a human action as the sign of something else, the inner meaning of what is to be done. We treat the expression of the face and the movement of the hand as themselves actions, or parts and aspects of actions."[49] The pseudoscience of physiognomy purports to offer literal proof for a series of crude metaphorical assertions. In actuality, however, the face can no more be separated from the things it supposedly represents than a photograph can be separated from its subject. The face is an action rather than a representation; the photograph is a representation *and* something else, what Barthes describes in *Camera Lucida* as "literally an emanation of the referent."[50]

A Familiar Strangeness

For Douglass the photographic image is revolutionary in that it reverses the relationship between original and copy, so that it is the subject who must copy his or her "immortal likeness"; for Poe the photographic image is revolutionary in that it does away with the relationship between original and copy altogether, presenting the viewer with a "perfect identity of aspect with the thing represented." The two viewpoints are related in that, as Rudolf Arnheim notes, the photograph "furnish[es] the guarantee for [its] similarity by being, so to speak, a creation of the object itself."[51] Arnheim is referring to the photograph's dual semiotic status as both an iconic sign—one that operates through resemblance—and an indexical one—one that operates through causality.[52] In collapsing the difference between icon and index the camera might be said to challenge the very basis for mimetic representation. According to the Platonic model, "an imitation can be deemed to exist only where there is a perceived difference from, as well as similarity to, the object being imitated."[53] In a photographic economy, however, representation is a matter not of imitation, nor even of duplication, but of something else altogether, something that can only be understood according to a reflexive model. As André Bazin observes in "The Ontology of the Photographic Image," photography "shares, by virtue of the process of its becoming, the being of the model of which it is the reproduction; it *is* the model."[54]

Although the difference between the photograph and what it shows seems to go without saying, the fact that the photographic image is seemingly inseparable from its referent makes it difficult to define exactly what that difference is. The photograph's confusion of original and copy leads Stanley Cavell to contend that "[a] photograph does not present us with 'likenesses' of things; it presents us, we want to say, with the things themselves."[55] The consequences for mimesis of photography's confusion of "likeness" and reality are as fundamental as the consequences for typicality of the mass-reproduced modern American subject. For a world increasingly seen as the product of photographic images is a world in which, as Jean Baudrillard puts it in characteristically hyperbolic terms, "[t]he possibility of metaphor is disappearing in every sphere. . . . [since] for there to be metaphor, differential fields and distinct objects must exist."[56] In a world in which nothing can be distinguished from anything else, metaphor—which depends upon there being a difference between two separate things just as mimesis depends upon there being a difference between the thing and its reproduction—becomes increasingly hard to imagine.

This study examines what Jean Baudrillard calls "the possibility of metaphor" in photographic fiction—that is, novels that explicitly engage with the photographic production of American identity. These texts, paradoxically, are fundamentally metaphorical. Yet it is precisely their dense figuration that marks them as photographic, in the sense that their seemingly limitless metaphorical conceits work to erase rather than uphold the very thing that makes metaphor possible—the boundary between the literal and the figurative, the boundary between one thing and another, and, finally, the boundary between the thing and its representation. Studies of the relation between photography and fiction have tended to oscillate between historical accounts of the emergence and popularization of the camera and readings that either compare fiction to photography or focus on fiction's use of photographic imagery. What such studies have overlooked is the question of how photography transforms the way novelists actually think about the possibility of analogy itself. Because the issue of how technology shapes fiction is such a vexed and complex one, critics tend to evade the question of causality by simply offering up novelists' frequent insistence that they have modeled their work on the camera as proof that fiction is comparable *to* the camera. Yet the claim to photographic accuracy is itself, of course, simply a metaphor. With that in mind, I want to suggest that the relation between photography and American fiction is one not *of* likeness but *about* likeness; that the American novel is not like the camera but is concerned with the problem of likeness—both in a physical and in a representational sense.

As I see it, the photographer—known in the nineteenth century as "the likeness man"—is the producer of images that, ironically enough, threaten to put an end to likeness altogether. American fiction is photographic not because the writers I examine take photography as a formal model, in other words, but because their conception of American history and identity is persistently articulated through the discourse of photography. For this reason I examine the work of Hawthorne rather than that of Harriet Beecher Stowe, who famously declared her desire to "daguerreotype" Uncle Tom; James rather than Norris, whose work would eventually, so William Dean Howells believed, possess "something of the impartial fidelity of the photograph"; Faulkner rather than John Dos Passos, who explicitly identified sections of the *U.S.A.* trilogy as written with "the camera eye"; Zora Neale Hurston rather than Eudora Welty, who claimed that "being ready to click the shutter at the crucial moment, was the greatest need I had."[57]

In treating with suspicion novelists' claims that their work is analogous to photography I take what we might think of as a modernist approach to literature. Friedrich A. Kittler associates the onset of modernism with Stephan Mallarmé's declaration that "one does not make poetry with ideas, but with *words*," an aesthetic Kittler understands as signaling that there can "no longer [be] any translation from one medium, literature, to another, such as painting."[58] Yet despite the impossibility of literature approximating the method of painting or photography, paying attention to writers' habit of drawing analogies between the mediums is important for what it tells us about analogy itself. "Media," Kittler has famously declared, "determine our situation."[59] But how exactly do they determine a form that is both part of the media yet also partly a reflection upon it, "the news that stays news," in Ezra Pound's well-known formulation. What makes fiction's treatment of photography such a compelling version of the narrative traced by Kittler is that it brings into focus society's persistent need to understand the fact of media determinism through analogies *with* the media. Seltzer outlines the situation with precision: "The difference between media analogy and media apriori is the difference between media copying, doubling, or 'revealing' our situation, on the one side, and media 'determining' our situation, on the other: the difference between analogy (we are like the machines we make) and cause (we are made by them). This tension between likeness and determination is irreducible."[60] The media thus presents us with a "proliferating series of likenesses [in] which discrete events blur into 'like' events, such that likeness and analogy replace cause."[61]

We see this substitution of likeness for determination in the critical insistence on reading the photographic analogies in realist fiction—the fact that characters are constantly described as seeing the world around them "like a film"—as proof that this fiction is photographic, what we might describe as the slippage from impression to composition. In her recent study *Fiction in the Age of Photography,* Nancy Armstrong exposes this slippage by offering a model of the relationship between fiction and photography based on the moebius strip:

> [F]iction authorized only those images that met the visual expectations of its readership, expectations that fiction itself had delineated. If the process by which fiction and photography authorized each other in the name of realism appears to be a circular one, that is because realism could not have achieved its power to tell the truth in any other way. I find it difficult to imagine how such a thoroughgoing change as the one for which I am arguing could occur . . . [except] in both domains at once and through a process of continuous circulation.[62]

Victorians believed that fiction was realistic because of photography, and that photography was realistic because of fiction. To recast this tautology in terms more appropriate to my own concerns: the proof that photography determined fiction is that fiction is like photography; the proof that fiction is like photography is that photography determined fiction.

Armstrong's circular formula neatly demonstrates what we might call the disappearing origins of photographic fiction; if we look closely enough we find that every fictional movement from 1839 to 1945 has claimed to be modeled on the camera. My purpose in this book is not to debunk these claims so much as to document how the relation between fiction and photography changed the way writers thought about the entire question of likeness in the first place. Hence I engage only briefly with the history and practice of photography and not at all with actual photographic images. My concern throughout is with the ways in which writers and critics have understood the medium of photography rather than with individual examples of it. To map the relation between photographic discourse and the larger media ecology of the period I offer an extended history of photographic fiction—from the middle of the nineteenth century to the middle of the twentieth. I do so in order to place fiction's relation to photography in the context of both the representational form photography largely superseded—painting—and the representational form that in turn largely superseded it—the cinema. The narrative offered in the following pages moves from the nineteenth century's fascination with photographic referentiality to the twentieth century's impatience with the still image. As we shall see, the camera offers writers a measure with which to understand the extent to which the media had transformed the modern world; a rhetorical mode—ekphrasis—with which to depict that world; and, finally, a means of reflecting on the formal issues of analogy, likeness, and resemblance raised by the very question of whether and why fiction might adopt photography as a model.

My opening chapter identifies Hawthorne as the first American novelist to recognize the ways in which the invention of the camera rendered obsolete traditional theories of representation. As we saw in the case of Poe, early responses to the photograph marveled not at its reproducibility—the most popular form of photography in the mid-nineteenth century, the daguerreotype, could not be reproduced—but at the fact that the image could not be distinguished from its subject. In the tautological definition offered by one of the medium's inventors, Nicéphore Niépce, the photograph was "nature herself." The consequences of this profound transformation in the mimetic order—an order that depends on a perceptible difference between original and copy—can clearly be seen in *The House of the Seven Gables*. Here, Hawthorne imagines photography in exactly the terms laid out by Niépce. The result is a novel committed to displaying the redundancy of representation in a world in which copy and original cannot be told apart.

By the late nineteenth century this redundancy would become the defining feature of modern life as the endless circulation of photographic images threatened to render everyone and everything the same. My second chapter argues that James understands this situation in terms of a crisis of resemblance, a crisis in which people, periods, even places cannot be told apart. In a series of works that explicitly engage with photography—"The Real Thing," *The Awkward Age*, *The Sense of the Past*, *The Aspern Papers*, and *The Golden Bowl*—James depicts a society in which the unvarying typological signs of identity used to differentiate people by class, race, and nationality have become exchangeable, reproducible, even imitable.

While the modernist late fiction of Henry James compulsively returns to the question of likeness, the unabashedly modernist fiction of William Faulkner might well be characterized as compulsively pursuing the question of difference. This pursuit takes as its subject the paradoxical consequences of the one-drop rule, which, by defining race as a matter of blood, necessarily disrupted the link between appearance and identity. My third chapter argues that in *Go Down, Moses*, *Light in August*, and *Absalom, Absalom!* Faulkner locates race in a series of illusory yet imaginable spaces drawn from the discourse of photography: the stereoptican, the film still, the composite photograph. These technologies reveal the inadequacy of conceiving of history as a record of visible traces. I make the case that Faulkner ultimately abandons the question of referentiality for the question of resemblance, offering in *Absalom, Absalom!* the blank Sutpen face as the most appropriate figure for the paradoxical invisibility of racial difference.

The relationship between race and the photographic formation of the modern American is further explored in my fourth chapter, on Zora Neale Hurston's *Their Eyes Were Watching God.* Hurston's text is typically seen as being concerned with establishing an authentic African American voice. I argue, however, that the novel is equally interested in exploring the role played by visual resemblance in the propagation of racial identity. Early in the novel Janie discovers that she is black while looking at a photograph of herself and the white children of the family with whom she grows up. Hurston's heroine is at first unable to recognize the only black girl in the photograph as herself, thereby setting the pattern for the novel, which narrates a series of scenes in which Janie is mistaken for someone else. Janie's experience completes the crisis of resemblance I trace in this book, in which the blankness of the reproducible American face represents the redundancy of representation in a world in which image and copy can no longer be told apart (in the case of Hawthorne), the erasure of the distinctions between one person and another (in the case of James), the impossibility of establishing racial difference (in the case of Faulkner) and the structure of the racial stereotype (in the case of Hurston).

Nothing Had Happened

The result of photographic multiplication, I am arguing, is not to differentiate one person from the next but to increase the resemblances between them.[63] There is something inevitable, then, that in Crane's "The Five White Mice" the New York Kid's sense of the unlikely resemblance between a Boston barber and a Mexican teenager ultimately extends even to himself. The Kid's identity turns out to be both reproducible—

alongside him in the alley is "the other Kid—the 'Frisco Kid: there were two Kids" (762)—and stereotypical—he imagines the news of his death provoking hysteria in his mother and sister but failing to disturb "the invincible calm of his hard-mouthed old father" (768). His eventual adversary adheres to his cultural script just as closely: "His sombrero was drawn low over his eyes; his serape was flung on his left shoulder; his back was bent in the supposed manner of a Spanish grandee" (767). The two young men, in a familiar moment of modern reflexivity, see themselves as a certain type and therefore modify their behavior so as to conform still more closely *to* that type.

This sense of following a script extends not merely to the characters of "The Five White Mice" but to the story's form. This is how the Kid anticipates his seemingly inevitable death being reported back home: "The story would be a marvel of brevity when first it reached the far New York home, written in a careful hand on a bit of cheap paper, topped and footed and backed by the printed fortifications of the cable company. But they are often as stones flung into mirrors, these bits of paper upon which are laconically written all the most terrible chronicles of the times" (768). All that will be left of the New York Kid's experience will be a brief telegram, his obituary sandwiched between advertisements for the cable company. The fact that the singular fact of the New York Kid's death will inevitably be announced through mass reproduction leads the narrator to imagine a shattering of mimesis itself. This shattering is ultimately the subject of "The Five White Mice," a story that is itself a staging of a cultural cliché—a Mexican standoff (a term first coined in the 1890s and popularized, it seems reasonable to imagine, by Crane's story itself).

This reflexive structure suggests that Crane's fondness for stereotyped characters and situations is a sign of his commitment to exposing the conventions of realist fiction, conventions that the New York Kid himself seems able to see through: "His hand was also at his hip. He was gripping there a revolver of robust size. He recalled that upon its black handle was stamped a hunting scene in which a sportsman in fine leggings and a peaked cap was taking aim at a stag less than one eighth of an inch away" (767). The foreshortened distance between hunter and prey represents, needless to say, the narrowness of the space separating the Americans from the Mexicans. But there is another, more compelling, reason behind Crane's seemingly perverse decision to focus on the holster's logo at the critical moment of his story. The sportsman aims at a stag less than one eighth of an inch away not, obviously enough, because this represents the range of this particular revolver, but because realism—literary or otherwise—is always a matter of metonymic condensation. "Following the path of contiguous relationships," Roman Jakobsen writes, "the realist author metonymically digresses from the plot to the atmosphere and from the characters to the setting in space and time. He is fond of synecdochic details."[64] Crane arrests this digression precisely by reflecting upon it, so that the images that run through the Kid's mind at the moment he imagines he is to die are precisely the synecdochic details that characterize realist fiction. Synecdoche, which operates through condensation, has replaced metaphor, which operates through comparison.

This equality between the story and its form could be said to mirror the equality between the various characters, and leads to what is perhaps the strangest of the New York Kid's impressions: "And now, here is the unreal real: into this Kid's nostrils, at the expectant moment of slaughter, had come the scent of new-mown hay, a fragrance from a field of prostrate grass, a fragrance which contained the sunshine, the bees, the peace of meadows, and the wonder of a distant crooning stream. It had no right to be supreme, but it was supreme, and he breathed it as he waited for pain and a sight of the unknown" (768). Here, we might say, is Kaplan's unreal real. Yet what makes the moment while he waits for the unknown feel unreal to the New York Kid is precisely the fact that it feels so familiar—the smell of home (or, given that the Kid is from New York City, what *signifies* home—the scent of new-mown hay). And it is this collapse of the familiar—home, a barbershop—onto the unfamiliar—a Mexican alley, a knife-wielding opponent—that marks the Kid's experience that night. For when he finally breaks the standoff by pulling his gun, his adversary cries out like "a man who suddenly sees a poisonous snake. Thus the Kid was able to understand swiftly that they were all human beings. They were unanimous in not wishing for too bloody a combat. There was a sudden expression of the equality" (770). One Mexican turns out to have a face exactly like a Boston barber, another to have a fear exactly like the Kid's; the men are mirror images of one another—stereopticon images, even: "He had been seduced into respectful alarm by the concave attitude of the grandee. And, after all, there had been an equality of emotion—an equality! He was furious. He wanted to take the serape of the grandee and swaddle him in it" (770). The Kid has been fooled: the Mexicans were as frightened as he was, and thus no real threat to him after all.

It is this sense of equality that leads the narrator to end the story with the extraordinary comment "Nothing had happened" (771). The New York Kid's decision to draw his gun convinces the Mexican to retire, and the standoff ends peacefully. Yet although the New York Kid saves the lives of his friends, they see his actions as the result of sobriety rather than courage; the only difference between the 'Frisco Kid and the New York Kid, according to the third member of the group, Benson, is that one had been drinking and the other had not:

> "Kid shober 'cause didn't go with us. Didn't go with us 'cause went to damn circus. Went to damn circus 'cause lose shakin' dice. Lose shakin' dice 'cause—what make lose shakin' dice, Kid?"
>
> The New York Kid eyed the senile youth. "I don't know. The five white mice, maybe."
>
> Benson puzzled so over this reply that he had to be held erect by his friends. Finally the 'Frisco Kid said: "Let's go home."
>
> Nothing had happened. (771)

"The Five White Mice" thus follows the characteristic Crane scenario as outlined by Howard Horwitz, in which a character's belief that she is different from the people around her is the very sign of her unoriginality. As

Horwitz observes: "Crane's characters live certain scripts quite vitally. This is what it means to be a type."[65] Unable to distinguish between the insulted Mexican and the Boston barber who shaved him years before, or even, more radically still, between the Mexican facing him and himself, the New York Kid realizes in the supreme moment of his life that he is just like everyone else. "Nothing had happened" can thus be taken as the watchword for photographic fiction, for in a world governed by photographic reproduction—in which everyone and everything is typical of everyone and everything else—nothing *can* happen—since every experience is as reproducible as a photograph, and nothing is not born a cliché.[66]

The face itself is redundancy.

GILLES DELEUZE AND FELIX GUATTARI, *A Thousand Plateaus*

CHAPTER ONE

Nature Herself

Hawthorne's Self-Representation

WITH LOUIS DAGUERRE'S unveiling of the daguerreotype in January 1839, the dream of nature reproducing herself without the aid of human hand or eye seemed finally on the verge of being realized. Because the subject of the photograph seemed to emerge spontaneously—early operators of the daguerreotype, when the exposure time was up to an hour, would simply set up the camera and walk away—the image was often characterized as a peculiar form of self-portrait. "The picture took itself," declared author Edward Everett Hale; "[t]he artist stands aside and lets you paint yourself," echoed Ralph Waldo Emerson.[1] In the days following Daguerre's announcement the British scientist William Fox-Talbot was to describe his own very different photographic process—which produced reproducible images he called calotypes—in very similar terms: "[The] fixing upon paper of the image formed by a Camera Obscura, or rather, I should say, causing it to fix itself."[2] Even Daguerre himself, despite his legendary gift for self-promotion, proved unable to identify who was responsible for the images he exhibited. "The DAGUERREOTYPE" he announced to the public in September 1839, "is not merely an instrument which serves to draw Nature; on the contrary it is a chemical and physical process which gives her the power to reproduce herself."[3] In Daguerre's eyes, the photograph was both a drawing of nature and a drawing by nature.

The confusion about how the photographic image was produced resulted in an equal confusion about what the photographic image actually was. The following list of definitions compiled by Daguerre's partner Nicéphore Niépce in 1832 demonstrates the difficulties involved:

1. Painting by nature herself
2. Copy by nature herself
3. Portrait by nature herself
4. To show nature herself
5. Real nature
6. True copy of nature[4]

According to Geoffrey Batchen, Niépce—the man credited with producing the first photographic image—could not decide between *physante* (nature herself) and *autophuse* (copy by nature) as an appropriate name for his invention. Niépce's two terms identify a second fault line running through early definitions of the photograph, which treat the new technology as if it were both the real thing *and* its reproduction, a contradiction reflected in the fact that Niépce's tautological formulation—"nature itself"—tended to be reproduced in articles on photography alongside rather than in place of the term "copy."[5] This confusion was not, however, simply a product of the fact that the daguerreotype produced only one image of its subject, since Fox-Talbot's process—which could be used to generate multiple copies—was talked about in exactly the same terms. Fox-Talbot reported that, when looking at a calotype of a piece of lace at the distance of a few feet, viewers responded to the photographer's question of whether the image was a good representation by assuring him "[t]hat they were not so easily deceived, for that was evidently no picture, but the piece of lace itself."[6] The problem contemporary observers of photography faced was that the photograph seemed to belong to its subject in a way completely different from other forms of representation. Photography confused the real thing with its reproduction, rendering the image and its subject consubstantial.

As Susan Williams details in *Confounding Images*, her study of how photography influenced antebellum fiction, Daguerre's invention prompted an extraordinary outpouring of American writing. Periodicals such as *Godey's Lady's Book* published numerous stories in which photographic portraits either become surrogates for their subject or replace that subject altogether. Nathaniel Hawthorne's 1851 *The House of the Seven Gables*, Williams suggests, provided the model for this new genre, since it is a novel in which engravings, paintings, and photographs "seem to reproduce their own copies, both in mental fabrications and in characters who become their doubles."[7] I want to propose, however, that Williams's depiction of Hawthorne's novel depends upon a model of original and copy superseded by the invention of the camera. This chapter argues that the doubling of characters, events, and objects in Hawthorne's text should be read according to a metonymic rather than a mimetic logic. The prominent role Hawthorne affords the daguerreotype is a sign, in other words, not of the triumph of mimesis but of the threat posed to it. *The House of the Seven Gables* is constructed out of a series of reflexive images, rhetorical figures whose paradoxical form cannot be accounted for by the mimetic logic of original and copy. Hawthorne's novel thus depicts antebellum America not as a place where the subject is being replaced by a representational double, but as a place where the subject is entirely constituted by representation. As we shall see, the resulting crisis of resemblance poses a serious challenge to fiction itself.

The engravings, paintings, and photographs that circulate through

The House of the Seven Gables are not mimetic copies of a preexisting subject but metonymic signs that stand in *for* the subject, thereby helping determine how that subject conceives of himself. For there to be a double, there needs to be an original. But the invention of the camera heralds the beginning of a world in which distinguishing between original and copy is no longer possible. According to Roland Barthes, the photograph "is never distinguished from its referent (from what it represents), or at least it is not *immediately* or *generally* distinguished from its referent (as is the case for every other image)." Because "the Photograph always carries its referent with itself . . . [photography] has something tautological about it: a pipe, here, is always and intractably a pipe."[8] This chapter maps Barthes's tautological model onto Hawthorne's *The House of the Seven Gables*, a novel composed of a series of reflexive signs that, rather than copying the world they depict, appear to be an actual part of that world: the Pyncheon house, the Pyncheon map, and, most disturbingly, Judge Jaffrey Pyncheon himself. These "ekphrastic emblems" challenge the distinction between original and copy in ways analogous to early photography.[9] It is hardly surprising, then, that the exemplary form of this circular structure should be a series of photographs. The images taken by Hawthorne's itinerant young daguerreotypist, Holgrave Maule, are simultaneously the most visible signs that the world depicted in *The House of the Seven Gables* is one in which subjectivity has been transformed into a sign for itself and the reason for that transformation. The governing logic of this world—and hence the governing logic of the novel—is redundancy, its watchword "nature herself." For there is something remarkably superfluous about the events depicted in the text, where nothing seems to happen that has not already happened: Pyncheons act like Pyncheons, Maules act like Maules, and even the marriage of Maule and Pyncheon at the end of the novel, though it appears to overturn the past, can be read as conforming to photographic fiction's defining logic: nothing had happened.

The redundancy of the plot of *The House of the Seven Gables* conforms to the model of the realist novel outlined by Leo Bersani, a form in which everything is reduced "to a parade of sameness. For example, it would not be wholly absurd to suggest that a Balzac novel becomes unnecessary as soon as its exposition is over. The entire work is already contained in the presentation of the work, and the characters merely repeat in dialogue and action what has already been established about them in narrative summaries."[10] The superfluity of realism's attempt to duplicate the visible world—what Mark Seltzer calls "the realist tautology"—is laid bare by the commitment to redundancy displayed by *The House of the Seven Gables.*[11] And it is this superfluity—for which no better emblem could be imagined than Holgrave's photographs—which render the text photographic: the presentation of the same thing over and over again.[12] We shall see this same structure in the otherwise very different novel I discuss in my last chapter, Richard Wright's *Native Son*, a text whose depiction of photographic identity produces a similar "parade of sameness." What this unlikely similarity suggests is that photography's influence on fiction disrupts the familiar narrative of American literary history, in which the romantic and sentimental novel gives way to the realist text, which in turn gives way to the modernist text and so on. For the impact photography has on fiction is to turn every text into a realist one—not in the sense of a concern for verisimilitude but in the sense of a formal redundancy. When representation cannot be separated from its subject, after all, representation itself becomes unnecessary in precisely the manner Bersani identifies in Balzac. It seems appropriate, then, that Balzac claimed that his realist technique foreshadowed rather than followed the daguerreotype.[13]

Minute Fidelity

To read *The House of the Seven Gables* as exemplifying Balzacian realism is to go against both Hawthorne's own account of his novel and critical tradition. In his preface Hawthorne famously declares the text to be a Romance in an attempt to free himself from being judged according to what he sees as the Novel's "minute fidelity" to reality.[14] Despite being set in a real house in a real town, despite being based on real people and real events, the novel no more represents the town of Salem, Hawthorne contends, than it represents "the clouds overhead" (3). Hawthorne admits that "[t]he Reader may perhaps choose to assign an actual locality to the imaginary events of this narrative," but he himself, he assures us, has "buil[t] a house, of materials long in use for constructing castles in the air" (3). Indeed, Hawthorne explicitly warns of the danger of comparing fiction too closely with the world in which it is set, since this "exposes the romance to an inflexible and exceedingly dangerous species of criticism, by bringing his [the writer's] fancy-pictures almost into positive contact with the realities of the moment" (3). As Alan Trachtenberg has pointed out, Hawthorne's eschewal of the realist aesthetic typically associated with photography—"minute fidelity"—is itself couched in the language of photography—"fancy-pictures" brought "into positive contact with the realities of the moment."[15] Indeed, despite Hawthorne's insistence that his novel was not realistic, contemporary responses to *The House of the Seven Gables* celebrated what they saw as the text's photographic accuracy. Oliver Wendell Holmes praised the novel for being "true as the daguerreotype," while Henry T. Tuckerman, in a review in the *Southern Literary Messenger*, declared that "[s]o life-like in the minutiae and so picturesque in general effect are these sketches of still-life, that they are daguerreotyped in the reader's mind."[16]

That contemporary critics described Hawthorne's self-proclaimed unrealistic novel in photographic terms should caution us to treat analogies between photography and fiction with suspicion. The definition of photography supplied in *The House of the Seven Gables*, moreover, would appear to align the medium with the Romance rather than with the novel.[17] Holgrave tells the youngest Pyncheon, Phoebe, that although photography is given "credit only for depicting the merest surface, it actually brings out the secret character with a truth that no painter would ever venture upon" (91). The "secret character" to which Holgrave is referring belongs to Phoebe's relative the Judge, whose attempts to mask his hardhearted nature beneath a sunny public disposition are undone by the series of daguerreotypes taken of him as part of his campaign to be elected Governor of Massachusetts, images that uniformly portray him as "hard and stern" (91). Holgrave's definition of photography conforms to the account of the romance offered by Nina Baym: "[T]he romance assumes that behind or beneath the actual world is an unseen world of motive and meaning, which actually controls the shape of the visible."[18] It contrasts, however, with Hawthorne's *own* views on the medium. Writing to his fiancée, Sophia Peabody, in December 1839—just three months after the first daguerreotype was taken in the United States—the novelist expressed his desire for "something in the intellectual world analogous to the Daguerrotype [sic] . . . in the visible—something which should print off our deepest, and subtlest, and delicatest thoughts and feelings, as minutely and accurately as the above-mentioned instrument paints the various aspects of Nature."[19] Ironically enough, Holgrave's daguerreotypes fulfill Hawthorne's desire for a photography of depth rather than of surface, printing off the Judge's "deepest" character in just the manner the novelist longed for and that the camera itself could not provide.

How are we to account for the discrepancy between Holgrave's and Hawthorne's definition of photography? Moreover, why would Hawthorne represent photography as exposing "an unseen world of motive and meaning" when his own view of the medium corresponded to the "minute fidelity" he associated with realism? One answer has been supplied by Walter Benn Michaels. Characterizing photography as "almost universally acclaimed in the 1850s as the perfection of mimesis," Michaels claims that Hawthorne's hostility toward mimesis was motivated by the novelist's contempt for mass production, which Hawthorne thought of as the endless production of the "realistically unreal."[20] Rather than reading the repetitive form of the novel as "realistic," in Bersani's terms, Michaels sees it as conforming to the requirements of the romance: "[T]he point of the romance is neither to renew the past nor to break with it; it is instead to domesticate the social dislocation of the 1840s and 1850s in a literary form that imagines the past and present as utterly continuous, even identical, and in so doing, attempts to repress the possibility of any change at all."[21] One problem with Michaels's powerful reading is that—Hawthorne's own characterization notwithstanding—the camera was "almost universally acclaimed" as mimetic only *after* the publication of *The House of the Seven Gables*. As Jennifer Tucker has recently demonstrated, "the argument that photography gave Nature the power to reproduce herself . . . was [only] eroded" in the 1850s.[22] Moreover, in taking Holgrave's definition of the mystical powers of the daguerreotype at face value, Michaels overlooks the fact that the images of Judge Pyncheon in the novel are only, to borrow a formulation from Paul Gilmore, "apparently revelatory"—since they merely show what is already on display.[23] For the "secret character" revealed by Holgrave's daguerreotypes is visible throughout the text. Unusual for a Hawthorne novel, everything is made apparent from the beginning in *The House of the Seven Gables*—from the secret character of the Judge to Holgrave's identity as a Maule. But photography, ultimately, is *not* the agent of this uncovering, since Holgrave's images neither reveal new information, nor allow us to see their subjects in a new way.

The reason why Holgrave's account of the camera is exactly the opposite of Hawthorne's own is because the daguerreotype helped produce a world in which people's "deepest, and subtlest, and delicatest thoughts and feelings" are no longer buried within them but readable on their faces. As we shall see, the Judge's "secret character" is anything but secret, being continually—one could even say obsessively—exposed by Hawthorne's narrator. The "secrets" supposedly revealed by Holgrave's various portraits of Judge Pyncheon—that his subject is cruel and selfish, that he closely resembles his ancestor, Colonel Pyncheon, and, at the end of the novel, that he has died—are all known by the reader well before the images are taken; indeed at times it seems that disclosing this information is all the novel ever does. In this respect *The House of the Seven Gables* could be said to follow the formula for the nineteenth century novel proposed by D. A. Miller, in which "the secret subject is always an open secret." As Miller explains, "Even when a character's subjectivity may be successfully concealed from other characters, for us, readers of the novel, the secret is always out."[24] This is why the many secrets of *The House of the Seven Gables* seem inadequate when they are finally revealed.[25] For just as the Judge's "secret character" is anything but secret, so the "secret" of the missing document hidden behind the Colonel's painting proves worthless; the "secret spring" that reveals the document is already known by both Clifford (who has forgotten it) and Holgrave (who never used it); and the "awful secret" of the Judge's death is told and retold throughout the last third of the novel. Moreover, Holgrave himself certainly has no need of a daguerreotype to reveal the truth about Judge Pyncheon; as Cathy N. Davidson has pointed out, all he need do is consult Maule family history.[26] Even the ingenuous Phoebe is able to see the Judge for who he is on their first meeting. Instinctively avoiding his proffered kiss, Phoebe notes the fierce frown that involuntarily crosses her uncle's "dark, full-fed physiognomy" (118). "To know Judge Pyncheon," the narrator solemnly assures us, "was to see him at that moment" (128). As we shall see, however, such moments are what make up the novel.

One of the curious aspects of *The House of the Seven Gables* is that the text makes a number of references to the public's faith in the Judge's benevolence while offering few examples of this faith. What we *are* given is town gossip, which repeatedly mocks the Judge for his excessively benign aspect. The narrator tells us that suspicion of the Judge circulates strictly "behind the original's back" (122), though he is more than happy to pass this suspicion on to the reader, repeatedly attributing his extravagant images of the Judge's hypocrisy to stories he has heard around town. Hawthorne justifies his approach by claiming that "[i]t is often instructive to take the woman's, the private and domestic view of a public man" (122), yet he never seems to take any other view.[27] Indeed, in a sense Hawthorne *cannot* take any other view, for the world depicted in *The House of the Seven Gables* is one in which the difference between private and public is rapidly eroding. According to the narrator, "the wild babble of the time, such as was formerly spoken at the fireside" has now become public record, so that gossip now "congeal[s] in [the] newspapers" (17). The breakdown of the distinction between public and private suggests that we need to rethink the implications of the fact that the Judge takes "his idea of himself from what purports to be his image, as reflected in the mirror of public opinion" (232). For since all opinion in the novel—no matter how private—is public from the beginning, *every* character's opinion of himself in *The House of the Seven Gables* is formed by this mirror—from Hepzibah to Clifford to Holgrave himself.

Holgrave's images thus do not expose the secrets *in* the novel because these secrets are wholly on the surface and are public knowledge. They do reveal, however, the secret *of* the novel: its commitment to the pseudoscience of physiognomy. Hawthorne's characters, despite the text's protestations, are what they appear to be, rendering his narrator's frequent judgments *of* these characters as redundant as Holgrave's daguerreotypes. As noted in the introduction to this book, photography and physiognomy were closely linked in the decades following Daguerre's invention, despite the fact that one seemed to deal in depth, the other in surfaces. As Alan Trachtenberg points out, early photographers responded to the fact that physiognomy "treated the exterior surface of persons as signs or expressions of inner truths, of interior reality . . . [by] develop[ing] a rationale which held that the true daguerrean artist looked through surfaces to depths."[28] Holgrave's celebration of photography's ability to capture the "secret character" of its sitters can thus be allied, paradoxically, with physiognomic logic. This reading is as unlikely, perhaps, as claiming *The House of the Seven Gables* as realism rather than romance; indeed it expressly ignores the narrator's own conclusion to his story—that "little faith is due to external appearance" (285). Because the narrator's view dovetails so closely with Holgrave's belief in photography's ability to expose inner character, it can easily be read as summing up the position of the novel. Yet, as I hope to prove, the narrator's judgment runs counter to the logic of the novel itself, which places *all* its faith in external appearance. Even Holgrave's images of the

Judge ultimately depend on the very physiognomic logic they supposedly overturn, since how can Holgrave conclude that the Judge's "hard and stern" appearance in the daguerreotype is a true sign of his character unless he believes that appearance at times does correspond to identity?

Tom, Dick, and Harry

Proof of the Judge's character can be found not just by looking at Holgrave's daguerreotypes but by looking at the oil painting of the Colonel hanging in the House of the Seven Gables. The uncanny resemblance between this image and the Judge prompts Holgrave to tell Phoebe that the Colonel "appears to have perpetuated himself, and still walks the street,—at least, his very image, in mind and body" (185). Holgrave's observation is curious, in a sense, for it seems to be a condition of his faith in photography that this likeness between the Judge and his rapacious ancestor is *only* visible in the Judge's daguerreotypes. If the Judge is the very image of the painted Colonel when walking the streets of Salem, after all, then the daguerreotypes reveal nothing that an observer could not merely see for her- or himself. Indeed, Hawthorne appears to go out of his way to emphasize the correspondences between this painting and Holgrave's photographs. For just as the daguerreotype is the almost arbitrary product of nature—"I misuse Heaven's blessed sunshine by tracing out human features, through its agency" (46), Holgrave rather confusingly explains to Phoebe, his definition recalling the muddled attempts at classification offered by Daguerre and Fox-Talbot—so too has the painting been transformed by centuries of direct light. The light brings out the character of Colonel Pyncheon with "a kind of spiritual relief" (58) and seemingly transforms him into the double of his descendant the Judge.

The fact that both the painting of Colonel Pyncheon and the photograph of Judge Pyncheon expose the men's "secret character" suggests that the daguerreotype's truth-telling ability is less mysterious than Holgrave makes out, since it is simply a matter of exposing this character to the sun. The truth will out, as it were. This suggests that both painting and photograph are not exactly doubles of their subjects in the traditional fictional sense. As I suggested in my introduction, the theme of the double belongs to an earlier, prephotographic, Gothic tradition—to the romance rather than to the novel. This is the world depicted in Hawthorne's last work *The Marble Faun*, a world, as Edgar Dryden puts it, "of pure representations, a world of re-creations, of pictures, sketches, statues, and words that 'phantomize' presence by pointing to the absence of the persons and objects that they signify."[29] In *The House of the Seven Gables*, however, representation can never be completely separated from its subject. For if Holgrave's images are "nature itself," so, in a sense, is the painting, which by the time Holgrave sees it is as much a product of the sun as his daguerreotypes.

Another way of putting this is that in *The House of the Seven Gables* even painting functions photographically. The representational consequences of this move from painting to photography can best be seen by briefly examining a text equally obsessed with the question of family resemblance: Herman Melville's *Pierre*. The novel, published just a year after *The House of the Seven Gables* and also set in a "high-gabled old home," explores the tension between Pierre's condition as the only surnamed Glendinning and the fact that he is his father's and grandfather's namesake, and thus, as Dryden points out, "the copy of a copy."[30] The contradiction between the narrator's celebration of Pierre's "rare and original" character and his insistence that "there never yet was an original man" is reflected in Pierre's oxymoronic status as an American aristocrat.[31] Proud of his ancestry, yet desperate to "live on himself" (261), Pierre is almost torn in two by the contradictory demands of his time. Even his "unequaled renunciation" (172) of his family title in atonement for what he believes was his father's refusal to recognize that he had a daughter is cast as repetition: Pierre's decision to pretend that his newly discovered sister is his wife—to explain their living together—is anticipated by his playful pretence that his mother—who closely resembles him—is his sister.

The seemingly endless repetitions of the novel are a reflection of the reproducible nature of life in a society in which everyone can have their picture taken. Pierre reflects on the "infinite readiness [with which] the most faithful portrait of any one could be taken by the Daguerreotype, whereas in former times a faithful portrait was only within the power of the moneyed, or mental aristocrats of the earth. . . . when every body has his portrait published, true distinction lies in not having yours published at all. For if you are published along with Tom, Dick, and Harry, and wear a coat of their cut, how then are you distinct from Tom, Dick, and Harry?" (254).[32] An aspiring writer, and hence "public property," Pierre is besieged with requests for his portrait, which provokes him to exclaim to his publicist, "To the devil with you and your Daguerreotype!" (254). Pierre's fear of the camera is a fear of losing what distinguishes him from everyone else, since, as Philip Fisher notes, "[e]very face becomes a portrait once the camera exists."[33] Fittingly, then, *Pierre* is "the story of [a] face" (37), a face whose "dark similitude" (42) torments Melville's hero until he matches it to a painting of his father made before he married Pierre's mother. His belief that Isabel—the bearer of the "familiar . . . yet inexplicable" (41) face—is his sister is undermined, however, by her later discovery of a resemblance between herself and the subject of another very different painting, "The Stranger."

Identity in *Pierre* is thus both dependent on likeness and endangered by it. For since Pierre believed that his father must also have been Isabel's father simply because of the likeness between their two faces, nothing prevents him believing that her father might be the man painted in "The Stranger," despite the fact that the painting possesses "an unequivocal aspect of foreignness" (351). Even more disturbingly, Pierre realizes that "there [might be] no original at all to this second portrait; it might have been a pure fancy-piece" (352). Indeed, even if the subject does exist, the painting might lie. After all, there are in existence two "strangely dissimilar" (72) portraits of Pierre's father, their differences partly attributable to the fact that they were painted some years apart but also to "the wide difference of the styles of those respective, semi-reflected, ideal faces, which, even in the presence of the original, a spiritual artist will rather choose to draw from than the fleshy face" (72). And if paintings can lie, then so can faces. For since "never was there a child born solely from one parent" (259), it is impossible to be certain that the "strangely translated, and intermarryingly blended" (112) likeness to his father that Pierre sees in Isabel's face offers any true guide to who she is at all.[34]

Pierre's belief that he can resolve Isabel's compound face into its constituent parts proves mistaken. For not only are people's faces "strangely like, and yet unlike" (124) their ancestors, people show different faces to different people at different times. Likeness proves unable to guarantee identity precisely because everything can be seen to be like everything else, a condition reflected in the fevered metaphorical style of the novel—its unconvincing analogies and excruciating similes. *Pierre* depicts what Wai Chee Dimock identifies as "a world of likeness, a world of kinship and only kinship."[35] This is a world Pierre comes to think of as "deface[d]" (107), a world in which everything is ultimately "blank" (109) since—like the "dumb blankness" of Ishmael's white whale—it is ultimately like all things, and thus never quite itself.[36] This blankness extends, ultimately, to Pierre himself, who unravels in much the same way as the novel itself. Melville's novel is ultimately the story of "he who was once Pierre Glendinning" (185), a man unable even to sign his name since he cannot produce the same signature from moment to moment, a man whose reflection ends up becoming "unfamiliar" (62) to him. Pierre, we might say, is Tom, Dick, and Harry rolled into one, since he winds up endlessly different from himself—and thus just like everyone else. Melville's hero does not need to have his photograph taken to become a photographic subject since in the age of the camera everyone already is a photographic subject regardless of whether or not they have been actually photographed.

The Democracy of Art

Despite Pierre's contempt for the camera the crisis of resemblance detailed in *Pierre* is in many ways a photographic one. Yet it is crucial, ultimately, that this crisis takes place through painting. The lack of a causal relationship between the painted portrait and its subject robs Pierre of his faith in likeness, since the resemblance Isabel believes she sees between herself and "The Stranger" might be nothing more than a creation of the artist. Photography's mass production of images, on the other hand, produces a distinctly different representational vertigo, memorably articulated by the much-photographed Walt Whitman near the end of his life: "I meet new Walt Whitmans every day. There are a dozen of me afloat. I don't know which Walt Whitman I am."[37] Whitman's bafflement in the face of his own image fulfills Oliver Wendell Holmes's 1863 prediction that the camera would transform how people looked by "show[ing] every aspect of life in the same individual, from the earliest week to the last year of senility. . . . Each new picture gives us a new aspect of our friend; we find he had not one face, but many."[38] The characters in *The House of the Seven Gables*, by contrast, always know who they are, since their photographs are always the same. This difference is partly, of course, the result of improvements in photographic technique, the masklike faces of the early daguerreotypes giving way to the detailed portraits of the later nineteenth century. In another sense, however, the endless photographic difference remarked upon by Whitman and Holmes and the endless photographic similitude outlined by Hawthorne are two sides of the same coin, since they have to do with the essential publicness of photographic identity.

As we have seen, what dumbfounded nineteenth century observers about the passage from painting to photography—and denied the latter the status of art—was the camera's seeming elimination of the artist. The artist's absence completely transforms the question of the resemblance between the subject and his representation that so bedevils Pierre. Rudolf Arnheim provides the best guide to this transformation: "[The photograph] furnish[es] the guarantee for [its] similarity by being, so to speak, a creation of the object itself."[39] A photograph might or might not look like its subject, yet even allowing for photographic manipulation there is no denying that this is what the subject looked like at the moment that the picture was taken. As E. J. Marey was to put it later in the nineteenth century, photographic images are in the "language of the phenomena themselves."[40] How can "nature herself" not look like herself? Yet it is the very fact that photographs allowed their subjects to speak in their own language—what critics identified as the photographic subject's ability to "represent themselves" before the camera—that made photography such a public medium.[41] In 1839, months before the first daguerreotypes would be displayed in America, the essayist N. P. Willis triumphantly declared that in the age of photography "[a]ll nature shall paint herself—fields, rivers, trees, houses, plains, mountains, cities shall all paint themselves at a bidding, and at a few moments' notice. Towns will no longer have any representative but themselves." What is striking about Willis's formulation is its reformulation of parliamentary politics: the camera will allow things to speak for themselves and thereby eliminate the need for others to speak for them, a development he called "the democracy of art."[42] Democracy is thus not a matter of everyone being represented but of everyone representing themselves.

A world in which everyone represents him- or herself is, needless to say, an incessantly public world, a world in which everything is made visible. Cheap, convenient, and portable, the photographic image allowed the ordinary person access to his or her own image: the *Daily Tribune* in 1853 estimated that three million daguerreotypes were annually produced in America. The immediacy and easy availability of the photographic image almost completely wiped out portrait painting, transforming the family portrait from a sign of distinction to a sign that its subject was like everyone else. As Britain's *Photographic News* declared in 1861: "Photographic portraiture is the best feature of the fine arts for the million that the ingenuity of man has yet devised. It has in this sense swept away many of the illiberal distinctions of rank and wealth, so that the poor man who possesses but a few shillings can command as perfect a lifelike portrait of his wife or child as Sir Thomas Lawrence painted for the most distinguished sovereign of Europe."[43] Many Americans believed that the Constitution had already "swept away" those "illiberal distinctions of rank and wealth," and hence they viewed photography not as a technology for achieving equality but as a technology for representing it. The belief in photography's essential Americanness was buttressed by the fact that—as we have seen—the image was thought to allow its subject to "represent" himself. Hence Emerson's sense that in the photographer's studio "[t]he artist stands aside and lets you paint yourself" prompted him to declare the daguerreotype "the true Republican style of painting."[44] No wonder, then, that the photographer Holgrave should be a self-declared republican.

Democracy and the photograph seemed like a natural fit partly because both held out the dream of fair and just representation. The photograph could, according to the photographer Marcus Root, allow the sitter to "represent himself" by acting, paradoxically, as its subject's own personal "representative"; in other words, the photographic image could serve as a better representative of its subject than the subject could of him- or herself precisely by allowing the subject to be seen as he or she truly was—even when he or she was not present.[45] There is something rather curious, however, about attributing to the camera the power to transform the subject into a representative of him- or herself. Unlike painting, which attempts to sum up a life, photography offers a view of its subject merely as he or she was at the moment of stepping in front of the camera.[46] Hence photography manuals, in the manner of Root's *The Camera and the Pencil*, recommended ways in which photography might match painting's supposed universality, advising that the photographer "pose his professional subjects in mental guises and physical poses reflective of their calling whether they be politicians, orators or actors. The subject will then project a truthful expression of his personality."[47] As Trachtenberg puts it, the photographic subject in the mid-nineteenth century had to "perform themselves," to don "a role and a mask [in] accord with one's self-image."[48]

Photography was quickly recognized as a potential aid to physiognomists, since the camera gave people the chance to study their own faces for the first time and to stare at others. "Daguerreotypes, properly regarded, are the indices of human character," claimed *Littell's Living*

Age, a sentiment that was widely shared.[49] Photographers insisted that their portraits would prove an infallible guide to modern society, for if character was readily discernible in the face then reproducing the faces of the republic would serve as an invaluable index to American society. Root believed, for instance, that the camera performed a vital social role in showing "[t]he pure, the high, the noble traits beaming from the faces and forms" of the upper classes; as he put it, "[W]ho shall measure the greatness of their effect on the impressionable minds of those who catch sight of them at every turn?" And if exhibiting the faces of the great and the good was sure to inspire virtue, exhibiting the faces of those lower down the moral scale was sure to protect against vice. The camera provided "valuable security for social order," Root suggested, by ensuring "that men shall ultimately be known for what they really are."[50]

Root's trust in photography's X-ray vision was of a piece with his faith in physiognomy. "The face is to a man what the dial is to a clock, or a table of contents to a book, viz., the index of the soul," he declared. "Measurably every one talks by means of his own countenance . . . the language of the face is immutable and universal."[51] Root's commitment to physiognomy inevitably results in tautology: photographic images of the good necessarily display the marks of virtue; images of the vicious necessarily display the marks of vice. Carol Armstrong has pointed out that physiognomy offers one of the clearest examples of the circular logic of positivism, in which "x is an instance of X, therefore X can be extrapolated from x, and x is evidence of X."[52] This tautological method has clear affinities, she suggests, with mid-nineteenth century thinking about photography. For since the photograph is "a document drawn up by the pencil of Nature, the photograph is a guarantee of its own verity; hence, its evidentiary status is ontological, in the nature of its being an image. Everything, in short, rests on its tautological naturalness."[53] Physiognomy promises that, to the skilled observer, people are as they appear; photography promises that, in front of the camera, people appear as they are.

The anxiety physiognomy needed to allay, of course, was that—as

Holgrave's images of Judge Pyncheon make clear—the purportedly virtuous subject did *not* always look so in the daguerreotype. The situation is complicated in *The House of the Seven Gables* still further by the fact that Holgrave's "hard and stern" portraits of the Judge can be seen not only as a reflection of the Judge's "hard and stern" character but of the technological limitations of early daguerreotypes. Due to long exposure times, daguerreotype images of the 1840s—the era in which Hawthorne's novel is set—tended to erase the sitter's face of all expression; to produce, that is, hard and stern images. As Root sadly notes, daguerreotypes often displayed "flat, meaningless maps of the face."[54] The daguerreotype's failure to accurately reproduce the countenance of its subject led Emerson to issue this complaint, two years after expressing his delight at the self-reproducing power of photography:

> Were you ever daguerreotyped, O immortal man? And in your zeal not to blur the image . . . did you feel every muscle becoming every moment more rigid; the brows contracted into a Tartarian frown, and the eyes fixed as they are fixed in a fit, in madness, or in death? And when at last you are relieved of your dismal duties, did you find the curtain drawn perfectly, and the coat perfectly, and the hands true, clenched for combat, and the shape of the face and the head?—but, unhappily, the total expression escaped from the face and you held the portrait of a mask instead of a man?[55]

Trusting to the photograph to accurately depict what we look like, Emerson argues, is as foolish as expecting to prevent a river from flowing by plunging your hands into the water. Instead of the image representing the subject as he or she truly is, the daguerreotype offers "the portrait of a mask instead of a man."

In order to avoid reproducing masks instead of men, Root advised the photographer to begin the sitting by putting his subject "into a *mood*, which shall make his face *diaphanous* with the expression of his highest and best, i.e. his *genuine*, *essential self*." In so doing, Root promised, the photographer would "be able to pierce through the ofttimes thick mask of the material *outward* and discern the inner, spiritual self."[56]

The sheer proliferation of the meanings of the term "mask" in Root's work points, once again, to the redundancy of the physiognomic model: either the supposedly virtuous subject looks virtuous, or, if he does not, his virtue is covered by a mask attributable either to the failings of the photographer or to the demands of public life.[57] The tautology of Root's thinking mirrors the redundancy lurking behind Holgrave's conviction that photography exposes the "secret character" of its subjects. For if the daguerreotype inevitably turns the man into a mask, and public life inevitably demands that the man wear a mask, then Holgrave's images display the Judge as he truly is not by showing the man behind the mask, but by showing the mask to be the man.

This One Old House Was Everywhere

Attempting to work out who people are in *Pierre* is a matter of discovering who they look like; who they look like is established not by comparing them to living people but to painted portraits. The fact that paintings are handmade is thus crucial to Melville's novel, since the problem of resemblance centers on the relationship between the artist and what he makes. Attempting to work out who people are in *The House of the Seven Gables* is a matter of telling who people are from *what* they look like (since who they look like turns out to be obvious to everyone); what they look like is established by comparing them to their own photographed image. The fact that photographs are seemingly made by their own subjects is thus crucial to Hawthorne's novel, since the problem of resemblance centers on the relationship between the subject and his representation—which might be said to make him. Resemblance in *The House of the Seven Gables*, as opposed to *Pierre*, is thus a public matter, since the democratization of representation has allowed all things and people to "represent" themselves—a seemingly necessary task in the photographic age. For whereas a character in Melville's novel compares herself to "The Stranger," in Hawthorne's novel characters must present themselves *to* strangers.

What does a world in which things "represent" themselves look like?

One answer is provided by Fox-Talbot's description of the calotype for the Royal Academy in 1839. Giving his paper the grand title "Some Account of the Art of Photogenic Drawing, or, the Process by which Natural Objects May Be Made to Delineate Themselves without the Aid of the Artist's Pencil," Fox-Talbot declared that his much-photographed house, Lacock Abbey, was "the first [building] that was ever yet known *to have drawn its own picture*."[58] To that end the photographer labeled his images with captions such as "Lacock Abbey Self-Represented in the Camera Obscura." Carol Armstrong reads Fox-Talbot's depiction of his self-generating images as "a kind of heraldic emblem for the 'self-representation' of photography"; intended as examples of what the medium can do, Fox-Talbot's images refer as much to themselves as they do to the actual subjects pictured.[59] Yet Fox-Talbot's descriptions are the product not simply of his need to advertise his new technology but of his sense of the distinctive self-producing nature of the photograph. Despite the differences between his invention and the daguerreotype, Fox-Talbot celebrates his invention in the very same terms as Daguerre celebrated the daguerreotype: as an image that produced itself.

Fox-Talbot's images of his own house can be read as a model for *The House of the Seven Gables*, a novel that contains and is named after a house that not only functions as a kind of sign manual but that also can seemingly reproduce itself. The house dominates the novel from the opening sentence. Only one chapter, "The Flight of Two Owls," is not actually set within the house and its garden, and even this chapter's account of the train that speeds Hepzibah and Clifford Pyncheon away from Salem might as well be an account of traveling up and down Pyncheon St. since all Hepzibah sees out of the train window is a vision of her family home. Hawthorne's narrator sardonically observes that Hepzibah's mental fixation on the House of the Seven Gables makes it seem as if "[t]his one old house was everywhere! It transported its great, lumbering bulk, with more than railroad speed, and set itself phlegmatically down on whatever spot she glanced at" (258). The house's ability to propagate itself within the text is only matched by its ability to reproduce itself outside the text—as a figure for the novel itself. "The chief, perhaps, of the dramatis personae, is the house itself," Hawthorne's editor E. A. Duyckinck observed in a review in *The Literary World*, a reaction anticipated by Hawthorne himself, who told his publisher James T. Fields in January 1851 that "[m]y House of the Seven Gables is, so to speak, finished; only I am hammering away a little on the roof, and doing a few odd jobs that were incomplete."[60]

The reflexivity of Hawthorne's representation of the act of writing *The House of the Seven Gables* is nicely captured by Herman Melville's praise for the novel in a letter to his friend in 1851:

> With great enjoyment we spent almost an hour in each separate gable. This book is like a fine old chamber, abundantly, but still judiciously, furnished with precisely that sort of furniture best fitted to furnish it. There are rich hangings, wherein are braided scenes from tragedies! There is old china with rare devices, set out on the carved buffet; there are long and indolent lounges to throw yourself upon; there is an admirable sideboard, plentifully stored with good viands; there is a smell as of old wine in the pantry; and finally, in one corner, there is a dark little black-letter volume in golden clasps, entitled "Hawthorne: A Problem."[61]

Melville's extended simile imagines *The House of the Seven Gables* as a book contained within a house that is itself a figure for a book about a house. His rendering of the reading of the novel as a tour through the house, moreover, reproduces what was an actual physical possibility. Henry James visited Salem in 1904 precisely in order to see the seventeenth century house that had inspired Hawthorne's novel, only to turn away in disappointment when he realized that "the shapeless object by the waterside wouldn't do at all, not the least little bit."[62] Considering his propensity for thinking of his work in terms of a house, Hawthorne might well have approved of sightseers tramping over the actual House of the Seven Gables. In an 1850 letter to Fields, for example, Hawthorne describes "The Custom House" as merely "an entrance-hall to the magnificent edifice" that was *The Scarlet Letter*, while his preface to "Mosses from an Old Manse" asks the reader to imagine himself as a guest, who, having completed a tour of the Old Manse, "has finally been ushered into my study. There, after seating him in an antique elbow-chair, an heirloom of the house, I take forth a roll of manuscript and entreat his attention to the following tales."[63] Melville's extraordinary image of *The House of the Seven Gables* as a house that contains itself thus reproduces Hawthorne's own metaphors for his work. The various houses that provide both the titles and the subjects for three of his books—the Old Manse, the Custom House, the House of the Seven Gables—are also signs for these works, works of which Hawthorne speaks as if they were actual houses. To compound things, the houses actually are real places; indeed, in the cases of the Custom House and the Old Manse, they are the very places where the books that describe them were either conceived or written.

The House of the Seven Gables is thus both a text that speaks about a house and a text that is spoken of as a house.[64] Furthermore, the house in *The House of the Seven Gables* operates as a figure both for the text in which it appears and for the characters who live within it. Not only is the house an "emblem of mind" (193), the Pyncheons' minds are emblems of the house—Hepzibah's, we are told, is "impregnated with the dry rot of its timbers" (59). The narrator's confession that the mansion "has always affected me like a human countenance" is thus in keeping with the circular relation between humans and houses detailed in the novel.[65] The novel repeatedly insists that the Pyncheon house is a metonym for the Pyncheon family, its exterior seeming to express "the long lapse of mortal life . . . that [has] passed within" (5). Appropriately, then, Hawthorne's account of this history is itself figured as a house: "With a brief sketch, therefore, of the circumstances amid which the foundations of the house was laid, and a rapid glimpse at its quaint exterior, as it grew black in the prevalent east-wind—pointing, too, here and there, at some spot of more verdant mossiness on its roof and walls—we shall commence the real action of our tale" (6). The text here explicitly compares itself to the house, which is both a synecdoche for the circular structure of Pyncheon history and the determining fact *of* that history. Hawthorne's narrative is like the house that is its subject because it is a synecdochic figure for Pyncheon history. Offering the reader a "brief sketch" of this history rather than a complete account—despite the fact that the latter would possess "a certain remarkable unity" (5)—is equivalent, according to the narrator's logic, to reading this history from the Pyncheon house.

Hawthorne's account of his compositional method pits fiction—which works through abridgment—against history—which works through enumeration. Following the dictates of fiction's metonymic method rather than history's mimetic one, the first chapter of *The House of the Seven Gables* recounts those events that the narrator considers representative of the family chronicle he is about to unfold: a Pyncheon drowning in his own blood, the opening of the Pyncheon cent-shop, the return of Colonel Pyncheon. These particular events are chosen, it seems, because they have all occurred more than once. Yet, paradoxically, because Pyncheon history is almost entirely composed of a series of repeated incidents, *every* moment in this history can be seen as representative of all other moments, for every moment shares the same structure of repetition.[66]

The repetitive, reflexive form of *The House of the Seven Gables* identifies the novel as a photographic text—a realist novel by Bersani's definition, and a significant break from the painterly aesthetic governing *Pierre*, in which representation breaks down altogether. Hawthorne's novel depicts a highly public, mediated world in which everyone must constantly represent a visible idea of themselves. The contours of this world have been sketched by Sharon Cameron, who characterizes Hawthorne's representational practice in terms of the metonymic depiction of houses as people and people as houses, a strategy of reduction that finds its ultimate form in Hawthorne's tendency to depict "the self . . . distilled to a representative bodily organ." This reduction is an inevitable consequence of Hawthorne's attraction to allegory, a genre that is especially likely to address itself to bodily innards such as a character's "heart" and "mind." Identity in Hawthorne thus follows a synecdochic logic, in which parts are treated as wholes, and "characters aspire to be 'representative men.'"[67] Cameron offers the example of the protagonist of Hawthorne's 1838 story "Peter Goldthwaite's Treasure," whose decision to tear down his own house in search of buried gold is described by Hawthorne's narrator as "parallel to the feat of the man who jumped down his own throat" (539). "This image of self-containment—of a body absorbing itself to depict a body's absorption in itself, its delusion that it could contain itself—is both tautological and characteristic," Cameron suggests, of the fact that "in Hawthorne's allegories, what (part of) the human body stands for is the human body."[68] Curiously, Hawthorne renders synecdoche redundant by positing an exact equivalence between the rhetorical figure and the thing for which it stands.

Like the Pyncheons (and like Pierre), the eponymous hero of "Peter Goldthwaite's Treasure" lives in a "rusty, moss-grown, many-peaked" (523) house, a house he is convinced harbors buried treasure. He proceeds to tear his house down to "nothing but a shell,—the apparition of a house,—as unreal as the painted edifices of a theatre" (537) until he finally happens across the treasure, "an incalculable sum, enough to purchase the whole town, and build every street anew" (540). Unfortunately, Peter's fortune proves illusory, consisting of outdated currency obtained by the elder Peter Goldthwaite who had been forced to mortgage the house. Hawthorne's protagonist is saved from ruin, however, by the property developer John Brown—a benign forerunner to Judge Pyncheon. Brown tells Peter to forego his project of building a new house on the foundations of the old one, telling him to be content with "building castles in the air, where house-lots are cheaper" (522). Hawthorne would reproduce this phrase in his description of *The House of the Seven Gables*, a novel he constructs on the site, so to speak, of "Peter Goldthwaite's Treasure." For just as Judge Pyncheon is an exact reproduction of his ancestor Colonel Pyncheon, Peter Goldthwaite is represented as an exact reproduction of *his* ancestor, who bears the same name. Catching sight of himself in a mirror, Hawthorne's protagonist "partly imagined that the former Peter Goldthwaite had come back, either to assist or impede his search for the hidden wealth. And at that moment a strange notion glimmered through his brain, that he was the identical Peter who had concealed the gold, and ought to know whereabout it lay" (528–29). This "phantom . . . of the mind" (532)—which seems as much presentiment as it does recollection—haunts Peter throughout his search for the treasure and leads him to believe that it is a question not of finding but of remembering where the money is hidden. And although this belief is mistaken, Peter's uncanny sense that he is merely repeating the mistakes of the past is not. His methodical destruction of his home in order to find the money to build himself a new home is equivalent to his ancestor's mortgaging of the house for a pile of worthless bills. There seems no way out of this structure of equivalence, the circularity of Peter Goldthwaite's actions exemplifying the convoluted structure of history itself, in which the past is revived by the very attempt to banish it.

Like Peter Goldthwaite, the Pyncheons are convinced that their many-gabled house contains hidden treasure. What lies buried in the Pyncheon mansion is not cash, however, but a corpse. Hawthorne spends an entire chapter exulting over the dead body of Judge Pyncheon, who dies suddenly near the end of the novel while waiting in the House of the Seven Gables for his cousins Hepzibah and Clifford. The idea of substituting a dead body for Peter Goldthwaite's dead bills had occurred to the novelist as early as 1842, according to an entry in his *American Notes*: "A man seeks for something excellent, but . . . finds something horrible—as for instance, he seeks for treasure, and finds a dead body."[69] Hence it comes as no surprise that the discovery of the corpse in *The House of the Seven Gables* follows the same trajectory as the unearthing of old bills in "Peter Goldthwaite's Treasure." In the story, although Peter's house appears sound to his neighbors, "a terrible consumption was preying on its insides" (535); in the novel, a terrible consumption preys on the inside not only of the Pyncheon house but of their bodies as well. *The House of the Seven Gables* repeatedly depicts the relation between past and present as one body incorporating another body—an image that inevitably recalls Melville's figure of *The House of the Seven Gables* as a book inside the very house it describes. The house is said to "include the home of the dead and buried wizard" (9) Matthew Maule—from whom the Judge's Puritan ancestor, Colonel Pyncheon, stole the land to build the house in the first place—while the purported last act of this supposed wizard—the theft of the Pyncheon deeds to eastern Maine—is figuratively expressed by town gossip as the shoveling of "miles and miles of the Pyncheon lands . . . into Maule's grave" (196). Pyncheon land is thus home to Maule's dead body; Maule's dead body home to Pyncheon land. In this reflexive structure, an interior ends up containing the exterior that contains it.

The strange tautological shape of Pyncheon family history, in which the same decline is experienced by each generation, is expressed through a variety of such reflexive tropes. Another way of saying this would be that the Pyncheons—like Peter Goldthwaite—find a way of jumping down their own throat. This is particularly fitting because the curse Matthew Maule places upon the Pyncheons after they have stolen his land is that God will give them their own blood to drink, a curse that takes both literal form—the Judge, like many of his ancestors, dies by drowning in his own blood—and metaphorical. Hence Holgrave, a tenant of the Pyncheons, can describe the House of the Seven Gables as a tomb built of "the crystallizations on its walls of the human breath, that has been drawn and exhaled here" (184). Indeed the dead bodies supposedly buried under the foundations of the House of the Seven Gables—such as the corpse of the deposed Matthew Maule, reputed to have corrupted the water of Maule's Well in the house's garden—seem to be part of the very fabric of the house itself. Hawthorne's narrator assures us that the "black stain of blood" that is the figurative legacy of Colonel Pyncheon cheating Matthew Maule out of his lands can still be scented by "conscientious nostrils" (23), while the timbers of the house are described as "oozy, as with the moisture of a heart" (27).

Life in the Pyncheon house is in large part a matter of self-consumption. This might be why the only item that actually seems to be consumed in the house—the very rare chicken egg Hepzibah serves Clifford—is eaten despite the fact that this might "sacrifice the continuance, perhaps, of an ancient feathered race" (153). There is more than a touch of cannibalism to the eating of the egg, just as there is more than a touch of cannibalism to the brood of birds themselves—especially the chicken, who is described as looking "small enough to still be in the egg, and, at the same time, sufficiently old, withered, wizened, and experienced, to have been the founder of the antiquated race. Instead of being the youngest of the family, it rather seemed to have aggregated into itself the ages, not only of those living specimens of the breed, but of all its forefathers and fore-mothers, whose united excellencies and oddities were squeezed into its little body" (151). It is hard not to see Hawthorne's account of the chicken and the egg as a kind of humorous image for his reflexive theory of history.[70] Pyncheon reproduction, whether of the feathered or the human variety, possesses a centripetal rather than a centrifugal force, tending toward an intensification rather than a proliferation of the race. The aggregation of "all its forefathers and fore-mothers" that gathers in the chicken is paralleled by the consumption of one Pyncheon by another—Clifford's eating of the egg, a moment that might be said to conflate Peter Goldthwaite's jumping down his own throat with the Pyncheons' drinking of their own blood.

This Is Death

The relation between the self-consumption of the world depicted in *The House of the Seven Gables* and the camera has to do with the popular nineteenth-century view that the photographed world was a dead world. When, for example, the critic Cuthbert Bede attempted to define the modern world in his 1855 *Photographic Pleasures,* he called it a "used-up age, when the heads of people have been placed before us, in all kinds of plates, and with every variety of dressing."[71] No wonder, then, that Holgrave justifies staying in the House of the Seven Gables by claiming that it is perfect for his photographic "studies," since photography's uncanny ability to turn the living into the dead finds an obvious parallel in the house's depiction of the living as made up of the dead. The ubiquity of the photograph promotes an increased self-awareness, producing a world in which people conceive of their own identity in terms of the need to constantly represent themselves. *The House of the Seven Gables* portrays this endless process of self-representation as one in which the living are constantly producing their own corpses. Indeed, Hawthorne's circular structure and tropes expose what the novelist saw as the self-consuming structure of contemporary life precisely by enacting this structure.

The novel thus fulfills Willis's prophecy that what he called the "black magic" of the camera would ultimately force all other forms of representation to devour themselves: "Vanish aqua-tints and mezzotints, as chimneys that consume their own smoke, devour your-selves. Steel engravers, copper engravers, and etchers, drink up your aquafortis, and die!" By allowing things to represent themselves as themselves, photography would do away with the need for representation altogether, since, "by virtue of the sun's patent, all nature, animate and inanimate, shall be henceforth its own painter, engraver, printer, and publisher." Willis's account of the first daguerreotypes conflates the notion of self-reproduction with that of self-representation. Because the image seems to produce itself, Willis can speak of towns representing themselves as if before a court of law. And having no representative but themselves, "fields, rivers, trees, houses, plains, mountains, cities" will be known for what they are. Thus in the age of the daguerreotype "[n]one but himself shall be his parallel."[72] The camera does not double the world—if anything, indeed, it does the opposite, removing the need for a "parallel" world of representation by locating representation in the subject himself.

Willis's extraordinary celebration of houses representing themselves, things measuring themselves, and people paralleling themselves are the very images we find in Hawthorne's novel. These images are the product of a photographic era, one in which people turn themselves into advertisements for themselves, so that every word they utter, every article they wear, and every action they perform has as its end the effect upon their fellow citizens.[73] Barthes describes this world with remarkable precision in *Camera Lucida*: "[T]he age of Photography corresponds precisely to the explosion of the private into the public, or rather into the creation of a new social value, which is the publicity of the private: the private is consumed as such, publicly."[74] As a character in James's 1902 story "Flickerbridge" puts it: "We live in an age of prodigious machinery, all organized to a single end. That end is publicity—a publicity as ferocious as the appetite of a cannibal. The thing therefore is not to have any illusions—fondly to flatter yourself, in a muddled moment, that the cannibal will spare you. He spares nobody. He spares nothing."[75] Hawthorne's Judge Pyncheon is one of this cannibal's first victims—the only difference being that his commitment to publicity can be seen as a form of self-consumption. The Judge's insistence on presenting himself as just like everyone else has eaten him away from the inside out, so that he is all surface. One image for this is cannibalism; another, equally grizzly, is that of a kind of living death. This is why Holgrave's images of the Judge, which depict him as corpselike in his rigidity, illustrate not the Judge's "secret" character so much as his *only* one.

What the photographic subject "represents," then, is his own extinction, the end of the very self who can be represented. The deathlike images produced by the first photographic techniques are fitting emblems for their deathlike subjects; indeed, they are as much the product of the sitter as of the daguerreotype, since—as we saw in Emerson's account of sitting for his photographic portrait—the photographed subject must imitate the stillness of the corpse in order for the image to appear.[76] Early daguerreotypes were, in other words, curious things, images that allowed the sitter to reproduce and thus, in Willis's terms, to represent themselves, but at the price of turning the sitter into their own corpse. This meant, naturally enough, that the dead made for the best subjects. The nineteenth century's high death rate greatly stimulated the demand for photography and helped cement the relationship between death and the daguerreotype—funeral processions would often stop at the local daguerrean gallery before heading off to the cemetery. In keeping with this practice, Holgrave's final image of the Judge shows him slumped dead in the very chair in which his ancestor the Colonel passed away more than two centuries before. The photographer takes the image in order to break the news of the Judge's death to Phoebe. As Michaels puts it, "The daguerreotype, always a representation of death, is [at this moment] also death's representative."[77] This reading does not, however, do complete justice to the fact that the Judge is a representative of death *before* his dead body is photographed. As Hawthorne sees it, to become a public figure—to become an image in the public eye—is to become a corpse.[78] For a life lived wearing the mask demanded by public life is, *The House of the Seven Gables* suggests, indistinguishable from death, so that the Judge's corpse can be described as "the true emblem of the man's character" (230). The photograph thus exemplifies both the deathlike pose associated with the daguerreotype *and* the deathlike identity the novel associates with public life.

Holgrave's various daguerreotypes of the Judge conflate what Trachtenberg regards as the two most distinctive products of the daguerreotype era: memorial pictures of the departed and likenesses of the great.[79] Indeed, because Hawthorne sees public life as a kind of living death, Holgrave's pictures of the living and of the dead Judge are, to all intents and purposes, the same: the "hard and stern" figure of the one mirroring the stiff and lifeless figure of the other. Somewhat paradoxically, the correspondences between the two images are established through Phoebe's differing reactions to them. Shown the first of these photographs, a puzzled Phoebe accuses Holgrave of having photographed not the living Judge but the painting of Colonel Pyncheon. "I know the face," she tells the photographer, "for its stern eye has been following me about, all day. It is my Puritan ancestor, who hangs yonder in the parlor. You have found some way of copying the portrait without its black velvet cap and gray beard, and have given him a modern coat and satin cravat" (92). Phoebe shows no such confusion, however, when confronted with the second image, exclaiming "This is death!" (302) the moment Holgrave hands her the daguerreotype of her uncle's corpse. Such certainty is a result of the fact that Phoebe associates the daguerreotype with death from the very beginning, complaining to Holgrave that his images escape life altogether by continually "dodging away from the eye" (91). Her insistence that Holgrave's images are a kind of fashion show for the dead anticipates the fact that she will later be shown an actual photograph of the dead. Indeed, we might say that it is *because* her uncle is dead that Phoebe so easily recognizes his photograph.

The repeated association of death and the daguerreotype prompts Cathy N. Davidson to observe in her groundbreaking reading of *The House of the Seven Gables* that "every photograph is, ineluctably, a photograph of the dead."[80] The formulation points to the fact that there is something intrinsically redundant about Holgrave's photograph of the dead Judge. Indeed, as an 1849 entry in Hawthorne's *American Notes* attests, the novelist himself conceived of his representation of the Judge's dead body in photographic terms, imagining a scene in which a "sunbeam comes through a round-hole in the shutter of a darkened room, where a dead man sits in solitude" (293). The Judge's dead body is imagined in photographic terms, in other words, even before it is photographed. Holgrave's ostensible reason for taking a photograph of the dead Judge is to protect Clifford Pyncheon from being accused of his murder. Yet the image, as Milette Shamir notes, "will not be put to use by either the police or the press."[81] Although Phoebe urges Holgrave to "throw open the doors!" of the House of the Seven Gables, Holgrave decides to keep the evidence to himself. Instead, the public contents itself with simply listening to Holgrave's account of what has happened: "Many persons affirmed that the history and elucidation of the facts, long so mysterious, had been obtained by the daguerreotypist from one of those mesmerical seers, who, now-a-days, so strangely perplex the aspect of human affairs" (311). Since Holgrave has already proven that he is himself a mesmerical seer, the reason for the public's faith in his testimony is perfectly circular. His photograph of the dead Judge is as superfluous as the rumor of how he came to know the story of the Pyncheon family—the facts of which, so this account has it, he got from himself.

The redundancy of the explanation for the Judge's mysterious death sheds important light on the other mysterious event with which *The House of the Seven Gables* ends: Holgrave's instantaneous conversion from radical to conservative. Although often disparaged by critics for its unlikeliness, the photographer's about-face is entirely in keeping with what I am characterizing as the tautological logic of the novel. Holgrave comes to Salem as a committed believer in progress, a revolutionary who wants "the moss-grown and rotten Past . . . to be torn down, and lifeless institutions to be thrust out of the way, and their dead corpses buried, and everything to begin anew" (179); he leaves Salem married to Phoebe, proud to be a property owner, and declaring that "hereafter, it will be my lot . . . to build a house for another generation" (307). Far from signaling a simple change-of-heart, however, Holgrave's behavior can be understood as in accordance with his revolutionary view of the world, which sees history as doomed to repeat itself. Although his graphic description of a world in which the dead determine the actions of the living explicitly echoes Thomas Paine, Holgrave's outburst to Phoebe represents less a call to overturn this state of affairs than an acknowledgement of the impossibility of change:

> We read in Dead Men's books! We laugh at Dead Men's jokes, and cry at Dead Men's pathos! We are sick of Dead Men's diseases, physical and moral, and die of the same remedies with which dead doctors killed their patients! We worship the living Deity, according to Dead Men's forms and creeds! Whatever we seek to do, of our own free motion, a Dead Man's icy hand obstructs us! Turn our eyes to what point we may, a Dead Man's white, immitigable face encounters them, and freezes our very heart! And we must be dead ourselves, before we can begin to have our proper influence on our own world. (183)

Holgrave's disgust with the past is grounded upon his belief that the dead do all they can to reproduce themselves in the present, thus turning the present into a repetition of the past. Wills and precedents create a situation in which the past "reproduc[es] itself in successive generations, with one general hue, and varying in little, save the outline" (240). Yet Holgrave's desire to bury the past is hopeless precisely because—as he recognizes—the past is what makes up the present; as Michaels puts it,

Hawthorne "imagines the past and present as utterly continuous, even identical."[82] The model of history on display in *The House of the Seven Gables* is thus equivalent to the realist model of representation it exemplifies, a "parade of sameness" in which everything is already known.

The only way of breaking the historical cycle in which the Pyncheons and Maules are caught is thus, paradoxically, by completing it: Phoebe falls in love with Holgrave precisely because the curse put on the house of Pyncheons by the Maules—that they will drown in their own blood—is once again fulfilled. This is why Gillian Brown describes the conclusion to *The House of the Seven Gables* as staging a kind of "tautological turn," a turn anticipated by Holgrave's tautologous language, the "dead corpses" of history he claims to want to put in the ground.[83] Holgrave's despair at the influence of the dead is somewhat contradicted, after all, by the fact that he happily rents a room in a house he thinks of as inhabited by the dead, spends much of his time trying to work out what has happened to the dead, and takes photographs that are accused of looking like the dead. Holgrave's critique of history's circular structure is thus, almost by default, reflexive rather than revolutionary, in that it describes the very text—the dead man's book—that gives it voice. Indeed, *The House of the Seven Gables* is a dead man's book not just because it is full of dead men, photographed or otherwise; not just because in it the dead haunt the living, and the living are taken for dead; not even because it tells the same story—the bloody death of a Pyncheon—over and over again. *The House of the Seven Gables* is a dead man's book because the novel takes itself for dead, consuming itself through endless repetition, through a commitment to tautology, and to an elaboration of a series of reflexive tropes. Instead of burying corpses, in other words, the novel endlessly (re)produces them.

Typology of Looking

I have been suggesting that the self-consuming nature of life in the Pyncheon household exemplifies the self-reflexive structure of *The House of the Seven Gables* and that this structure is itself a response to what

Hawthorne saw as the self-consuming nature of life in the age of photography, an age in which "the private is consumed as such, publicly." The photographic nature of this public consumption has been described by a number of critics. Williams, for example, points out that the mid-nineteenth century witnessed an increasing permeability between the public and the private realm, one sign of which was the hanging of private portraits in public galleries and of portraits of celebrities in private homes.[84] Hawthorne himself observes this development in a letter to Horatio Bridge written a few months after the novelist had published a biography of Franklin Pierce in an attempt to aid his friend's bid for the presidency in 1852: "Should he fail, what an extinction it will be! He is in the intensest blaze of celebrity. His portrait is everywhere—in all the shop-windows, and in all sorts of styles—on wood, steel, and copper; on horseback, on foot, in uniform, in citizen's dress, in iron medallions, in little brass medals, and on handkerchiefs; and it seems as if the world were full of his not very striking physiognomy."[85] Many of these portraits would have been daguerreotypes, since tiny photographs of politicians were often made for lockets, brooches, watchcases, and campaign badges.[86] By the self-consuming logic of the insistently public and endlessly photographed world depicted in *The House of the Seven Gables*, then, Pierce had been extinguished even before he took political office.

The interpenetration of public and private life in antebellum America is reflected in the world depicted in *The House of the Seven Gables*, a world in which privacy is impossible. Despite the utter seclusion in which Hepzibah and Clifford Pyncheon live, for example, the Judge informs them that "[y]our neighbors have been eye-witnesses to whatever has passed in the garden. The butcher, the baker, the fishmonger, some of the customers of your shop, and many a prying old woman, have told me several of the secrets of your interior" (236). The public gaze even determines Hepzibah's own view of herself. Her "forbidding scowl" (34), which frightens off potential customers from her cent-shop, is regarded by the public of Salem and by Hepzibah herself as proof of a bad temper. In fact, Hepzibah's unfortunate expression is merely the product of her shortsightedness—the result of squinting at herself in the mirror in order to judge whether the public's opinion of her character is correct. Ironically, her horror at what she sees in the mirror provokes the kindly Hepzibah to act kinder still.

The public gaze leads Hepzibah to misjudge herself in much the same way as it does the Judge, who, as we have seen, takes "his idea of himself from what purports to be his image, as reflected in the mirror of public opinion" (232). These misjudgments suggest that the fishbowl in which the Pyncheons live cannot be understood according to the familiar realist model of surveillance and spectacle, in which the subject is "visible, legible, and governable."[87] Karen Haltunnen has described mid-nineteenth-century America in terms of "a typology of looking," in which "one looks at idealized images in order to learn how to appear to others, thereby becoming a standard oneself."[88] These images were often supplied by the camera. In 1850, for example, photographer Mathew Brady began publishing his *Gallery of Illustrious Americans*, issuing twelve daguerreotypes of "representative" Americans each month to subscribers; subjects included presidents, senators, generals, an artist, a historian, and a poet. In a sense, however, Brady's model is fundamentally different from the situation outlined by Haltunnen. For whereas the photographer accepts the fundamental nature of typology, which depends upon the idea of representativeness, Haltunnen's "typology of looking" is not, strictly speaking, a typology at all, since it imagines a society in which *every* member is ultimately representative of every other.[89]

It is Haltunnen's rather than Brady's model that we find in *The House of the Seven Gables*. Consider, for example, one of the novel's most inconsequential characters—Uncle Venner. Facing the constant threat of the poorhouse, Uncle Venner decides to offer Holgrave his services as a photographic model and proves such a success that the daguerreotypist decides to display his friend's portrait at the entrance to his studio. Uncle Venner's value is that he represents the public Holgrave is trying to reach—not in the political sense in which the Judge represents them, but in his very person. The narrator observes that Uncle Venner's poverty has transformed him into someone who is "partly himself, but, in good measure, somebody else; patched together, too, of different epochs; an epitome of times and fashions" (62). Uncle Venner's patchwork philosophy is represented by his patchwork clothes, which themselves represent the various eras in which they were originally worn.[90] The photogenic Uncle Venner is thus a representative figure before he steps in front of the camera, a walking synecdoche for the various "times and fashions" he has lived through. He already embodies, in other words, the peculiar representative function of the photograph; he is representative, we might say, of representativeness itself.

As Henry James pointed out in his 1879 study of Hawthorne, the characters in *The House of the Seven Gables* are "all types . . . of something general"—the wicked uncle, the itinerant young man, the naïve and good-hearted young woman.[91] Hawthorne's use of types brings together, in somewhat unlikely fashion, both the characters of printing and the earliest photographic plates—both of which were known as types. Frank Kermode has brilliantly observed that printed characters were engraved with an instrument called a puncheon, which was tapped with a maul; photographic plates, meanwhile, were "types," both in the sense that they were thought to be engraved by light, and in the sense that they were the source of endless identical copies.[92] The history of the Pyncheon family is thus recorded in the language of typology from the very beginning. As I see it, Hawthorne's reliance on easily recognizable types reflects the insistent publicness of identity in the novel. The narrator tells us that Holgrave "might fitly enough stand forth as the representative of many compeers in his native land" (181), and the daguerreotypist himself tells Phoebe that he "represent[s] the old wizard [Maule]" (316). Holgrave represents his ancestor both in terms of his identity and in terms of his actions; like the Pyncheon chicken, he is the exemplary type of himself. This model is reproduced throughout the novel. The Judge, for instance, is described as "perfectly represent[ing] the person and attributes" (240) of the Colonel, who is himself a "representative of hereditary qualities" (19). Indeed, the characters not only represent institutions such as the family and the nation, they are themselves represented by the clothes they wear and the things they own. Clifford's dressing-gown is described as "translat[ing] the wearer's untold misfortune, and mak[ing] it perceptible to the beholder's eye" (105), while the Judge's "gold-headed cane . . . had it chosen to take a walk by itself, would have been recognized anywhere as a tolerably adequate representative of its master" (56).

The synecdochic logic I have associated with both Pyncheon history and the Pyncheon house is thus constitutive of Pyncheon identity. Indeed, the Judge's ability to represent himself through his possessions extends—in somewhat circular fashion—to his own face, the smile on which is "a good deal akin to the shine on his boots" (117). The logic of Hawthorne's figure is that the Judge's face represents the Judge, as if he has turned himself into a metonymic sign for himself. The self-representative, self-consuming world depicted in *The House of the Seven Gables* finds its ultimate expression in the Judge's face. "A susceptible observer," the narrator suggests, would undoubtedly regard this face "as affording very little evidence of the genuine benignity of soul whereof it purported to be the outward reflection" (116). This is not a matter of penetration, however, but simply of reading what lies on the surface. Indeed, the lineaments of the Judge's character, which the book spends so much time detailing, are represented not simply as readable *on* the Judge's face, but as that face itself; character and countenance, in other words, are depicted as the very same thing:

> The purity of his judicial character . . . the snowy whiteness of his linen, the polish of his boots, the handsomeness of his gold-headed cane, the square and roomy fashion of his coat, and the fineness of its material, and, in general, the studied propriety of his dress and equipment; the scrupulousness with which he paid public notice, in the street, by a bow, a lifting of the hat, a nod, or a motion of the hand, to all and sundry his acquaintances, rich or poor; the smile of broad benevolence wherewith he made it a point to gladden the whole world;—what room could possibly be found for darker traits,

> in a portrait made up of lineaments like these? This proper face was what he beheld in the looking-glass. This admirably arranged life was what he was conscious of, in the progress of every day. Then, might not he claim to be its result and sum, and say to himself and the community,—"Behold Judge Pyncheon there"? (228)

Every action performed, every opinion held, even every article of clothing worn by the Judge goes into the composition of his "proper face," the face that greets him every time he looks in the mirror. Pointing to his many charitable acts as evidence of his benign nature, the Judge asks the public to "behold Judge Pyncheon" both in his own person, and in the acts themselves. His public acts make up his body, and his body is a public act.

This vitriolic account of the Judge's public character is typical of the novel as a whole; as I suggested above, if there is anyone in Salem taken in by the Judge, we do not get to see them. What we do see, over and over again, is the fact that the inevitable outcome of attempting to turn one's own life into a kind of advertisement for itself is to be transformed into a corpse:

> With [money], and with deeds of goodly aspect, done in the public eye, an individual of this class builds up, as it were, a tall and stately edifice, which, in the view of other people, and ultimately in his own view, is no other than the man's character, or the man himself. Behold, therefore, a palace! Its splendid halls and suites of spacious apartments are floored with a mosaic-work of costly marbles; its windows, the whole height of each room, admit the sunshine through the most transparent of plate-glass; its high cornices are gilded, and its ceilings gorgeously painted; . . . Ah! but in some low and obscure nook,—some narrow closet on the ground-floor, shut, locked and bolted, and the key flung away,—or beneath the marble pavement, in a stagnant water-puddle, with the richest pattern of mosaic-work above,—may lie a corpse, half decayed, and still decaying, and diffusing its death-scent all through the palace! (229)

Hawthorne's lurid and pedantic image anticipates Melville's description of the novel as a house that contains itself—only here it is the Judge's life that is compared to a house containing the very life to which it is being compared. The reflexive figure introduces a simple if rather unsettling binary—the Judge's public life is a building, his private life is a "decayed, and still decaying" corpse—that the events of the novel turn into literal fact: the Judge ending up as an actual corpse inside an actual building—a corpse that is immediately photographed. In Holgrave's final photograph, then, the Judge can be seen as the corpse he was all along. Yet to view the ending of the novel as the transformation of a metaphorical corpse into a material one would be to impose a linear narrative upon an event that is ultimately circular—even tautological. For all that happens at the end of the novel is all that has ever happened in the House of the Seven Gables: a "half decayed, and still decaying" body decays in a decaying house.

Dead Corpses

The world depicted in *The House of the Seven Gables* is a world where the relation between copy and original has disintegrated, a dead world where all life is public and representation makes the man. Maurice Blanchot's essay "Two Versions of the Imaginary" provides a guide to this world by asking whether "the strangeness of a cadaver is also the strangeness of the image." According to Blanchot, both the photograph and the corpse display "the present thing in its absence," a doubled relation he expresses in terms of resemblance: "at this moment, when the presence of the cadaver before us is the presence of the unknown, it is also now that the lamented dead person *begins to resemble himself*. . . . if the cadaver resembles to such a degree, that is because it is, at a certain moment, preeminently resemblance, and it is also nothing more. It is the equal, equal to an absolute, overwhelming and marvelous degree. But what does it resemble? Nothing." The corpse presents us with an image of a "resemblance that has nothing to resemble."[93] The dead body is, in other words, resemblance *in general*; it resembles nothing precisely because it resembles resemblance itself. And it is the corpse's tautological status that causes it to resemble the photographic image, which can be called a likeness not because it is "like" its subject but because it allows us to see the way in which identity is itself a product of likeness.

The Judge's corpse might be said to behave according to Blanchot's logic. "Even though the cadaver is tranquilly lying in state on its bier," Blanchot delights in imagining, "it is also everywhere in the room, in the house. At any moment, it can be elsewhere than where it is."[94] Toward the end of Hawthorne's novel the Judge's dead body, like Blanchot's corpse, is everywhere; it is also "elsewhere than it is," since it appears in the daguerreotype Holgrave produces in order—bizarrely—to shield Phoebe from seeing the actual corpse. The Judge's dead body is as exposed as the Judge's "secret character"—a character that, as we have seen, is itself figured as a body. And although this metaphorical body is buried under the "palace" of the Judge's public character, it can be detected as easily as the Judge's benevolence can be proved a fraud:

> Now and then, perchance, comes in a seer, before whose sadly gifted eye the whole structure melts into thin air, leaving only . . . the decaying corpse within. Here, then, we are to seek the true emblem of the man's character, and of the deed that gives whatever reality it possesses to his life. And, beneath the show of a marble palace, that pool of stagnant water, foul with many impurities, and, perhaps, tinged with blood,—that secret abomination, above which, possibly, he may say his prayers, without remembering it,—is this man's miserable soul! (230)

Hawthorne's narrator calls our attention to an observer whose visionary gifts allow him to see the corpse beneath the palace at the very moment that the narrator is showing us the corpse beneath the palace; this same corpse is then described in bloody detail all over again.[95]

The Judge's body reappears yet again a few pages later, this time on the train carrying Hepzibah and Clifford away from Salem. In the course of a crazed conversation with an old man sitting opposite him, Clifford finds himself describing the very situation from which he and his sister are fleeing. "There is a certain house within my familiar recollection," he tells his increasingly baffled interlocutor: "Whenever my thoughts recur to this seven-gabled mansion, immediately I have a vision or image of an elderly man, of remarkably stern countenance, sitting in an oaken elbow-chair, dead, stone-dead, with an ugly flow of blood upon his shirt-bosom! Dead, but with open eyes! He taints the whole house, as I remember it" (261). The Judge's body, it seems, taints not only the house in which he rots but the novel in which he constantly reappears. The repeated appearances of this body reflect that fact that modern inventions such as the electric telegraph have, according to Clifford, made everything public—even the bodies of the dead. He tells his by-now appalled listener to imagine a man fleeing an old house in which there is, inevitably, "a dead man, sitting in an armchair, with a blood-stain on his shirt-bosom." Were the fugitive to arrive "in some distant town, and find all the people babbling about that self-same dead man" (262), the man might as well have never left the house in the first place. The world of instant communication is an insistently public one, and what is made public are the "dead corpses" of the past.

Clifford's crazed complaint is yet another reflexive figure—he is himself the man on the run, and his account of his situation ends up driving him and his sister from the train in fear of being apprehended. By describing his own plight Clifford helps brings it about, since his listener begins to suspect him of the very crime he recounts and thus threatens to expose Clifford in exactly the same manner as the murderer is exposed by the telegraph. In a very real sense, then, to describe is to enact in Hawthorne's novel, since every action *in* the novel takes the form of a description *of* the novel.[96] The text could be said to follow the same reflexive logic, constantly reflecting back on the narrative of which it is comprised. In this way *The House of the Seven Gables* could be said to come as close to approximating the peculiar form of the photograph—its conflation of the real thing and its representation—as it is possible to imagine a novel doing. Made up of descriptions of itself, the novel offers a series of examples of representations that are themselves indistinguishable from the thing they represent. For in repeatedly describing the actions of the wealthy man who "build[s] a great, gloomy, dark-chambered mansion, for himself to die in," Clifford could be said to reproduce the House of the Seven Gables as effectively as Hepzibah's hallucination that the house is following her and her brother down the train tracks. The moral of Clifford's story is that the rich man "lays his own dead corpse beneath the underpinning . . . and hangs his frowning picture on the wall" (263). The two actions—burying yourself and representing yourself—follow the same logic. There is no space in *The House of the Seven Gables* not defined by images since in the age of photography we repeatedly represent ourselves to ourselves and to others, continually live in and through represented states. It makes little sense in such a world to insist upon a rigid boundary between copy and original, for we are all, Hawthorne seems to suggest, representations of ourselves—advertisements of and for our own lives.

Capt. Spaulding (*Groucho Marx*): I used to know a fellow who looked exactly like you by the name of Emanuel Ravelli. Are you his brother?

Ravelli (*Chico Marx*): I am Emanuel Ravelli.

Capt. Spaulding: You're Emanuel Ravelli?

Ravelli: I am Emanuel Ravelli.

Capt. Spaulding: Well, no wonder you look like him. But I still insist there is a resemblance.

Ravelli: Heh, heh, he thinks I look alike.

THE MARX BROTHERS, *Animal Crackers*

CHAPTER TWO

Resembling Oneself

James's Photographic Types

ADMIRING THE Capitol building in 1905, Henry James noted that he had for company "a trio of Indian braves, braves dispossessed of forest and prairie." The men were dressed, he recounts in *The American Scene*, "in neat pot-hats, shoddy suits, and light overcoats, with their pockets, I am sure, full of photographs and cigarettes." This odd inventory leads to an even odder comparison: James proposes that the modern dress of the Native Americans "quickened their resemblance, on the much bigger scale, to Japanese celebrities, or to specimens, on show."[1] Like exhibits in a World's Fair, the men are regarded by James as if they were permanently on display—a condition, needless to say, with which turn-of-the-century Native Americans were not unfamiliar. But what the comparison attempts to demonstrate, despite its insistence on visibility, is the essential unknowability of the men: James is no more able to recognize them as individuals than he could recognize a Japanese celebrity.

James's insistence on seeing the Indian braves only in terms of spectacle is itself an example, ironically enough, of the very process of historical erasure *The American Scene* continually laments. According to James's appalled account, Washington D.C. is symptomatic of the nation as a whole in its devotion to a kind of ceaseless forgetting. And, as James recognizes, the Native Americans he reduces to the level of specimens are the most noticeable victims of this historical amnesia. In his quasi-photographic metaphor, the men with whom he shares the Capitol steps "project as in a flash an image in itself immense, but foreshortened and simplified"; an image, rather tautologically, of the self-erasing movement of American history itself. James imagines this image "reducing to a single smooth stride the bloody footsteps of time. One rubbed one's eyes, but there, at its highest polish, shining in the beautiful day, was the brazen face of history, and there, all about one, immaculate, the printless pavements of the State" (364). American history thus presents to the discerning observer a shining blank face—a blankness reflected in the enigma, as James sees it, of Indian braves reduced to the inconsequentiality of photograph-carrying tourists.[2]

The camera's role in what James sees as the State's principal business—the interminable removal of the marks of the past—is suggested, somewhat paradoxically, by the use of the term "printless" to describe the vacant surfaces of the government buildings and historical monuments that surround him. What Washington lacks are the prints made by time; what has produced this absence, James's image seems to suggest, are prints made by the camera. For not only do the photographs he imagines filling the pockets of the Indian braves not count as a record of the past, they actually work to hasten its loss. This is the lesson of a number of episodes in *The American Scene* similar to James's epiphany on the Capitol steps, all testifying to his bewilderment at "the constituted blankness" (30) of his home country.[3] This blankness extends even to historic Richmond, a place where, James laments, "there were no *references*." The "pathetic poverty of the exhibition" (282) on display at the Richmond Museum is not only proof of this strange deficiency, it also seems even to be responsible for it: "The sorry objects about were old Confederate documents, already sallow with time . . . together with faded portraits of faded worthies, primitive products of the camera, the crayon, the brush" (283). The Civil War photographs that supposedly inspired Stephen Crane to write *The Red Badge of Courage* leave James unmoved, his only consolation the dawning of the idea that in many ways defines *The American Scene*: that the failure of Richmond—and by extension America—to refer to its past is precisely the form in which that past is preserved. In continually erasing the past the camera operates, paradoxically, as the best witness *to* that past, since American history—as James sees it—is the record of its own forgetting. This explains why James continually expresses his sense of the impossibility of retrieving the American past in the language of photography: American life "registers itself on the plate with an incision too vague, and, above all, too uniform" to leave a historical trace, thereby dooming the observer's impressions "to fade, to pass away, to leave not a wreck behind" (334).

This chapter tracks James's depiction of this passing away across a variety of stories and novels: "The Real Thing," *The Awkward Age*, *The Sense of the Past*, *The Aspern Papers*, and *The Golden Bowl*. What connects these texts is their investment in photography, which appears as subject (in "The Real Thing"), historical marker (in *The Awkward Age*), point of comparison (in *The Sense of the Past* and *The Aspern Papers*), and metaphor (in *The Golden Bowl*). I argue that James's interest in the photograph is as much bound up with the challenge the medium posed to thinking about resemblance—what C. S. Peirce identifies as the photograph's iconicity—as with the challenge the medium posed to thinking about referentiality—what Peirce identifies as the photograph's indexicality. My intention is not to suggest that critics such as Laura Saltz are wrong to contend that "James did not like photography."[4] Yet although James did not believe that photography was an art, blamed it for transforming society, and frequently derided it in his work, his repeated invocation of the camera provides a crucial—and critically overlooked—clue to understanding what I see as the central representational question raised by James's work: the interpenetration of form and content, or, to put this another way, the fact that metaphors function as actual agents within James's texts.[5] As in Aristotle, those characters who make metaphor in James's world are masters of that world, since they are able to remake it. Surprisingly, however, James repeatedly links analogy, or what I shall be calling resemblance, to photography—despite the fact that the camera is seen as responsible for the literal referential world that metaphor struggles (sometimes unsuccessfully) to remake.

James's engagement with photography provides a model for understanding why he repeatedly treats what appear to be questions about referentiality—such as the fact that American history appears to possess "no *references*"—as questions about resemblance. For what is ultimately at stake in James's professed inability to distinguish past from present is an inability to distinguish one American from another. He persistently complains in *The American Scene* that "there are no 'kinds' of people" in the United States but only "people . . . all of one kind" (37). Such a "scant diversity of type" forced him to move to Europe, since it "left [him] short, as a story-seeker or picture-maker" (335). Just as American history is all the same, so American identity is all of one type; Americans lack the representative or typological character necessary for the production of art, which requires that "everything should represent something more than what immediately and all too blankly met the eye."[6] This blankness *does*, however, end up providing James with a subject—the crisis of resemblance he outlines (on a thematic level) and attempts to evade (on a formal one) in his late work—by which I mean the work published after the 1892 short story "The Real Thing." This crisis is the product of the endless circulation of photographic images in modern society, a circulation that threatens to render everyone and everything the same. And although *The American Scene* traces this crisis back to America, such a diagnosis is ultimately self-canceling, in the sense that the form this crisis takes is the undoing of the very distinctions *between* people of different races and nations.

The most dramatic sign of this collapse of difference, James notes in his 1898 essay "The Question of the Opportunities," is the English language itself, at least as spoken in America: "Homogeneous I call the huge American public, with a due sense of the variety of races and idioms that are more and more under contribution to build it up, for it is precisely in the great mill of language . . . that the elements are ground into unity."[7] James believes he escaped this homogeneity by fleeing America; however, despite the fact that four of the five texts I examine in this chapter take place in the city that was James's home for much of his life, London, all four can be said to be a product *of* this homogeneity. As we shall see, these texts detail the collapse of the ability to make distinctions either between national identities (in the case of "The Real Thing" and *The Golden Bowl*) or historical periods (in the case of *The Awkward Age, The Aspern Papers,* and *The Sense of the Past*). My last chapter argued that photography's troubling of the distinctions between the image and its subject provided Nathaniel Hawthorne with a compelling model for what he saw as the reflexivity of American life, in which everyone had become indistinguishable from his or her own representation. This chapter argues that photography's troubling of the distinctions between one subject and another provided James with a compelling model for what he saw as the homogeneity of American life, in which everyone had become indistinguishable from one another.

Typical Americans

James's belief that American life was unfit for fiction is somewhat surprising in light of the fact that the generic Jamesian plot pits naïve Americans against sophisticated Europeans. One way of making sense of this contradiction is to read the Americans in his work according to the terms set out by Mark Seltzer's characterization of the most typical American in all of James's work—Christopher Newman, the protagonist of the 1877 novel *The American.* According to Seltzer, Newman represents "not so much the idea of the typical American as [he] does the idea of the American *as* the typical—of Americans as typical, general, and reproducible."[8] The American citizen is typical, in other words, of the American citizen. By this reasoning, the crisis of resemblance provoked by photography—the crisis whereby everyone comes to look like (and hence is a type of) everyone else—is the very sign of American identity in James's fiction, indeed almost its very principle. The unmistakable sign of this crisis of resemblance is the blankness of the faces of James's fictional Americans. Newman's face, for example, is said to possess "that typical vagueness which is not vacuity, that blankness which is not simplicity, that look of being committed to nothing in particular . . . so characteristic of many American faces."[9] This blankness is reproduced in countless other James texts—most memorably perhaps on the face of the philanthropic Miss Birdseye in *The Bostonians*, who has "no features" at all, so that her "sad, soft, pale face . . . looked as if it had been soaked, blurred, and made vague by exposure to some slow dissolvent," or, even more tellingly, on the "lithographic smoothness" of the face of the public speaker Mrs. Farrinder.[10]

The empty faces of James's Americans reproduce what he sees as the empty face of America itself. *The American Scene* complains that the absence of the marks of history—church spires, antiquated buildings, distinguished citizens—renders the American city as bereft as a painting with a "fine blank space" (280) in the middle: "the effect is, for all the world, as if, with the body and the limbs, the hands and feet and coat and trousers, all the accessories of the figure showily painted, the neat white oval of the face itself were innocent of the brush" (280). Paradoxically, this blankness is constitutive of American identity, as if becoming American robbed the subject of his or her own face. In James's formulation, becoming an American citizen is a physical procedure, a somewhat occult process of "conversion" in which the recognizable European immigrant becomes the indistinguishable American.

James's firsthand experience of this process—recorded in his visit to Ellis Island—ultimately leaves him unable to say what the new American looks like at all: "The great thing, at any rate, was that they were all together so visibly on the new, the lifted level—that of consciously not being what they *had* been, and that this immediately glazed them over as with some mixture, of indescribable hue and consistency, the wholesale varnish of consecration, that might have been applied, out of a bottomless receptacle, by a huge white-washing brush" (97).[11] This endless making of Americans results in what James sees as the "criminal continuity" (432) between the variously undifferentiated regions of the United States and its supposedly homogeneous population. Indeed, the process of American conversion is so relentless it acts on the subject even when he or she already *is* American. The immigrants James finds in "serene and triumphant possession" of Boston, for example, act upon the novelist as "a sponge saturated with the foreign mixture and passed over almost everything I remembered and might still have recovered" (172). James finds himself experiencing the *same* amnesia as the immigrant, only in his case, paradoxically, the native identity he loses is American. Such is the homogenizing force of America that its newly converted citizens are able to strip away what is different about the returning American, turning their observer into another version of themselves.[12]

Recent interest in the question of visuality in James has tended to be guided by what Seltzer identifies as the familiar realist tropes of "scrutiny and surveillance."[13] Such an approach stresses the complicity between power and vision in James's work and reads him in the context of texts such as Jacob Riis's *How the Other Half Lives*.[14] James's ability to survey the world and to render that world metaphorically breaks down, however, in the face of the modern American. The trip to Cambridge, Massachusetts, recorded in *The American Scene*, for example, leaves the novelist asking a question that had become increasingly familiar in the age of mass immigration: "what might be becoming of us all, 'typically,' ethnically, and thereby physiognomically?" Yet James's query is prompted not by a recognition of the diversity of the "ingenuous youths" he witnesses in Harvard yard but by what he sees as their uniformity. "*Whom did they look like the sons of?*" (50), he wonders, the young men's remarkable similarity to each other seemingly disabling James's famous power of analogy altogether. Indeed, the Harvard undergraduates who so perplex him not only look like each other but also like all the other Americans James has encountered on his tour, since they all possess what he archly calls "the unmitigated 'business man' face" (51). "No impression so promptly assaults the arriving visitor of the United States," James complains, "as that of the overwhelming preponderance" (51) of featureless faces, as if the blankness of American history he noted in Washington—the "printless pavements of the State"—was mirrored on the reproducible countenance of its citizens.

The commonly held wisdom that the face, in the words of Charles Baudelaire, was "the emblem of character, the stamp of fate" is thus paradoxically affirmed by the absence of expression on the American face.[15] The depiction in *The House of the Seven Gables* of the mask-like face produced by early daguerreotypes represented, I argued in the previous chapter, a commitment to the taxonomic reasoning of physiognomy—in which character determines the cast of the face. In the years following the publication of Hawthorne's novel dramatic improvements in photographic technique led to photography being both championed and criticized for its ability to produce highly detailed portraits. James's position was clear from the outset: he declared in 1865 that the photographic image "lacks the supreme virtue of possessing a character. It is the detail alone that distinguishes one photograph from another."[16] Limited to merely reproducing what is in front of it, the camera lens, in James's view, is unable—like America itself—to perform what his 1884 essay "The Art of Fiction" argues is the fundamental task of representation: a "selection [of events] . . . whose main care is to be typical." Fiction necessarily "boils down" events, the artist's task being "to give all the sense . . . without all the substance . . . to summarise and foreshorten."[17] The problem with the photograph, as James sees it, is that it gives the substance without the sense, particularity rather than typicality. The detail made possible by the more accurate photographic portraits of the 1850s and 1860s misrepresent their subjects, in this view, as fundamentally as did the "flat, meaningless maps of the face" produced by the daguerreotypes of a decade before.[18]

Condemning photography for its inability to distinguish what was meaningful from what was not remained a popular critical pastime throughout the second half of the nineteenth century. Many critics of photography believed that the medium could become an art only by suppressing its tendency to reproduce the world in all its detail. Charles Caffin's 1901 *Photography as a Fine Art*, for example, argues that "[t]he painter obtains his synthesis by elimination of the unessential and massing of the most important features. The photographic artist does practically the same."[19] G. H. Lewes's 1865 study *Principles of Success in Literature* goes so far as to characterize what it sees as photography's indiscriminate reproduction of "unessential details" as a kind of "offensive and tasteless" democracy of vision.[20] The antebellum celebration of the daguerreotype as an agent of American democracy I outlined in my last chapter was thus increasingly replaced after the Civil War by warnings that the ceaseless photographic reproduction of the American subject was making it increasingly more difficult to say what that democratic subject looked like. In "[sweeping] away many of the illiberal distinctions of rank and wealth," in the words of the 1861 article from *Photographic News*, the photograph was also sweeping away the visual characteristics that distinguish one person from another.[21] For James in particular, this problem was bound up with democracy's leveling of rank—*The American Scene* speaks of "the huge democratic broom" (44)—and hence inseparable from the question of American identity. The photograph, like America itself, is unselective and therefore of no use to the artist.

The Real Thing

James's insistence on the photographic uniformity of the American citizen represents a somewhat perverse response to the age of mass immigration. His representation of American identity as a mass produced article, moreover, belies his own dependence upon reproducible stereotypes. As

Sara Blair has pointed out, James's famous "international theme" is the product of his reliance on such well-worn figures as "the atavistic Italian, the Negro servant, the culturally exhausted European, the Jewish usurer, and even the 100 percent American."[22] That these stereotypes possess a photographic provenance is the lesson of James's most well known examination of the effects of the camera, his short story "The Real Thing."[23] The story is most often read as a somewhat transparent allegory of James's contempt for the camera. I want to read "The Real Thing" not as a parable about the gulf between photography and fiction, however, but as a parable about the relationship between the reproducible photographic image and the reproducible types that are the subject of James's fiction.

"The Real Thing" begins with its unnamed narrator recounting a moment of imaginary rather than photographic vision: "When the porter's wife (she used to answer the house-bell) announced 'A gentleman—with a lady, sir,' I had, as I often had in those days, for the wish was father to the thought, an immediate vision of sitters."[24] Unfortunately for the narrator, the gentleman and lady turn out to be not prospective sitters but prospective models. A down-at-heel genteel couple, they arrive at the narrator's door as a last resort, having been told that he is a struggling painter who makes a living illustrating popular novels. The Monarchs' embarrassed failure to declare their situation is compounded by the narrator's failure to recognize it. "There was nothing at first to indicate that they might not have come for a portrait" (229), he protests, adding that the couple looked as if they "had ten thousand a year" (234).[25] That the narrator should be so easily deceived by appearances puts him at odds, strangely enough, with the logic of his own narrative. He declares "an innate preference for the represented subject over the real one" (236), the reason for his preference sounding as if it has been lifted from an Oscar Wilde play: "[T]he defect of the real one was so apt to be a lack of representation. I liked things that appeared; then one was sure" (236–37).

The problem the Monarchs pose for the narrator is that they are too much like aristocrats to be used as models for aristocrats; they are "the real thing" (243)—a gentleman and a lady. It is the fact of their authenticity, the narrator insists, that renders his drawings of them "second-rate" (258). Critics have tended to follow Leon Edel in reading the story as proof that for James "[t]he real thing . . . remains simply the real thing; only the imagination transfigures"; "The Real Thing," in other words, displays James's disdain for "the real thing."[26] Yet what the story ultimately demonstrates is the impossibility of clearly distinguishing between the real thing and its representation—for the simple reason that the real thing is always a matter *of* representation. As Bruce Henriksen points out, insisting on an allegorical interpretation of the story inevitably leads to critics confusing James with his narrator and thus to "[r]eproducing the narrator's limited vision." Recent attempts to avoid this critical trap owe much to Catherine Vieilledent, who persuasively reads "The Real Thing" as "really produc[ing] what the artist vainly tried to do."[27] The story, in other words, is not an allegory about the defects of the real thing so much as an allegory about the creation of "The Real Thing"—an allegory, that is, about writing itself. The narrator's repeated references to "the real thing" thus metonymically signal his own aesthetic project; he ends his story, after all, admitting that if the Monarchs have indeed ruined his illustrative talents he is "content to have paid the price—for the memory" (258). Hence "The Real Thing" can be read not so much as an account of the ways fiction differs from photography—a conclusion that, as nuanced as her reading is, Vieilledent ends up supporting—as a depiction of the ways fiction is shaped by photography.

Vieilledent is surely right to read the constant references to "the real thing" as metonymic signifiers of the story itself. Identifying the diegetic meaning of the phrase, however, is less simple. The Monarchs insist that they are ideal for the narrator's needs because they have already worked as models for a number of photographers. But, as he quickly discovers, "the very habit that made [them] good for that purpose unfitted [them] for mine . . . do what I would with it my drawing looked like a photograph or a copy of a photograph" (243–44). Just as in *The House of the*

Seven Gables, photography has confused the distinction between copy and original, so that a drawing of a photograph and a photographic image can be considered equivalent. This photographic similarity extends to the Monarchs themselves. The narrator reflects that Mrs. Monarch "had no sense of variety . . . She was always a lady certainly, and into the bargain was always the same lady. She was the real thing, but always the same thing" (244). The problem is not only, in other words, that the Monarchs are the real thing but also that they are always the *same* thing. The situation is complicated still further by the fact that the story offers two competing candidates for the real thing: the photographic image and the Monarchs themselves. Indeed, it is never completely clear whether the Monarchs are the real thing because they have been photographed, or whether they have been photographed because they are the real thing:

> "We've been photographed—*immensely*," said Mrs. Monarch.
>
> "She means the fellows have asked us," added the Major.
>
> "I see—because you're so good-looking."
>
> "I don't know what they thought, but they were always after us."
>
> "We always got our photographs for nothing," smiled Mrs. Monarch.
>
> "We might have brought some, my dear," her husband remarked.
>
> "I'm not sure we have any left. We've given quantities away," she explained to me.
>
> "With our autographs and that sort of thing," said the Major.
>
> "Are they to be got in the shops?" I inquired, as a harmless pleasantry.
>
> "Oh yes, *hers*—they used to be."
>
> "Not now," said Mrs. Monarch with her eyes on the floor. (235)

The photographers give the Monarchs their images for free because they wish to use Mrs. Monarch's image to advertise their trade, much as Holgrave places an image of Uncle Venner at the entrance to his daguerreotype studio in *The House of the Seven Gables*. But while Mrs. Monarch's representative qualities are evident in her photograph, her husband's are evident in his own person. The narrator snobbishly observes that "It would have paid any club in process of formation and in want of a stamp to engage him at a salary to stand in the principal window. What struck me at once was that in coming to me they had rather missed their vocation; they could surely have been turned to better account for advertising purposes. . . . I could imagine 'We always use it' pinned on their bosoms with the greatest effect" (233). Major Monarch's presence in a shop window, the narrator suggests, will exercise much the same attraction as did Mrs. Monarch's image on the side of a photographer's booth.

As compelling as this image of the Major is, the last thing "a perfect gentleman" would do, of course, would be to offer himself for display in a shop window. The Monarchs' identity as a lady and a gentleman is thus threatened, paradoxically, by the perfection with which they look the part; they are so much the type of the gentleman and lady that they cannot actually *be* a gentleman and a lady. The same paradoxical law governs their identity as celebrities. The Monarchs claim that their photographic images were well enough known for them to have "given quantities away."[28] What they are famous for, however, appears to be their photographed image; the Monarchs give away their photographs not because they are famous but become famous because they have given away so many photographs. They are famous, in the familiar formulation, for being famous, celebrities because they look like celebrities.[29] This would be ironic enough even without the narrator's observation that Major Monarch "would have struck me as a celebrity if celebrities often were striking. It was a truth of which I had for some time been conscious that a figure with a good deal of frontage was, as one might say, almost never a public institution. A glance at the lady helped to remind me of this paradoxical law: she also looked too distinguished to be a 'personality.' Moreover one would scarcely come across two variations together" (229). Looking like a celebrity, the narrator proposes, disqualifies one from actually being a celebrity (unless, presumably, one is a celebrity whom nobody knows—that is, a Japanese celebrity). The Monarchs are thus caught in a curious bind, in which the fact of looking like something is the very guarantee that this is the very thing that they are not.

The story as a whole scrupulously adheres to this "paradoxical law," in which the "type" of something looks more like the thing it represents than does the thing itself. What accounts for the narrator's inability to represent the Monarchs, according to the terms of this logic, is not the fact that they *are* the real thing—having been reduced to working as models they can hardly be said to be the epitome of a gentleman and a lady—but the fact that they so perfectly suggest the real thing. This is what Martha Banta means, I think, when she suggests that the story is about "the creation of images by which we come to recognition of certain types."[30] That the Monarchs *are* types is attested to by the fact that the narrator's friend Jack Hawley immediately regards them as "a compendium of everything he most objected to in the social system of his country" (254). The Monarchs' typicality explains why the narrator is able to picture their life in such detail. He tells us that the reason that he is so disappointed that the Monarchs have come to him as models rather than sitters is because "in the pictorial sense I had immediately *seen* them. I had seized their type" (231):

> I could see the sunny drawing-rooms, sprinkled with periodicals she didn't read, in which Mrs. Monarch had continuously sat. . . . I could see the rich covers the Major had helped to shoot and the wonderful garments in which, late at night, he repaired to the smoking-room to talk about them. I could imagine their leggings and waterproofs, their knowing tweeds and rugs, their rolls of sticks and cases of tackle and neat umbrellas; and I could evoke the exact appearance of their servants and the compact variety of their luggage. (235–36)

The narrator pictures the Monarchs' former life with photographic precision. Yet although he can visualize even the "exact appearance of their servants," he eschews such detail when it comes to drawing the Monarchs themselves. They ask him only to copy their figure, since "the reproduction of the face would betray them" (236). Such caution seems somewhat unnecessary, for Mrs. Monarch's "face was not charged with expression; that is her tinted oval mask showed friction as an exposed surface shows it" (230). This blankness of feature extends to her husband—the product, the narrator judges, of "the deep intellectual repose of the twenty years of country-house visiting" (235). Paradoxically, it is the reproduction of the Monarchs' blank faces that would expose them to their friends; that is the mark, in other words, of their individuality.

The narrator's drawings of the Monarchs could not then possess particularity—could not possess, that is, what we think we mean when we refer to "the real thing"—even if they allowed their faces to be reproduced. Possessing no visible features, the Monarchs can only be identified by their figures. To copy the Monarchs is thus to copy a type, or even, the narrator reflects, "to invent types that approached [their] own" (244). And it is the Monarchs' typicality that makes them the real thing, which makes it all the more ironic that the narrator spends much of the story attempting to persuade us of his dislike for types. He protests that "[t]he thing in the world I most hated was the danger of being ridden by a type" (244), claiming to have repeatedly quarreled with friends over the question: "I held that everything was to be sacrificed sooner than character. When they averred that the haunting type in question could easily *be* character, I retorted, perhaps superficially: 'Whose?' It couldn't be everybody's—it might end in being nobody's" (244–45). The danger posed by typology, the narrator contends, is the fact that it demands the sacrifice of specificity; representing types means abandoning the real thing and thus being left with nothing—or nobody.

The narrator's avowed position is thus the *opposite* from that of James, who saw typicality as a way of accessing the real thing. Yet, despite his misgivings, the narrator agrees to take on the Monarchs because of his need to "secur[e] the best types" for a "projected *edition de luxe* of one of the writers of our day—the rarest of the novelists" (237). This novelist—Philip Vincent—has, the narrator informs us, been "long neglected by the multitudinous vulgar and dearly prized by the attentive," a description that inevitably recalls another novelist with two first names whose work was to be collected in an illustrated *edition de luxe.*[31] The edition that the narrator is working on, he proclaims, is "practically an act of high reparation; the wood-cuts with which it was to be enriched were the homage of English art to one of the most independent representatives of English letters" (237). Philip Vincent represents English letters in much the same way, it would seem, that the Monarchs represent English society.[32] There is something highly appropriate, therefore, in the fact that the narrator's own name, which is carefully kept from the reader, is described as a metonym for the English language itself. In the middle of another disastrous modeling session by the Monarchs "there came at the door a knock which I immediately recognized as the subdued appeal of a model out of work. It was followed by the entrance of a young man whom I at once saw to be a foreigner and who proved in fact an Italian acquainted with no English word but my name, which he uttered in a way that made it seem to include all others" (247). The narrator "immediately recognizes" the knock at the door as belonging to a prospective model, just as he has an "immediate vision" of sitters when he hears the Monarchs ring the doorbell. In this case, however, his assumption proves correct.

In contrast to the narrator's name, which stands in for the entire English language, the Monarchs' name obviously misrepresents their social status. Though at the beginning of the story the couple suggests a series of majestic metaphors—"When she [Mrs. Monarch] stood erect," the narrator assures us, "she took naturally one of the attitudes in which court-painters represent queens and princesses" (245–46)—by the end of the story they have been reduced to "a pair of patient courtiers in a royal ante-chamber" (253). "The Real Thing" performs a series of such reversals—"if my servants were my models," the narrator considers at one point, "my models might be my servants" (253)—all of which are the product of the story's founding paradox: that our belief in the value of the real thing is based upon the success with which something can represent itself *as* the real thing. Hence the narrator discovers what he suspected all along—that Philip Vincent's account of English letters and English society is best represented by an Italian and a cockney. The Italian Oronte "was sallow but fair, and when I put him into some old clothes of my own, he looked like an Englishman"; his other model, the working-class English woman Miss Churm, "could look, when requested, like an Italian" (249). The narrator's praise for the "native exuberance" (251) of his Italian model and the "mother-wit" of his cockney one suggests, however, that he fails to learn the lesson of his own models. Oronte and Miss Churm demonstrate that the successful representation of national "types" depends upon the plasticity rather than upon the ethnicity of one's models, yet the narrator persists in representing *them* via the most clichéd of characteristics. Consider, for example, how he comes to the conclusion that Oronte desires work as a model: "I hadn't then visited his country, nor was I proficient in his tongue; but as he was not so meanly constituted—what Italian is?—as to depend only on that member for expression he conveyed to me, in familiar but graceful mimicry, that he was in search of exactly the employment in which the lady before me was engaged" (248). In replacing the Monarchs with their supposed opposites, the narrator exchanges one set of "types" for another.

The narrator's commitment to cliché demonstrates that the reason he prefers represented subjects to real ones is because—despite his professed belief otherwise—he understands the world according to the ready-made rubric of typology. He admiringly relates how Oronte, with the blind judgment of the "instinctual" foreigner, guesses "from the shape of my high north window, seen outside, that my place was a studio and that as a studio it would contain an artist" (248). The anecdote reveals that "The Real Thing" is itself very much "ridden by a type"—the stereotype.[33] Such is the power of national and racial typology that James's narrator can ignore the very moral of his story and continue to adhere to stereotypes about Italian identity, safe in his belief that Oronte behaves the way he does because he is Italian and that Italians behave the way Oronte does.

The link between the endlessly reproducible photograph and the national stereotypes James relies upon for his supposed allegory of the camera's resistance to representation should by now be clear. First used in the printing industry in the late eighteenth century to mean "a series of unvarying casts made from one mold," by the mid-nineteenth century the term stereotype had become closely associated with photography. As early as 1851, for example, the Californian photographer Robert H. Vance would define the unreproducible daguerreotype as "the stereotyped impression of the real thing."[34] This was partly due to the photograph's endless reproducibility but also to the sense that the ubiquity of the camera was beginning to impose a kind of uniformity upon the world itself. In Nancy Armstrong's bold account of this process, the rapid proliferation of photographic images fueled a compensatory need to receive new information in utterly familiar ways. As the subject matter increased in scope and variety, the kind of shot grew more predictable, so that photographs become either normative (family portraits) or disfigured (mug shots). Identity thus becomes a matter of the position an individual occupied within a differential system of images; formal stereotypes begat national and racial ones.[35] It is in this sense, then, that James's story identifies photography with the real thing—not because he imagines the camera in opposition to representation but because he imagines representation as constitutive of the real thing. In the photographic age English people are best represented by Italians and aristocrats by cockneys because Englishness and aristocracy, like everything else, are a matter of a fixed number of reproducible elements. Representation itself—which is, finally, the true subject of "The Real Thing"—depends upon the stereotype; "the real thing" has become "the same thing."

A Unique Revival

"The Real Thing" marks a significant shift in James's thinking about representation. The texts that follow James's 1892 story display a sense of the reproducibility of people and of periods less apparent in earlier works equally concerned with questions of vision and visuality—such as 1886's *The Princess Casamassima.* I am suggesting that this shift is partly the result of James's sense that the camera has transformed how the world looks, so that very different things—itinerant Italians, English aristocrats—have come to look the same. This transformation provides the subject matter for James's 1898 novel *The Awkward Age*, as is clear from the novel's opening scene, which consists of a detailed examination of the startling similarities between a young English girl, Nanda Brookenham, and her grandmother, Lady Julia. The comparison is first noted by Mr. Longdon upon his return to London society after an absence of thirty years. Having decided to accompany his new friend, Gus Vanderbank, back to his home for a nightcap, Mr. Longdon immediately notes that his host lives surrounded by "many, too many photographs."[36] In the middle of describing to the young Van the incomparable beauty of Lady Julia—the woman with whom he fell in love thirty years before—Mr. Longdon picks up one of these photographs, an image of Van's friend, Nanda:

> "Lady Julia was exquisite, and this child's exactly like her."
>
> "If Julia's so like her, *was* she so exquisite?" he [Van] hazarded.
>
> "Oh yes; everyone was agreed about that." Mr. Longdon kept his eyes on the face, trying a little, Vanderbank even thought, to conceal his own. "She was one of the greatest beauties of her day."
>
> "Then *is* Nanda so like her?" Vanderbank persisted, amused at his friend's transparency.
>
> "Extraordinarily. Her mother told me all about her."
>
> "Told you she's as beautiful as her grandmother?"
>
> Mr. Longdon turned it over. "Well, that she has just Lady Julia's expression. She absolutely *has* it—I see it here." He was delightfully positive. "She's much more like the dead than like the living." (30–31)

The two men describe with precision the contours of the crisis of resemblance I am arguing is brought on by the circulation of the photographic image. In Mr. Longdon's circular reasoning, Lady Julia's granddaughter must be beautiful because her grandmother was always thought so. But if there is no general consensus that Nanda is pretty—Van is never completely convinced that she is—and if Nanda exactly reproduces her grandmother, then Mr. Longdon can no longer be sure that Lady Julia *was* beautiful, or even that he knows what beauty is. The fact that Nanda looks "more like the dead than the living" only underscores the photographic nature of this crisis, since, as we saw in the previous chapter, the photographed subject was often described as corpselike in appearance.

The problem outlined by the two men is exacerbated by the fact that the resemblance between Nanda and Lady Julia is as seemingly perfect as the resemblance between a photograph and its subject: "It's *she* again, as I first knew her, to the life; and not only in feature, in stature, in color, in movement, but in every bodily mark and sign, in every look of the eyes . . . She's *all* Lady Julia. There isn't a touch of her mother. It's unique—an absolute revival" (94–95). Nanda's photographic-like reproduction of Lady Julia takes the form of an oxymoron: a unique revival. But despite the fact that Nanda's photograph identifies *who* she looks like—the dead—this image proves of no use in actually identifying *what* she looks like. Van tells his friend that Nanda "has no features. No, not one" (31). In a sense, however, this only confirms her familial identity. Her brother, Harold, for example, is described as having a "smooth fair face" (39), while her father's countenance has "no significance, no accent" (52).[37] The difficulty Van and Mr. Longdon encounter in trying to characterize Nanda's appearance is due not simply to the blankness of her face but also to their insistence that she exactly resembles her dead grandmother. Van admits that he has long been puzzled by "the curious character of her [Nanda's] face":

> "I have always found in it a recall of the type of the period you must be thinking of. It isn't a bit modern. It's a face of Sir Thomas Lawrence—"
>
> "It's a face of Gainesborough?" Mr. Longdon returned with spirit. "Lady Julia herself harked back."
>
> Vanderbank, clearly, was equally touched and amused. "Let's say at once that it's a face of Raphael."
>
> His old friend's hand was instantly on his arm. "That's exactly what I often said to myself of Lady Julia's." (95)

The two men speculate not only that historical periods, like racial "types," possess representative faces, but that these faces are—at least in part—the creation of art.[38] Yet believing in a representative face and describing what this face looks like prove two different things. Vanderbank and Mr. Longdon struggle to place the "type" of Nanda's face, moving backward from the early nineteenth century to the late eighteenth to the early sixteenth with a rapidity that seems to disable the entire process of identifying facial "types." The fact that Nanda and Lady Julia are ultimately seen as possessing "a face of Raphael" implies that Lady Julia's beauty was as anachronistic as Nanda's—despite the fact that the older woman was regarded by everyone as "one of the greatest beauties of her day." So when Van suggests that, with regards to Nanda and Lady Julia, "[t]he situation's reproduced" (36), he is not exactly correct—since Nanda is *not* regarded as a great beauty. The standards of beauty have changed, it seems, despite the fact that no one knows what those standards are.[39]

What has produced this change, James's novel seems to suggest, is the very photographic reproduction that allowed for the comparison between Lady Julia and Nanda in the first place. The fact that Mr. Longdon discovers the exact resemblance between Nanda and Lady Julia by looking at Nanda's photograph is thus far from accidental. It is also something of a cliché, in the sense that the camera was believed by many nineteenth century observers to possess the power to uncover physical similarities invisible to the naked eye. The following claim in an 1867 essay in the periodical *Littell's Living Age* is typical in this regard: "A good photograph often possesses a subtlety of resemblance which brings out characteristics of race or mental capacity scarcely seen in the original, but which undoubtedly exist. Unexpected family likeness is at times suddenly revealed in the photograph in a startling degree."[40] As Oliver Wendell Holmes explains in his essay "Doings of the Sunbeam," family likenesses are easier to spot in photographs than in life due to "the fact that we bring many of these family portraits together, and study them more at our ease."[41] The photograph thus conflates two different forms of likeness: that between the individual and the image, and that between the individual and his or her ancestors. Roland Barthes observes about photographs of himself that he "spontaneously call[s] them 'likenesses,' because they conform to what I expect of them. All I look *like* is other photographs of myself."[42] Barthes's distrust of photographic likeness is based on the fact that, as he sees it, the camera offers "the truth of lineage," whereas what he wants is what he identifies as the "irreducible" individual. When we speak of the subject of the photograph as being "like" someone, in other words, we are either condemning her or him to the repertoire of images—where, as Barthes wearily puts it, "no one is ever anything but the copy of a copy"—or imprisoning her or him in a social role.[43] This is, of course, what is really at stake in the question of what Nanda looks like. As Van points out, the important question is "[h]ow *will* she look, what will be thought of her, and what will she be able to do for herself? She's at the age when the whole thing—speaking of her appearance, her possible share of good looks—is still, in a manner, in a fog. But everything depends on it" (32). Everything depends upon it because without being considered beautiful Nanda cannot be married, and unless Nanda is married her mother's social circle—the success of which is dependent upon the kind of "good talk" inevitably compromised by the presence of a young unmarried girl—will collapse. Such a society has little use for Barthes's "irreducible" individual or, at least, does not believe Nanda to be one.

The reason Nanda's "possible share of good looks" remains unclear is because, as Van points out, London society recognizes only "staring, glaring, obvious, knockdown beauty, as plain as a poster on a wall, an advertisement for soap or whisky" (31). This is the kind of beauty possessed by the slow-witted Fanny Cashmore, a woman praised by Mrs. Brookenham for "show[ing] things . . . as some fine tourist region shows the placards in the fields and the posters on the rocks" (107). Fanny's face betrays her feelings the way a photograph advertises a tourist spot's features, her helplessness as open to scrutiny as the images Mr. Longdon handles in Van's apartment. Her constant self-exposure thus offers, in Mrs. Brookenham's appropriately photographic metaphor, "a flash of insight into history" (107) because the modern world is the world of advertisements, which demands "cash over the counter and letters ten feet high" (32).[44] In an age when the photograph has made everything visible, people must put themselves on permanent display simply to be seen. This condition of permanent exhibition not only renders the Native Americans James spies in Washington, D.C., exemplary figures of modernity, it also erases the differences between people that allow for the recognition of such resemblances in the first place.

Like Apollo

For James, as for Hawthorne, the present is bathed in what *The American Scene* describes as "the air of unmitigated publicity, publicity as a condition, as a doom, from which there could be no appeal" (11). And for James, as for Hawthorne, this publicity results in two contradictory yet complementary effects: an extension of the self that also represents, curiously enough, its extinction. Hence when the preface to *The Awkward Age* identifies publicity as the novel's principal subject, repeatedly promising—in a term obviously borrowed from photography—to treat the question of "Nanda's *exposure*" (8), James could be said to be directly confronting the problem of identity in the photographic age.[45] The challenge repeated photographic exposures pose to James's fiction is not the danger offered by the real thing to the project of representation—since, as we have seen, in the photographic age the real thing is always a matter of representation—but simply that when all the world can be seen, everything begins to look all the same, thereby disabling the comparison of one thing with another that makes representation possible in the first place.

This circularity provides *The Awkward Age* with both its theme and its structure. When, for example, Mr. Longdon, having ascertained from Van what people think of Nanda's looks, then attempts to find out from Van's friend, Mitchy, what people think of Van's looks, the answer he receives exposes the circularity of identity in the photographic age.

Mitchy casually refers to Van as Apollo, which provokes this surprised question from Mr. Longdon:

> "Do you think him like Apollo?"
>
> "The very image. Ask any of the women!"
>
> "But do *they* know—"
>
> "How Apollo must look?" Mitchy considered. "Why, the way it works is that it's just from Van's appearance they get the tip, and that then, don't you see? they've their term of comparison. Isn't that what you call a vicious circle? I borrow a little their vice." (85)

The exchange might well stand as emblematic of the novel as a whole. According to Mitchy's diagnosis of the "vicious circle" of societal logic, women think Van "the very image" of Apollo, a figure whose features they are able to conceive of only after having seen Van.[46] The joke is compounded by the fact that Apollo is the very type of beauty itself; our notion of what Apollo looks like, in other words, changes according to the taste of the day. The grounds for determining male beauty are thus as tautological as those for determining female beauty: Van is thought to personify the beautiful simply because modern society believes the beautiful to be personified by Van.[47]

Mitchy and Mr. Longdon's exposure of the circularity of typological thinking is closely bound up with the fact of photographic reproduction. During their conversation about Van's appearance Mitchy tells Mr. Longdon that he is delighted to finally "talk with some one who can meet one's conception of the really distinguished women of the past!" In response, Mr. Longdon pedantically asks him

> "Are you sure you've got one?"
>
> Mr. Mitchett brightly thought. "No. That must be just why I appeal to you. And it can't therefore be confirmation, can it?" he went on. "It must therefore be for the beautiful primary hint altogether." (83)

Mitchy's attempt to confirm his conception of what "the really distinguished women of the past" looked like by asking Mr. Longdon ends with him confessing that such a conception must be provided by his interlocutor. Here again verifying the terms of a comparison proves impossible because the terms in question turn out to be derived from one another. This is not because "ladies" no longer exist but because, according to Mitchy, there are now "quantities" of them. Such an idea, Mitchy admits, is somewhat ridiculous; as he tells Mr. Longdon, "[F]ancy the 'lady' in her millions" (83).

Mitchy's vision of the "'lady' in her millions" is only possible, of course, in the era of photography—it is surely not a coincidence, after all, that the "too many photographs" in Van's apartment whose existence Mr. Longdon bemoans are all of women:[48]

> "Little Nanda?—have you got *her*?" The old man was all eagerness.
>
> "She's over there beside the lamp—also a present from the original." . . .
>
> "Do they give their portraits now?"
>
> "Little girls—innocent lambs? Surely, to old friends. Didn't they in your time?"
>
> Mr. Longdon studied the portrait again; after which, with an exhalation of something between superiority and regret, "They never did to me," he replied.
>
> "Well, you can have all you want now!" Vanderbank laughed.
>
> His friend gave a slow, droll head-shake. "I don't want them 'now'!"
>
> "You could do with them, my dear sir, still," Vanderbank continued in the same manner, "every bit as *I* do!"
>
> "I'm sure you do nothing you oughtn't." Mr. Longdon kept the photograph and continued to look at it. (27)

Van collects photographs with the same avidity as Mrs. Brook's son, Harold, palms five-pound notes. Indeed it does not seem too outlandish to suggest that the endless circulation of money, books, and photographic images detailed in *The Awkward Age* has produced a society in which distinguishing one person from another is as difficult as distinguishing one mass-reproduced object from another. This is the logic behind Harold's defense of his continual borrowing of five-pound notes from the guests at his mother's salon. When Mrs. Brook asks Mitchy—Harold's most frequent victim—if her son ever gave him back the five pound note he lent to him, her friend simply replies, "But which, dear lady?" (273). Mitchy treats Mrs. Brook's reference as ambiguous because Harold's five pound notes—like Harold's social interactions—are interchangeable: they all look the same. And when Van goes on to characterize Harold as being "as clear and crisp and undefiled as a fresh five-pound note" (227), the vicious circle is complete.

According to Tzvetan Todorov's well-known account of the novel, this vicious circle is the sign of modern society's loss of faith in referentiality. Todorov argues that the novel traces language's degeneration from the age of Mr. Longdon—when words possessed constant and commonly agreed-upon referents—to the awkward age of the present—in which words seem indistinguishable from their referents.[49] The sign of this crisis of reference is something Todorov himself was the first to notice—the fact that James's novel is almost completely free of metaphor. Todorov's startling observation underscores the homogeneity of the world depicted in *The Awkward Age*, since in order for comparisons to be made between one thing and another there must first exist a sense of the differences *between* them. Yet if "good talk" is not made up of metaphors, of what is it made up? The delight Van, Mitchy, and Mrs. Brook take in recognizing and completing each other's references suggest that good talk is the giddy, circular process of seeing one's own perceptions reproduced in one's friends—of seeing oneself, in other words, reflected in others. Hence there is something fitting about the fact that, although the characters in *The Awkward Age* rarely compare one thing to another, they are repeatedly compared *to* each other: Van to Mr. Longdon, Mr. Longdon to Aggie, Aggie to Lord Petherton, Lord Petherton to Harold, and Nanda, needless to say, to Lady Julia.

Such is the extent of the equivalence between people in the photographic age that James's characters are not simply compared to one another, they end up turning into versions *of* one another. Van, for example, imagines that he is becoming more like Mr. Longdon, while

Nanda recalls both her "old-mannered" grandmother *and* her "modern" mother, leading Van to note "a resemblance of expression" (133) between Nanda and Mrs. Brook just as Mr. Longdon observes Nanda to have "just Lady Julia's expression" (31). The contagious nature of resemblance documented in *The Awkward Age* extends even to the age itself. According to Michal Ginsburg, the novel proposes that no era is ever completely itself, that "every point in time is both 'modern' and inhabited by the past, . . . making absolute revival impossible and every age awkward."[50] Ginsburg's sense that James's historical model mirrors the model of identity offered by the novel offers a direct challenge to Todorov's reading of *The Awkward Age*, which depends upon a clear break between the past—when reference was transparent—and the present—when reference is opaque; photography has, in other words, collapsed the very distinction upon which Todorov's argument relies.

That the awkward age depicted in the novel *is* a product of photography seems clear enough, notwithstanding Mr. Longdon's insistence that Nanda's resemblance to her grandmother is "far beyond any identity in the pictures" (95). Van, after all, directly attributes his friend's sense of the closeness between Nanda and Lady Julia to "the three or four photographs that . . . you must have noticed at Mrs. Brook's. These things must have compared themselves, for you, with my photograph in there of the grand-daughter" (95). In Van's oddly passive formulation, photographs of Lady Julia compare themselves in Mr. Longdon's imagination with photographs of Nanda. The seeming autonomy granted these images anticipates the extraordinary moment at the end of the novel, in which a photograph of Van becomes the standard by which the living person is measured. The last scene opens with Nanda rearranging her books and photos in preparation for her three gentleman callers—Van, Mitchy, and Mr. Longdon:

> The friends in the photographs in particular were highly prepared, with small intense faces each, that happened in every case to be turned to the door. The pair of eyes most dilated perhaps was that of old Van present under a polished

> glass and in a frame of gilt-edged morocco that spoke out, across the room, of Piccadilly and Christmas, and visibly widening his gaze at the opening of the door, the announcement of a name by a footman and the entrance of a gentleman remarkably like him save as the resemblance was, on the gentleman's part, flattered. (281)

Cleaned, arranged, and turned to the door, Nanda's photographs give every sign of being on the verge of coming to life, and the announcement of Van's name completes the transformation. Indeed, the narrative itself obeys this inverted logic: "Vanderbank had been in the room ten seconds before he showed that he had arrived to be kind. Kindness therefore becomes for us, by a quick turn of the glass that reflects the whole scene" (281). The narrator, it seems, takes his cue from the appearance of his characters, just as his characters take their cue from the appearance of their photographs. Nanda's photographs of her friends, like Van's photographs of *his* friends, have reversed not only the relationship between copy and original, but also the relationship between narrated and narrator. This explains why the novel ends with three almost identical set pieces between Nanda and her suitors, set pieces so similar that "[t]here would have been for a continuous spectator of these episodes an odd resemblance between the manner and all the movements that had followed his entrance and those that had accompanied the installation of his predecessor" (293–94). The form of *The Awkward Age* thus contradicts what J. Hillis Miller sees as Nanda's—and hence James's—"final judgment" on the awkward age in which she lives: "Everything's different from what it used to be" (310).[51] For all that is different, we might say, is that now everything is the same.

The Question of Resemblance

According to Gilles Deleuze, American literature threatens the very possibility of resemblance by opening up what he calls a "zone of indistinction," a place where similitude is replaced by "slippage, an extreme proximity, an absolute contiguity." This threat is articulated most distinctly in Bartleby's refusal to work as a copyist, an act that becomes emblematic of American literature's departure from the European mimetic model. "It is no longer a question of Mimesis," Deleuze contends, "but of becoming," by which he means the hollowing out within the system of mimetic differences of an "ever expanding zone of indiscernibility or indetermination."[52] James's account of the photographic production of American homogeneity in *The American Scene* can be seen as one version of this "zone of indistinction," Harold's five pound notes and Van and Nanda's photographic images in *The Awkward Age* as another. I want to suggest that James's late fiction takes place within this zone, a space never more clearly outlined than in James's unfinished and largely unread 1914 novel *The Sense of the Past.* The novel tells the story of an American writer who swaps places, bizarrely enough, with his namesake and ancestor, a man he encounters one night in the London house he has recently inherited. As the writer, Ralph, tells his one confidant, the U.S. Ambassador, "[T]he whole affair . . . was that we should exchange identities; an arrangement all the more easy that he bears an extraordinary resemblance to me and that on my first meeting him I even made the mistake of taking for a wondrous reflection—in a glass or wherever—of my own shape."[53] Ralph's account omits the fact that he believes his forerunner to have stepped not out of a mirror but out of a highly unusual painting—one that pictures its subject with his back turned to the artist. Despite dating from the early part of the nineteenth century, the painting behaves somewhat like a photographic snapshot in that it seems the product of chance, as if its subject were caught unprepared. The pose seems to rule out the possibility of likeness altogether, prompting James's hero to ask, somewhat bewilderedly, "who in the world had ever 'sat' . . . in a position that so trifled with the question of resemblance?" (74).

Trifling with resemblance is in fact the business of *The Sense of the Past.* For the exchange of identities between Ralph and his ancestor can be read not simply as a literalization of the close parallels between the two men but as a literalization of other, very different parallels: between subject and image, and, somewhat more surprisingly, between one national subject and another. What Ralph wants—and what leads him to abandon not simply America but his chance of marriage to the fiercely patriotic Aurora Coyne—is to encounter history itself: "He wanted the hour of the day at which this and that had happened, and the temperature and the weather and the sound, and yet more the stillness, from the street, and the exact look-out, with the corresponding look-in, through the window and the slant of the light on the walls of afternoons that had been. He wanted the unimaginable accidents, the little notes of truth for which the common lens of history . . . was not sufficiently fine" (48–49). Ralph's contempt for what he calls the "common lens of history" is somewhat contradicted by the photographic language with which he expresses his longing for the past: the slant of the light, the stillness of the street. Yet, rather than being the conduit to a world long gone, the camera is explicitly identified in the novel as representative of the modern world Ralph is so desperate to leave behind. On first entering his new London house, Ralph is struck by the paucity of signs left by his ancestor: "He would have been particularly grateful for a portrait; but though there were in the house other framed physiognomies these were things . . . of a different order of reference, an order in which the friendly photograph for instance, whether of the late tenant of the place or of any other subject, played no part. The friendly photograph had been with us for half a century, but there was nothing there to Ralph's vision so new as that" (47). Nine Mansfield Square is devoid of the family photographs that filled so many other homes at the turn of the century and is so by design. The house offers what Ralph calls "a different order of reference," an order for which he can find no better name than "Jacobean"—though, as the narrator dryly informs us, "it wasn't, even though he had thought but of the later James" (63).

As in the other James texts I have examined, the centrality of photography to *The Sense of the Past* has to do with questions of resemblance rather than questions of reference. For the self-referentiality involved in the invocation of "the later James" speaks not simply to the highly mannered treatment of Ralph's journey back to 1820—James takes nearly two hundred pages to describe one afternoon, slow going even by his standards—but to the curiously circular form of American identity. This circularity is reflected in the fact that, as we learn from James's "Notes for *The Sense of the Past*," the painting with which Ralph changes places ultimately proves to be of Ralph himself, painted during his time-traveling adventures. The question that inevitably follows—if the picture is of Ralph, then with whom does he change places?—is answerable only in terms of American identity. The importance of Ralph's nationality to *The Sense of the Past* is attested to by the fact that the "common ground" (100) between him and his ancestor is their shared Americanness; resemblances between Americans outweigh, it would seem, differences between historical periods.

Once again what looks like a comparison between two separate things—in this case Ralph and his ancestor—is ultimately revealed to be a comparison of one thing with itself. Clearly, then, James's strident objections to what he sees as the absolute homogeneity of American identity did not prevent him from repeatedly adopting this homogeneity as the subject matter for his fiction. According to James, the paradox of modernity is that the break it constitutes with the past consists of its unstoppable rendering of people, places, and periods as equivalent to one another; in treating the past as absolutely different from itself, the present collapses history into the simplicity of then and now—the empty structure of nostalgia. This is the thinking that motivates Ralph's sense of the past, thinking challenged by the form of the novel itself; it is the thinking behind Todorov's reading of *The Awkward Age*, a reading challenged by the form of *that* novel; and it is the thinking responsible for the following claim by the narrator of *The Aspern Papers*, the claim critics most often point to as proof of James's disdain for photography: "[W]hen Americans went abroad in 1820, there was something romantic, almost heroic in it, compared with the perpetual ferryings of the present hour, when photography and other conveniences have annihilated surprise."[54] That this final observation playfully recycles James's world-weary observation in his essay "Venice" that "there is notoriously nothing more to be said" about the city since "[e]very one has been there, and every one has brought back a collection of photographs" serves to make clear the irony of the narrator's judgment.[55] For although the narrator is right to suggest that photography has introduced a difference between past and present, he is wrong about what constitutes that difference—which is, tautologically, the belief that there *is* a difference.

What makes the modern age of transatlantic trips and tourist photography different from the past, that is, is its sense that it *is* different from the past, a self-consciousness which that past itself lacked—since it did not think of itself as absolutely different from *its* past. The narrator's suggestion that the camera has "annihilated surprise" makes this very point: "It was a society less awake than the coteries of today—in its ignorance of the wonderful chances, the opportunities of the early bird, with which its path was strewn—with tatters of old stuff and fragments of old crockery" (77). The reason the prephotographic past was less "awake" than the present was because it failed to think of *its* past as something to be collected and displayed. Thus the narrator is disappointed that the woman in possession of the fabled papers, Julianne Bordereau, "appeared not to have picked up or have inherited many objects of importance. There was no enviable *bric-a-brac*, with its provoking legend of cheapness, in the room in which I had seen her" (77). Were *he* to have lived alongside rather than after Aspern, the narrator's anachronistic logic implies, he *would* have picked up the "tatters of old stuff and fragments of old crockery" Julianne Bordereau seems to have ignored. The final irony, of course, is that the narrator's gift for antiquing is itself a product of photography. For it is the mass media, as Niklas Luhmann points out, which in ceaselessly describing the "new" makes something else "old," thus forcing us to revalue "certain kinds of being old: they become oldtimers, classics, antiques, about which we can generate ever-new information, prices, interpretations."[56] The narrator is thus only able to believe in the essential difference between a prephotographic past and a photographically produced present, in other words, because the camera has itself "annihilated" the difference between past and present that allowed people to see the ways in which they resembled—and thus also the ways in which they did in fact differ—from each other.

The Modern Sense of Type

The problem photography poses for James is that it erodes the differences between people that make identity possible—as in "The Real Thing," in which everyone can be represented by everyone else—the difference between things that make analogy possible—as in *The Awkward Age*, in which there is an almost complete absence of metaphor—and the difference between periods that makes history possible—as in *The Sense of the Past*, in which the early nineteenth century duplicates the early twentieth. James's texts both represent and are the result of the crisis of resemblance I am arguing is constitutive of the photographic age. Yet if James's world is one in which everyone is becoming like everyone else, how are we to account for the metaphorical extravagance of the late works, in which everything is constantly being compared *to* everything else? It often seems as if a novel such as *The Golden Bowl*, for example, is composed of nothing *but* metaphor; as Michael Levenson observes, characters and events in the late novels receive metaphorical characterizations "which [are] not dependent on, derived from, or referable to any independent non-metaphoric judgment, but are often the *only* form of representation which the fiction offers."[57] And what happens when the distinction between literal and figurative breaks down is that another even more fundamental distinction goes with it. Leo Bersani's "The Jamesian Lie" puts the case with typical lucidity: because knowledge in James's work is "a kind of seeing which can dispense with the objects of vision . . . the reality of a thing depends on the quality of the treatment it gets."[58] Metaphors, that is, are what make James's world.

If, as Bersani suggests, the world represented in late James is a function of the metaphors used to describe it, then we might say that things possess reality in the novel only because they are said to resemble something else. Being like something else, in other words, is what allows something to be itself. In *The Golden Bowl*, for example, the young American heiress Maggie Verver comes to understand that her marriage to the Italian Prince is under threat not through anything that is said or done but through the fact that she becomes aware that her husband and his lover—her friend Charlotte Stant—have begun to treat her in exactly the same manner. Maggie begins to notice "a kinship of expression in the two faces—in respect to which all she as yet professed to herself was that she had affected them . . . in the same way." Having discovered this analogy between the way the Prince looks at her and the way Charlotte does, Maggie begins to think of their faces as if they were miniature portraits of the kind found in a medallion: "The miniatures were back to back, but she saw them for ever face to face."[59] Maggie's analogy rewrites physiognomic logic so that the faces of those around her are no longer understood in terms of how closely they correspond to what their owner is feeling and thinking but in terms of how closely they correspond to the face of someone else. What matters is not what the Prince's and Charlotte's faces look like, in other words, but the fact that they both look the same.

What Nancy Armstrong identifies as physiognomy's "principle of resemblance" thus continues to operate in *The Golden Bowl*, with the difference that rather than the resemblance being between a face and its owner, it is between one face and another.[60] This is as true of the Ververs as it is of the Prince and Charlotte: Maggie's response to the knowledge that she is being "treated" by Charlotte and the Prince is to hide her suspicions behind the "blank, blurred surface" (415) of her face, her impassive expression itself a mirror image of her father Adam's smiling inscrutable countenance.[61] The Ververs might be said to resemble one another perfectly in their refusal ever to refer to the fact of the Prince and Charlotte's adultery. Indeed, it is precisely by continuing to resemble their earlier selves—that is, by refusing to acknowledge that anything has changed—that the Ververs avoid having to refer to the parlous state of their respective marriages, and thus are able to keep those marriages intact. Maggie's ability to turn her face into a kind of mask prevents the

Prince and Charlotte from being able to find out whether she knows of their affair, which prevents them from continuing to regard her as the innocent they set out to deceive.[62] The knowing, cynical, plotting Maggie of Book Two thus obeys the same logic, paradoxically, as the ingenuous, naïve, trusting Maggie of Book One. "To remain consistent," the narrator archly observes about Maggie before her marriage, "she had always been capable of cutting down more or less her prior term" (303). Yet this could also stand as a description of the way in which Maggie triumphs: by refusing to compare the present state of her marriage with what she had earlier believed it to be. It is only by cutting down her prior term, in other words, that Maggie remains consistent and thus keeps hold of the Prince.

One objection to this account of Maggie's consistency is that the very thing Maggie learns through the course of the novel is how to see her life in metaphorical terms—how, that is, to put two terms into relation with one another. In the novel's most famous image the dawning knowledge of her husband's adultery takes the fantastic form of the pagoda described in the beginning to Book Two, a Book in which Maggie compares herself to any number of things: a spaniel shaking itself dry, an actress in the floodlights, a shipwrecked swimmer. The more knowledge Maggie gathers about the extent of her husband's infidelity, the more she is struck by her own resemblance to all manner of beings, a process that—in typical Jamesian fashion—is itself expressed in metaphoric terms. In comparison with what she thinks of as her husband's situation—"something made for him beforehand by innumerable facts, facts largely of the sort known as historical"—Maggie's situation feels to her like an advanced "post . . . in the fashion of a settler or a trader in a new country; in the likeness even of some Indian squaw with a papoose on her back and barbarous beadwork to sell" (548–49). Such is the creative force of Maggie's metaphorical imagination that she can compare herself to both an American settler and an American Indian without regard to the differences between these two subjects. Paradoxically, Maggie's metaphors rest on precisely the "cutting down . . . [of] her prior term" that in Book One signaled her inability to recognize resemblance, so that she can see herself as two very different things simultaneously.

James's image could be said to enact the very historical erasure he identifies as archetypically American in *The American Scene*. This American blankness is in fact precisely what allows James, at the end of that book, to wipe his own slate clean, as it were, and imagine himself as one of the Native Americans he catches sight of on the steps of the Capitol. James wonders what he would think of the ceaseless erasure of the past visible from his train window "if I had been a beautiful red man with a tomahawk." James's rather pat answer is that *were* he an Indian brave, "I shouldn't have been seated by the great square of plate-glass through which the missionary Pullman appeared to invite me to admire the achievements it proclaimed" (341–42). The Native American is thus debarred from witnessing his own erasure. James's analogy, like the comparison of Maggie to both settler and squaw, equates the victims of history with their obituarist, and in so doing *repeats* the very process of historical erasure he laments. Both images can be seen as the logical endpoint to the crisis of resemblance I have been tracing throughout James's work, in which the English are best represented by Italians and aristocrats by cockneys. We saw in "The Real Thing" and *The Awkward Age* that a world in which everyone looks the same is a world in which metaphor is no longer possible; in *The Sense of the Past* and *The Aspern Papers* that this crisis of language is also a crisis of history. *The Golden Bowl* turns this situation inside out. For in a world in which identity is a product of the endless circulation of photographic images, not only do "types and histories," in the words of Patricia McKee, "become misleading signs . . . the signs of type [become] effects [that the subject] herself can reproduce."[63]

McKee has in mind Maggie's friend Fanny Assingham, whose ability to construct her own racial type becomes apparent during an extraordinary exchange of glances between herself and the Prince near the beginning of the novel. Facing each other across Fanny's sitting room, the pair, James's narrator observes, might "in their positively portentous stillness, have been . . . sitting for their photograph" (63):

> Type was there . . . in Mrs. Assingham's dark, neat head, on which the crisp black hair made waves so fine and so numerous that she looked even more in the fashion of the hour than she desired. Full of discriminations against the obvious, she had yet to accept a flagrant appearance and to make the best of misleading signs. Her richness of hue, her generous nose, her eyebrows marked like those of an actress . . . seemed to present her insistently as a daughter of the South, or still more of the East, a creature formed by hammocks and divans, fed upon sherbets and waited upon by slaves. She was in fact, however, neither a pampered Jewess nor a lazy Creole; New York had been, recordedly, her birthplace and "Europe" punctually her discipline. (64)

The American-born Fanny resembles, according to James's unpleasant description, both a Creole and a Jew. And it is this odd suggestiveness that makes Fanny look so modern, so "in the fashion of the hour." Like Maggie, Fanny can resemble very different subjects at the same time. But whereas for Maggie this resemblance is metaphorical—a figure for her own newfound figurative ability—for Fanny this is literally what she looks like. The very modern Fanny exemplifies the photographic identity I have been arguing is integral to James's compositional method. Fanny, we might say, *always* looks as if she is sitting for her photograph, because to sit for one's photograph is always, as James sees it, to enter into relations of resemblance, and thus to collapse the barrier between the literal and the metaphorical.

This photographic identity extends to the other participant in this exchange of glances. Maggie marries the Prince because she and her father consider him "a representative" Italian, despite the fact that he is described as looking "like a 'refined' Irishman" (44) and thinks and speaks in English. The Ververs' typological view of the Prince is of a piece with their insistent commodification of him. Maggie tells him that the Ververs regard him as "an object of beauty, an object of price" (49), a view the Prince thinks reduces him to "one of the little pieces that you unpack at the hotels and put out with the family photographs" (50). The Prince is himself guilty, however, of conceiving of his identity in typological terms, believing that he is "somehow full of his race" (51): "Its presence in him was like the consciousness of some inexpugnable scent in which his clothes, his whole person, his hands and the hair of his head, might have been steeped as in some chemical bath" (51–52). James's extraordinary, quasi-photographic image of the racialized Prince introduces the notion that Maggie's husband refers the particular behavior of his "single self" to the ready-made identity supplied by the racial type he purportedly resembles. The only form in which the Prince's "single self" can manifest itself, in other words, is through exactly resembling his forebears; as the narrator observes, "It had been happily said of his face that the figure thus appearing in the great frame was the ghost of some proud ancestor" (69–70). If Fanny creates her own typology, the Prince willingly embraces his, justifying his actions by appealing to stereotypes of Italian behavior in a manner reminiscent of James himself in his portrayal of Oronte in "The Real Thing." To be "ridden by a type" is thus seemingly inescapable, since it is the very essence of representation itself—no better figure for which can be imagined than the endlessly reproducible photograph.

Seeing Again

My insistence on reading questions of national and racial identity in *The Golden Bowl* through the discourse of photography is partly a response to James's own insistence on coupling photography with his theory of composition in the novel's preface. James discusses two closely related issues in the preface: first, the relationship between the photographic frontispieces of the *New York Edition* of his complete work and the actual texts themselves; second, the relationship between the first edition of his fiction and the revised version contained in the *New York Edition*. In turn, two aspects of James's account of his search for the frontispieces are particularly arresting: the fact that his depiction of these images—taken by the well-known photographer Alvin Langdon Coburn—seems to represent a rethinking of his earlier dismissal of the photograph; and the fact that his account of what he calls the "hunt" for these images reproduces the imagery of *The Golden Bowl* itself.[64]

James's oft-quoted dismissal of Coburn's images as "mere optical symbols or echoes, expressions of no particular thing in the text, but only of the type or idea of this or that thing" (xi) is the product—as he himself admits—of his anxious desire to avoid having his fictional images compared to Coburn's photographic ones. Yet in relegating the frontispieces to what he sees as the generality of the type, James reverses his earlier claim that photographs are characterized by particularity, that "[i]t is the detail alone that distinguishes one photograph from another." That James seems to have changed his mind about the relation between photography and typicality is evident from a letter he wrote to Coburn in 1906 detailing where to find the places in London, Paris, and Rome the novelist imagined serving as photographic frontispieces. "Look for a grand specimen of the *type*," James told the photographer, "as once you get the Type into your head, you will easily recognize specimens."[65] What accounts for this reversal in James's thinking? In order to answer this question I want to track as closely as possible what James describes as the "hunt for reproducible subjects" (x) he takes with Coburn through London—a hunt that ended with the taking of the image of the antique shop that forms the frontispiece for volume one of *The Golden Bowl*:

> The problem thus was thrilling, for though the small shop was but a shop of the mind, of the author's projected world, in which objects are primarily related to each other, and therefore not "taken from" a particular establishment anywhere, only an image distilled and intensified, as it were, from a drop of the essence of such establishments in general, our need (since the picture was . . . also completely to speak for itself) prescribed a concrete, independent, vivid instance. (xii)

Despite James's insistence that Coburn not supply "a concrete . . . instance" of this "shop of the mind," the fact that the photographer *was* somehow able to take a photograph of a shop acceptable to James suggests that the novelist is engaged in rethinking exactly what a photograph is. The photographed shop, like the Monarchs, is both typical—and thus "not 'taken from" a particular establishment"—*and* concrete; it is, in other words, the type made particular—a paradoxical formulation we have encountered before, in Francis Galton's discussion of the composite photograph.

James reproduces this formulation in his description of the frontispiece to volume II of *The Golden Bowl*, for which he wanted, he advised Coburn, "some generalised vision of Portland Place" (xii). In this case, of course, there was no need to go on a hunt through London, since James had a particular street in mind. The task instead was to wait until the particular place became typical of itself; as James puts it, "The thing was to induce the vision of Portland Place *to* generalise itself" (xii). What such inducement might look like—what, indeed, might the difference be between a particular image and a generalized one—remains unsaid, and can hardly be attained by looking at Coburn's image, as arresting as it turned out to be. The problem takes us back to the paradoxical account of typicality in "The Real Thing"; back to the "vicious circle" of representation in *The Awkward Age*; back to the contradiction between James's rejection of the American as *too* typical for representation and his repeated representations of precisely that typicality in *The Sense of the Past*. For, almost inevitably, James's disavowal of photography in the preface to *The Golden Bowl* ends up binding together the camera and his theory of composition.

James's sense of the need to eschew the particular—to eschew what he had earlier thought of *as* the photographic—is closely related to his need to assure himself that Coburn's photographs fail "to keep . . . anything like dramatic step with their suggestive matter" (x). This image is reproduced a few pages later, in James's account of the gap between his present style and his earlier one. Rereading his first novels, the novelist finds that what he calls his "exploring tread . . . [had] unlearned the old pace and found itself naturally falling into another, which might sometimes . . . agree with the original tracks, but might most often . . . break the surface in other[s]" (xiii–xiv). The path taken by James's metaphor is worth reexamining. First, the novelist describes the search for photographable subjects as a "hunt"; second, he characterizes the gap between these images and his own writing in terms of the gap between hunter and hunted; third, he describes the gap between his old imaginative vision and his new one as the difference between old and new tracks made by the same person.

How are we to account for the fact that the image James uses to characterize the gulf between photography and fiction is the very same image he uses to characterize the relationship between his former artistic vision and his current one? In order to answer this we need to go back to *The Golden Bowl* itself. Not by chance, the image of walking in one's own footsteps is one of the governing metaphors of the novel. The idea of covering one's tracks is introduced early on in the novel, in Fanny's advice to Charlotte to hide from Maggie the fact that she knew the Prince before Maggie ever met him—indeed, had had an affair with him. The most effective way for Charlotte to cover her tracks, Fanny suggests, would be to marry, and thus "make new tracks altogether" (101). What Charlotte actually wants, of course, is to take up with the Prince where they left off, a plan she puts into motion, ironically enough, by asking him to join her on a "little hunt" (116) for a wedding present for Maggie. Like James's hunt with Coburn, this expedition ends up at the obscure antique shop, the result of the pair having deliberately kept away from the usual course taken by Adam and Maggie: "It had therefore been easy to settle, as they walked, that the tracks of the Ververs, daughter's as well as father's, were to be avoided" (110). In a move that is rather more satisfying on the level of imagery than it is on the level of plot, Maggie later uncovers the relationship between her friend and her husband as a result of unwittingly stumbling upon the antique shop containing the golden bowl while taking a walk guided only by what she thinks of as the Prince's "noble and beautiful associations" (431) with the past. There follows what the narrator describes as "the most extraordinary incident of all" (480): the shopkeeper, having called on Maggie in order to tell her that the golden bowl he sold her is cracked, recognizes the photographic portraits of the Prince and Charlotte on her mantelpiece. Maggie imagines this moment as the golden bowl having "turned witness" (437), though we might just as easily say that photography has—the knowledge Maggie gains being repeatedly described as an "exposure" (441). The Prince, whose relationship with Charlotte is uncovered because of his photograph, is finally reduced to the photographic print he feared he would become all along.[66]

What possible connection could there be between photography and Maggie's relentless pursuit of the Prince and Charlotte? The question comes back, once again, to the problem of resemblance. One of the most striking aspects of the various hunts that make up *The Golden Bowl* is that they end up becoming confused with one another. Just as Adam "move[s] about in Amerigo's very footsteps" (379), so Maggie walks in Charlotte's, "track[ing] her stepmother . . . from room to room" (520–21). When Maggie follows Charlotte to the garden's "ancient rotunda" (538) in the very next chapter, we seem back where we started, with the image of Maggie discovering the pagoda that opens Book Two, or, further back still, with the description of the Prince's thoughts "guid[ing] his steps" (43) through London that opens Book One. What is happening is that the novel is beginning to retrace its own footsteps, to rediscover its own images. Something of the same principle is at work in James's account of revision. The novelist's insistence that he is engaged not in rewriting his former works but simply in rereading them, for example, imagines his earlier texts as mutable forms, transformed by rereading into the texts they should have been: "What rewriting might be was to remain—it has remained for me to this hour—a mystery. On the other hand the act of revision, the act of seeing it again, caused whatever I looked at on any page to flower before me as into the only terms that honourably expressed it" (xvi). The triumph of the *New York Edition* is that it allows James's texts to be the works they potentially always were. In the case of his last work *The Golden Bowl*, however, no revision is necessary, since the original text and James's vision of what that text should be *already* resemble each other to the highest possible degree. Rereading *The Golden Bowl* is thus exactly the same as writing it. The perfect symmetry of original and revised text in turn mirrors the form of the novel itself, which resolves the epistemological problem it sets itself precisely by bringing its two volumes into perfect correspondence. Mitchy's "vicious circle" is no longer a vice so much as a compositional method.

Rereading his early fiction, James feels his former imaginative vision to be out of step with what he sees now; rereading *The Golden Bowl*, in contrast, the novelist feels as if "the march of my present attention coincides sufficiently with the march of my original expression . . . [so that] [i]nto his very footprints the responsive, the imaginative steps of the docile reader that I consentingly become for him all comfortably sink" (xii–xiii). James's figure traces a progression from his earlier work—whose relation to his current vision is as distant as that between Coburn's photographs and the texts they illustrate—to his most recent—whose relation to his current vision is as close as that between Book One and Book Two of *The Golden Bowl.* The footsteps chart what we might call a relationship of resemblance, a relationship that is particularly striking in that, as J. Hillis Miller observes, it "is not that what he sees now fits so well with what he wrote then but that what he sees now was so exactly anticipated by what he wrote then."[67] The validity of his work depends, in other words, on how closely it corresponds to his present vision, not on how successfully it realized his past ambitions. The model of history decried in *The American Scene* and depicted in *The Sense of the Past*—a model in which past and present reproduce one another—turns out to furnish the basis for James's late style.

The irony that James should end up defining his aesthetic in the very terms he uses to denounce modern American society is perhaps an inevitable one, given that his willingness to disregard the difference between the literal and the metaphorical gives these terms an extraordinary elasticity. But the correspondences between James's notion of rereading—the central term in his account of his own writing practice—and the discourses of photography and typology—which, I have been arguing throughout this book, should be seen as inseparable—go far beyond this. According to James's idiosyncratic definition, rereading is a matter of seeing something for a second time as if you were seeing it for the first time. It is thus structurally analogous both to the photograph—which offers a vision of something that has already been seen—and to the stereotype—which offers an account of the "already read."[68] No wonder, then, that James's fiction should depend on these two discourses quite so heavily, or that the challenge posed by the camera and by the changing face of turn-of-the-century America should pose such a dilemma for James's interest in resemblance.

Yet if we follow the logic of James's imagery to its end, what we find is that this interest in seeing the world in terms of resemblance is ultimately inseparable from eliminating resemblance altogether—a project later taken up by James's great disciple, Gertrude Stein.[69] James's final attempt to explain what he means by "re-reading" imagines himself seeing the writer he has now become perfectly anticipated by the man he once was, a vision of his past self "superimposed on my own as an image in cut paper is applied to a sharp shadow on a wall, match[ing], at every point, without excess or deficiency" (xiii).[70] The crisis of resemblance James associates with American identity—a crisis in which, thanks to photography, every period and everyone looks the same—is, in the last resort, the very principle of his own writing, in which every moment cannot not be the same, and thus every moment matches every other.

It is possible to record the historical physiognomic image of a whole generation and . . . to make that image speak in photographs.
AUGUST SANDER, *Face of Our Time*

CHAPTER THREE

Vanishing Race

Faulkner's Photographic Face

WHAT IS THE role of photography in determining who people are in a society in which identity is fundamentally determined by blood? This question is surprisingly central, this chapter argues, to William Faulkner's obsessive inventory of racial identity in the Jim Crow South. As Walter Benn Michaels points out, the law that governed that society—the one-drop rule—reduced "all the things that make [race] visible . . . to mere representations of a racial identity located elsewhere. At the same time, however, because race is invisible and cannot be reduced to any of its representations, any and everything can be understood as a representation of it. It is only because the thing itself is invisible that everything can be imagined as a way of seeing it."[1] Under the rule of Jim Crow, race is nowhere and everywhere at the same time. This formulation accurately describes the world depicted in Faulkner's fiction, in which the invisibility of race—the "blackness" of Joe Christmas and Charles Bon being a matter of blood rather than skin color—is precisely what makes it all-inclusive. Every act in Faulkner's novels, it sometimes seems, is determined by whether the character has "white" or "black" blood. Hence Faulkner's obsession with miscegenation, according to Michaels, should be seen not as a commitment to racial union, as critics have often suggested, but as a commitment to racial difference.[2] But because this difference cannot be seen, it can only be represented metaphorically—that is, through relations of likeness. As we shall see, the representation of racial difference in Faulkner is both a metaphor that is treated as literal fact, and a literal fact that is treated as metaphor.

According to Samira Kawash, the "problem at the heart of the modern idea of race . . . is that legal, physical, and social identities might fail to coincide, leaving open the gaping question of where the truth of race in fact resides."[3] Faulkner's fiction attempts to answer this question by locating race in a series of illusory yet imaginable spaces. These spaces, which include the compound image formed by a stereopticon viewer (in *Go Down, Moses*), the unlocatable moment when the still projected at a certain speed becomes the moving film (in *Light in August*), and the composite photograph formed by an image of the blank faces of an entire family (in *Absalom, Absalom!*), are persistently drawn from the discourse of photography. Yet not only are these images not exactly photographs, obviously enough, they also are not exactly ekphrastic descriptions of photographs. All three, rather, are both examples of ekphrasis—language's attempt to approximate the visible—and emblematic of ekphrasis's impossibility. This chapter proposes that this impossibility is itself a figure for Faulkner's necessarily doomed attempt to make race visible in the era of the one-drop rule—in other words, that ekphrasis's impossibility is precisely what makes it the perfect vehicle for Faulkner's fiction.

Because race in the era of the one-drop rule was invisible, photography's role in identifying racial identity in the Jim Crow South was necessarily reduced to confirmation rather than revelation. Indeed this is true of all modes of documentation; as Thadious Davis points out, "No one sensory test is capable of validating the existence of the Negro; even sight has traditionally been insufficient." This is why, she suggests, "the Negro [is] the metaphorical embodiment of all that is invisible in southern life."[4] I argue that the invisibility of race in Faulkner's fiction can be seen, paradoxically, in the blank faces of his characters, most notably those of the Sutpen family in his 1936 novel *Absalom, Absalom!* The Sutpens' shared absence of expression operates, ironically enough, as proof of their shared genealogy; like the faces of Colonel and Judge Pyncheon in *The House of the Seven Gables*, and of the Prince and Charlotte in *The Golden Bowl*, the faces of Faulkner's characters refer to one another rather than to their subject. As I see it, these faces no longer bear the traces of history precisely so that they might better register that history, which Faulkner imagines as one of invisibility, indeterminacy, and loss.

The blankness of what Faulkner repeatedly refers to as "the Sutpen face" both sets its subjects apart from society and makes them a synecdoche for that society, since southern history—like Henry James's America of thirty years before—is itself a record of constant erasure. That Faulkner thought this process of erasure was a product *of* photography is clear from his 1955 essay "On Privacy," which complains that the camera inevitably reduced its subjects "to one more identityless integer in that identityless anonymous unprivacied mass which seems to be our goal."[5] Like Hawthorne and James before him, Faulkner insists that the more visible the subject becomes, the more difficult it proves to distinguish one subject from another.[6] The emptiness of so many of the faces in Faulkner's fiction resembles the masklike faces of early photography described by Hawthorne and the blank faces of the American businessman described by James. Yet what makes Faulkner's account of the photographed face different from Hawthorne and James is his insistence that the crisis of resemblance brought on by the camera—a crisis in which everyone turns themselves into images *of* themselves and thus becomes indistinguishable from everyone else—is ultimately a crisis not of representation but of identity—that is, race.

In what follows, I track the various appearances of photographic imagery across a range of Faulkner's texts.[7] Faulkner's various descriptions of photographs, repeated use of photographic terms, and elaborate photographic metaphors operate as a moving record of loss (in his early stories "Beyond" and "The Leg"); as a means of collapsing the differences between periods, places, and people (in the first version of *Sanctuary* and in "The Bear"); and as a way of detailing the erasure of the subject itself (in *Light in August*). My ultimate focus, however, is on *Absalom, Absalom!*, and specifically on the four daguerreotypes seen, handled, alluded to, or imagined by the novel's four narrators. What these photographs actually show differs according to which narrator is speaking, but the images themselves can be enumerated as follows: the image of Bon seen by Rosa in Judith's room; the image of Judith given to Bon by his fiancée; the image of Bon's wife and child found on his dead body (a photograph that replaces the one of Judith); the two images of the Sutpen family described by Quentin (that might well be one image described in two different ways). I will be arguing that the repeated references to these images in *Absalom, Absalom!* should be read not as evidence that Faulkner was interested in the photograph as a technology for restoring the past but as evidence that he was interested in the camera's ability to depict the ways in which the past is lost. Jean-Paul Sartre's famous comparison of Faulkner's vision to "that of a man sitting in an open car and looking backward" thus gets Faulkner's vision of history backward, as it were.[8] For rather than watching the wreckage of the past pile up behind them in the manner of Benjamin's angel of history, Faulkner's characters, we might say, look on as history vanishes in front of them.

Invisible Inscriptions

The reason Faulkner consistently articulates his conceptions of history and identity through the figure of the photograph is closely bound up with the camera's association with referentiality. According to Roland

Barthes, "Reference . . . is the founding order of Photography."[9] Fiction, however, deals not in reference but in representation; even its most explicit attempts to render the visual world—the rhetorical trope of ekphrasis—are in the end nothing more than, as Murray Krieger puts it, the "illusionary representation of the unrepresentable."[10] Photographic ekphrasis is different from other forms, however, in that it explicitly draws attention to its own impossibility; no trope, then, could be more appropriate for the task of depicting the past as a record of what cannot be seen. Hence there is something photographic—in Faulkner's terms—about the fact that his protagonists typically imagine the world as an enormous repository for a history that is sensed rather than seen. Both the air and the earth of Yoknapatawpha record the lives lived in and on them in the form of marks that are invisible but somehow perceptible—like the one-drop rule's conception of race itself. "What is it?" Shreve asks Quentin about the South, "something you live and breathe in like air?" his question neatly illustrating both the inescapability and the intangibility of the past in Faulkner's world.[11]

Faulkner's insistence on the irretrievability of the past distinguishes *Absalom, Absalom!* from the glut of historical novels dealing with the South published in the mid-1930s. Characterized by a determination to reproduce every detail of antebellum life, novels such as Margaret Mitchell's 1936 *Gone with the Wind* were inevitably compared to the camera.[12] Faulkner, needless to say, despised such fiction, advising his publisher Random House that detailed accounts of "hoop skirts and plug hats" formed no part of his plan for *Absalom, Absalom!* His aim, he proposed, was to represent the ways history is told rather than that history itself, a method that would "get more out of the story itself than a historical novel would."[13] Yet hoop skirts and plug hats are not entirely absent from Faulkner's novel. For in order to represent the history of the South accurately, Faulkner must represent how that history had been told; he must depict, that is, the very nostalgia he was determined to avoid. And one of the principal ways that history has been told is through photography. "History," according to Georg Lukács, "vanishes in the presence of too many images."[14] For Faulkner, however, this vanishing *is* history: the record of the ways our attempts to preserve the past—for instance, by photographing it—inevitably erase it from view.

Rather than attempt to emulate the camera, Faulkner's task in *Absalom, Absalom!* was thus to depict the role played by the camera in the South's historical imagination. History, as Faulkner sees it, is a matter not simply of a series of things to be described or events to be related but of a sense of the relation between what happened and what was recorded. In place of a photographic rendering of the past, Faulkner's work depicts how photography determines the way that people experience the past. That the past is a product of rather than simply recorded by the camera explains why so many of the metaphors in *Absalom, Absalom!* are borrowed from photography. Mr. Compson's compelling account of Henry and Bon's trip to New Orleans, for example, imagines Bon taking "the innocent and negative plate of Henry's provincial soul and intellect and expos[ing] it gradually toward the picture which he desired it to retain, accept" (87). The picture to which Henry is being exposed is that of Bon's wife and child, a family in whose existence he is anxious not to believe—Bon being engaged to his sister, Judith. Yet even seeing Bon's family with his own eyes is not enough to convince Henry of their existence. Mr. Compson compares the trip to a "dialogue without words . . . fix[ing] and then remov[ing] without obliterating one line the picture, this background, leaving the background, the plate prepared and innocent again" (88). The metaphor of a photograph being as reusable as language itself is not without some historical justification—because of expense, daguerreotype plates were often used more than once in the early days of photography. Yet the notion of a reusable photograph seems to undermine the very point of the camera. Mr. Compson's trope imagines photography, paradoxically, as a technology for both preserving *and* erasing the past. Indeed the figure is itself repeated three or four times, so as to "resolve and become fixed" (88) in the reader's own mind as much as in Henry's: "exposures brief, so brief as to be cryptic, almost staccato, the plate unaware of what the complete picture would show, scarce-seen yet ineradicable" (88). In a manner emblematic of the working of the novel as a whole, Faulkner's metaphor deliberately confuses Henry's exposure *to* an image with the photographic exposure *of* an image.

Mr. Compson's contradictory formulation, whereby something is removed without being erased, can be extended to the entire narrative structure of *Absalom, Absalom!* The novel's four narrators continually revise and reimagine what has already been told, the effect on the reader being both to erase *and* to "fix" what has come before. We believe everything we are told in *Absalom, Absalom!*—rather like the way we believe everything we see in *Rashomon*—because we have no license to do otherwise. But believing everything is merely another name, of course, for believing nothing. Rosa's avowed aim in telling Quentin her story, to "*efface his* [Sutpen's] *name and lineage from the earth*" (6) is thus consistent with Mr. Compson's photographic metaphor, which suggests that to document a life is also to destroy it.[15] Rosa's unusual choice of terms to describe this reverse process—effacement—is particularly telling. *Absalom, Absalom!*, we might say, directly challenges Ralph Waldo Emerson's dictum "[e]very act of man inscribes itself in the memories of its fellows, and in his own manners and face," since for Faulkner history is a record of invisible inscriptions.[16] This is not to suggest that the face is any less revealing for Faulkner than it is for Emerson. Indeed the face acts as the agent of revelation in Faulkner's history of the Sutpen family, a role that, in Faulkner's first account of the Sutpens—the 1931 short story "Evangeline"—was previously allotted to photography. Paradoxically, however, what aligns the faces in Faulkner's work with his conception of the camera is that both physiognomy and photography erase rather than retain the marks experience leaves upon them.[17] Both face and photograph, that is, are the record of a vanishing.

Absence as Presence

"Like the photograph that tells us what is no longer before us," Eduardo Cadava suggests in his study of the work of Walter Benjamin, historical truth appears "in the traces of what is no longer present."[18] Conceiving of the photograph in this way allows us to think of Faulkner's model of history as photographic, in the sense that his work depicts the past as endlessly returning in the form of its own absence. The world in Faulkner's fiction is a kind of photographic plate, operating as a record of what has been lost. This insistence on the camera's paradoxical relationship to history runs throughout Faulkner's work. In the 1933 story "Beyond," for example, the narrator spends his time searching for his dead child in the afterlife guided only by a photograph of his son on horseback: "I have used this picture as a bookmark in the printed volumes where his and my ancestry can be followed for ten generations in our American annals, so that as the pages progressed it would be as though with my own eyes I watched him ride in the flesh down the long road which his blood and bone had traveled before it became his."[19] Faulkner depicts photography here as a sort of genealogical guide, one that affirms the relationship between the generations in a more immediate way than the names of the narrator's ancestors. The eye of the narrator moving down the page imitates the movement of the boy on the horse, a movement that itself suggests the metaphor of the family moving forward through history. The photograph, however, bears witness not to the enduring presence of the narrator's son but to his enduring absence; by picturing what is not present, the photograph continually reminds the narrator of what he has lost. Hence what the narrator fears most is the possibility of *finding* his son in the afterlife: "If I could believe that I shall see and touch him again, I shall not have lost him, and if I have not lost him, I shall never have had a son. Because I am I through bereavement and because of it" (796). All that remains of his son is loss, a loss announced—preserved, as it were—by the photograph. Hence what the narrator values about the photograph of his son is precisely its inadequacy as a substitute, since looking at the image serves only to remind the narrator of his son's death. Loss is the only thing the narrator has left and is thus what he wants to keep.

Faulkner's depiction of the photograph as a kind of certificate of loss anticipates Maurice Blanchot's suggestion that the photograph manifests "absence-as-presence." Barthes glosses this paradoxical formulation in *Camera Lucida* as follows: because the photograph shows us something that "*has been there*," the subject pictured in the image is, in a sense, retrievable only in the form of its absence.[20] Photography is thus a technology of loss, which makes it ideally suited to Faulkner's work, since according to John T. Matthews, the novelist conceived of writing precisely in terms of loss. Matthews maintains that for Faulkner, "[w]riting does not respond to loss, it initiates it; writing itself is as much a kind of loss as it is a kind of compensation."[21] Matthews bases his reading upon Faulkner's account of the "ecstasy" brought on by writing about Caddy climbing the pear tree in *The Sound and the Fury*, "the only thing in literature," the novelist claimed, "that would move me very much." All his work since, Faulkner maintained, was nothing but a failed attempt to "recapture that first ecstasy."[22] Yet because the episode of Caddy climbing the tree is itself a narrative of loss—what she sees at the top, her dead grandmother laid out in an upstairs bedroom, marks the end of Caddy's innocence—the achievement of "ecstasy" is, as Matthews points out, also its loss. In other words, the ecstasy of writing is an attempt to recapture not so much what is lost as the moment of loss itself. It is this that allows us to call Faulkner's writing "photographic."

Faulkner's interest in the relation between loss and photography can be traced back to one of his earliest stories, "The Leg." Written in 1925, though not published until nine years later, the story relates the hallucinations of an American soldier recovering in hospital after losing his leg in World War I. Like Melville's Ahab, the narrator is driven mad by the sensation that his missing limb is still attached to his body: "[T]he gap was still there, and sometimes at night, isolated by invisibility, it would become filled with the immensity of darkness and silence" (833). While feverish, he talks to the ghost of his dead friend George, warning his pal that the missing leg is still alive and pleading with him to kill it. A few months later, long after these hallucinations have ceased, the narrator is attacked out of the blue by a former acquaintance who is convinced that the narrator has seduced his sister, Everbe. Proof of this is furnished by a photograph of the narrator

> dated in Abington in June of the summer just past. At that time I was lying in the hospital talking to George, and I sat quite still in the blankets, looking at the photograph, because it was my own face that looked back at me. It had a quality that was not mine: a quality vicious and outrageous and unappalled and beneath it was written in a bold sprawling hand like that of a child: "To Everbe Corinthia" followed by an unprintable phrase, yet it was my own face, and I sat holding the picture quietly in my hand while the candle flame stood high and steady above the wick and on the wall my huddled shadow held the motionless photograph. (841–42)

The photograph confronts Faulkner's narrator with irrefutable evidence that he is guilty of a crime he believes he could not possibly have committed.

The contradictory evidence supplied by the photograph suggests that either the narrator or his attacker must be mistaken, or perhaps mad. Yet this reading seems untrue to the logic of Faulkner's story—the narrator's hallucinations that his amputated leg is walking around on the battlefield, after all, prove him to be no stranger to the notion that a body could be in two places at once. The need to account for the ambiguity of the narrator's history leads to a straightforward symbolic reading, in which the horrors he has seen on the battlefield so dissociate the narrator from his own experience that he struggles to recognize his photographed face as his own. Faulkner's story could thus be said to compare the temporal dislocation suffered by many veterans—whose past experience often seems more real to them than the present moment—with the experience of alienation felt by the subject confronted with his or her photographic image. The narrator is unable to establish which past belongs to him: his own somewhat hazy memory of lying semiconscious in a hospital bed—a memory that includes, disturbingly, a series of strange dreams vaguely corresponding to the events suggested by the photograph—or the photographic record of his attendance at the Abington fair. He is thus severed from his own history, a dislocation signaled by the description of the photograph as being held by his "huddled shadow." Such an experience is in keeping with what Barthes calls the temporal dislocation provoked by the photograph, whose subject can be said to exist in two times and therefore two places at once. According to Barthes, photography's referent "is not the same as the referent of other systems of representation" because the photographic referent is a "*necessarily* real thing"; as he puts it, "[i]n Photography I can never deny that *the thing has been there*."[23] This is precisely the dilemma faced by Faulkner's narrator: how to deny the undeniable—his own photographed image.

If in "The Leg" a photograph suggests that someone could be in two places at the same time, in the original 1929 version of Faulkner's novel *Sanctuary* a photograph opens up the possibility that two different people in two different places could have the same experience.[24] Horace Benbow, the novel's protagonist, is so haunted by a photograph of his stepdaughter, Little Belle, that one night he finds himself "driven . . . from bed to walk four and three quarter miles in the darkness" in order to look at it.[25] The reason for Horace's anxiety is his sense of the helplessness of the photographed subject—the fact that someone's image can be seen by anyone, at any time, for any purpose. In circulating beyond the reach of its subject, the photograph offers the possibility of a narrative outside of his or her control. What disgusts Horace is both his own desire and Little Belle's availability as an object for that desire—he is able to appropriate the photograph simply by removing it from his frame and stuffing it into his pocket. Detaching Little Belle's photograph from its frame does, however, leave a narrow imprint around the edge of the image, rendering the portrait both a material witness to the past—to the moment Little Belle stepped before the camera—*and* to the present—to the various ways in which the image intersects with the lives of its observers. Even the absence-as-presence of the photographic image offers its subjects no sanctuary.

The careful record of what happens to Little Belle's photographic image emphasizes what I see as the point of the novel: that the horrific violence depicted in *Sanctuary* is never simply a matter of who does what to whom but extends to all those who look at, recount, listen to, or read about the events depicted. Faulkner's decision to excise almost all the references to Horace's photograph of Little Belle in the substantially revised 1931 edition of the novel thus needs to be read as evidence not of the irrelevance of photography to the novel, but of its centrality. His decision to replace the fragmented narrative of the original with a linear, largely straightforward account of the rape of Temple Drake makes for a more readable novel but also for a cheaper and more sensationalist one. The grammatical slippages of the 1929 version—multiple subjects, indistinct objects, ambiguous pronouns—prevent the reader from isolating the horrific events the way he or she can in the later one. The confusion of actor and observer that provides the very subject of the novel—Popeye's rape of Temple with a corncob, which conflates acting with observing—thus extends to the viewing of the photographic image. The centrality of photography to the original novel's insistence that to read about horrific events is also to participate vicariously in them demands that Faulkner remove the scenes involving Little Belle's photograph from the 1931 edition, which deliberately distances its readers from the violence it takes such pleasure in representing. Faulkner turns a publishing failure into a success, but at the cost of shielding the reader from the horrific violence described in the novel.

Gazing at the photograph of his stepdaughter, the Horace of the 1929 edition finds that his own feelings of sexual attraction converge with Popeye's desire for Temple. Once back home Horace tramps back and forth in front of the photograph, the shadow he throws upon "the glossy surface of the portrait" alternately hiding and revealing Little Belle's "sweet, soft, secret face" (144). What agitates Faulkner's hero is the fact that the helplessness of the image reminds him of Temple's helplessness at the hands of Popeye:

> Then he was looking at the photograph, holding it in his hands. Enclosed by the narrow imprint of the missing frame Little Belle's face dreamed with that

> quality of sweet chiaroscuro. Communicated to the cardboard by some quality of light or perhaps by some infinitesimal movement of his hands, his own breathing, the face appeared to breathe in his palms . . . the small face seemed to swoon in a voluptuous languor, leaving upon his eye a soft and fading aftermath of invitation and voluptuous promise and secret affirmation. (220)

Horace's desire brings Little Belle's photograph to life, thereby mixing up not only past and present but also his stepdaughter with Temple Drake and, ultimately, Horace himself with Popeye. Still holding the photograph, Horace suddenly "plunged forward and struck the lavatory and leaned upon his braced arms while the shucks set up a terrific uproar beneath her thighs" (220). In a remarkable grammatical shift, Horace and Popeye become the same subject, exchanging places in exactly the same way they exchange glances earlier in the novel. The temporal confusion wrought by the absence-as-presence of the photograph leads to Horace being unable to separate his body from the image of Little Belle or from his imagining of Popeye. The scene rewrites the confrontation between the narrator and his "vicious and outrageous and unappalled" photographic image at the end of "The Leg" by extending photography's reach to society as a whole, which, in ceaselessly recording itself, turns every moment into an image to be circulated, exchanged, and observed.

The Stereopticon Whole

The camera in Faulkner's work functions as a technology not for recording and remembering but for binding together past and present, observer and observed. The resulting crisis is one in which nothing can be kept distinct, a crisis of differentiation as much as of representation. Framing the question in this way allows us to see the connection between Faulkner's repeated invocation of photography and his obsession with racial difference. For what photography offers him is not a means of picturing the subject so as to make his or her racial identity visible but rather a device for imagining a space traversed by different temporalities, localities, even epistemologies. This space represents his attempt to address what Kawash calls "the gaping question" opened up by Jim Crow: "where the truth of race in fact resides." Faulkner provides an unlikely but compelling answer to this question: the truth of race can be located in what the narrator of Herman Melville's *Billy Budd* calls "the deadly space between"—between different histories ("truth" in Faulkner is a matter of the convergence of several, often contradictory accounts); between physical states (characters are repeatedly caught between sleeping and waking, running and standing still); even between identities (not only the legally distinct if endlessly breached space between black and white but also the literal differentiation between one subject and another).[26]

Faulkner's 1940 story "The Bear" offers perhaps the clearest view of the first of these spaces, that formed by the convergence of a number of competing stories. "The Bear" tells the story of Ike McCaslin's realization of his kinship with the slaves formerly owned by his family. Ike comes to this knowledge through piecing together the relation between incest and property told in the accounting ledgers kept by his father, Buck, and his uncle, Buddy. The fact that Ike's family's financial records are in a very real sense also family trees is expressed through a somewhat astonishing photographic metaphor. Responding to Ike's assertion that both their family and the nation's history have been cursed by slavery, Ike's cousin, Carothers McCaslin "Cass" Edmonds "merely lifted one hand, not even speaking and not even pointing toward the ledgers: so that, as the stereopticon condenses into one instantaneous field the myriad minutia of its scope, so did that slight and rapid gesture establish in the small cramped and cluttered twilight room not only the ledgers but the whole plantation in its mazed and intricate entirety."[27] Cass's gesture encompasses the entire history that has driven Ike to repudiate his right to the McCaslin plantation. The room in which the young men speak is transformed into a stereopticon viewer, suturing times and places together to form what Ike refers to moments later as "the stereopticon whole" (285).

Faulkner's reference to a stereopticon represents a historically precise visual rendering of McCaslin family history. The technology was a late nineteenth-century variation on the popular parlor device the stereoscope; whereas the stereoscope offers its viewer the illusion that they were looking at a three-dimensional image by positioning two almost identical photographs side by side within a specially designed viewer, the stereopticon—which we have already encountered in Stephen Crane's short story "The Five White Mice"—projects images from two or more magic lanterns onto a screen to form one composite image. Both stereoscope and stereopticon challenge photographic referentiality by offering the viewer an image of something that does not actually exist: a three-dimensional view of a flat surface in one, a compound view of two or more discrete images in the other. The stereoscope's assault on referentiality has been expertly diagnosed by Jonathan Crary's *Techniques of the Observer*, which argues that the device came to supplant the camera obscura as the dominant model for visuality. Because the three-dimensional image seen by the viewer in the stereoscope was a psychological creation, Crary suggests that "[i]t shattered the *scenic* relationship between viewer and object that was intrinsic to the fundamentally theatrical setup of the camera obscura." Whereas the camera obscura both situated its viewer in a material space and presented its viewer with an actual image, the stereoscope only offered illusion. Yet this illusion, paradoxically, appeared more realistic, its three-dimensional space seeming to possess an "immediate, apparent *tangibility*."[28] As Oliver Wendell Holmes's ecstatic 1861 celebration of the medium "The Stereoscope and the Stereograph" observed, "[T]here is such a frightful amount of detail, that we have the same sense of infinite complexity which Nature gives us."[29]

Following Faulkner's lead, I want to suggest that the stereoscope and the stereopticon offer compelling models for "The Bear," which repeatedly brings two narratives together so as to form a "stereopticon whole." *Go Down, Moses* is in fact made up of a whole series of stereopticon-like doublings. In the story "Was," for example, Miss Sophonsiba's insistence on calling her brother's plantation by a different name makes it "sound as if she and Mr. Hubert owned two separate plantations covering the same area of ground, one on top of the other" (9). Miss Sophonsiba's stubborn refusal to accept that her plantation is named after her brother and not after Warwick, the English town she claims her family is from, offers a clue to understanding the repeated doublings of the text. For in the eyes of the owner and in the eyes of the slave the same piece of ground is in fact two different places, as if one were laid on top of the other. For the master, the land spells property; for slaves, it denotes their own status *as* property. This double discourse is inscribed in the pages of the ledger that Ike reads to his cousin Cass, which serves as a record of both financial transactions and family history on the plantation—appropriately enough perhaps for a system that treats human beings as goods to be bought and sold: "*Eunice Bought by Father in New Orleans 1807 $650. dolars. Marrid to Thucydus 1809 Drownd in Crick Cristmas Day 1832*" (255). Ike's father and uncle, the twins Buck and Buddy, write alternate entries, communicating with each other, Ike suggests, almost solely through the ledger: "the twins who were identical even in their handwriting, unless you had specimens side by side to compare, and even when both hands appeared on the same page (as often happened, as if, long since past any oral intercourse, they had used the diurnally advancing pages to conduct the unavoidable business" (251–52). The twins record a series of exchanges of money for people—either the cash paid for a slave or how much time the slave owes them. But the human price of this grotesque economy is equally visible, recorded in the various deaths recounted in the ledger: Eunice drowns herself on Christmas Day 1832; her daughter, Tomasina, dies giving birth to Tomey's Turl in June 1833. The reason Eunice commits suicide (a reason Ike realizes he has known all along) is because his grandfather is not only the father of Tomasina but also of Tomey's Turl. This horrifying fact is obliquely signaled by the fact that Ike's father, Buck, records Eunice's suicide in the ledger twice, his second entry written in response to his brother's incredulity:

June 21th 1833 Drownd herself

and the first [handwriting]:

23 Jun 1833 Who in hell ever heard of a niger drownding him self

and the second, unhurried, with a complete finality; the two identical entries might have been made with a rubber stamp save for the date

Aug 13th 1833 Drownd herself (256).

The ledger's double entries—Faulkner's use of the terms "the first . . . and the second" refers both to the almost identical handwriting of the two brothers and to the almost identical entries—reproduce the doublings of Ike's incestuous family history. Under the insane logic of the slave system, which treated a human being as a thing, rape was an economical as well as a sexual act: Carothers McCaslin first rapes his slave and increases his property, then rapes his slave daughter and further increases his property. The horror of this history turns the language of the ledger in upon itself, so that the doublings of Buck and Buddy ultimately collapse into tautology: "*His own daughter His own daughter*" (259).

Reading Buck and Buddy's ledger convinces Ike that the only possible means of atoning for the past is to repudiate his inheritance and leave the plantation to his cousin Cass. Yet he recognizes that his act is doomed to fail, since as he sees it there is nothing ultimately to repudiate, "because on the instant when Ikemotubbe discovered, realized, that he could sell it [the land] for money, on that instant it ceased ever to have been his forever . . . and the man who bought it bought nothing." (246). One of the men who bought this "nothing," Ike reflects, was Thomas Sutpen, who purchased "the fragment" upon which he was to build Sutpen's Hundred with "money or rum or whatever it was" (244). Faulkner's early story "Evangeline"—which tells in abbreviated form the story that eventually becomes *Absalom, Absalom!*—offers a slightly different account of this transaction, recounting how Sutpen "found the land or swapped the Indians a stereopticon for it or won it at blackjack or something" (583). The optical technology that Faulkner uses as a metaphor to express the doubled relation of the plantation is thus, according to the narrative offered in "Evangeline," potentially the very thing exchanged for the land in the first place. Indeed, the fact that Faulkner offers two almost identical accounts of the purchase of the plantation suggests that his compositional method can itself be compared to a stereopticon, which takes two almost identical images and condenses them into one.

Still Moving

The printed history recorded in the ledger reminds Ike of the prints he follows during the annual return to the wilderness to hunt for the bear Old Ben. In turn the killing of the bear symbolizes the destruction of the wilderness, a destruction signaled by the arrival of the very thing to which Ike has most often compared Old Ben—an onrushing train, which crosses the wilderness "as arrows travel, groundless, elongated, three times its actual length and even paler, different in color, as if there were a point between immobility and absolute motion where even mass chemically altered" (306). The unnatural speed of the train produces an optical illusion analogous to that created by the stereopticon, except that whereas the photographic technology produced a new space by blending two separate images, the train seems to produce a new time as well as space. The train's double duty as the actual technology that destroys the wilderness and as the symbol of the wilderness's own destructive powers is thus itself symbolized by the illusion it produces of a time traversed by both past and present, a space between stillness and motion. The image conflates past and present as surely as the photograph of Little Belle confused Horace and Popeye in *Sanctuary* and the stereopticon brought together the plantation and the ledger in "The Bear."

As J. Hillis Miller has observed, Faulkner repeatedly invokes the space *between* motion and stillness Ike glimpses as he watches the train go by: "Faulkner excels at presenting human consciousness as suspended in amazed outrage at its own situation, poised immobile and at the same time in terrific motion."[30] This is the condition Rosa describes in *Absalom, Absalom!* as that "dream-state in which you run without moving" (114), a space that belongs neither to photography nor even to cinema but to both and neither at the same time. Faulkner's attempt to locate the space *between* motion and stillness is clear from the following famously cryptic account of the artistic experience: "The aim of every artist," the writer proposes in an interview he gave just before he died, "is to arrest motion, which is life, by artificial means and hold it fixed so that 100 years later when a stranger looks at it, it moves again since it is life."[31] Faulkner offers a kind of compound of photography and film, imagining art as caught between stillness and motion, past and present.

This same oscillation can be found in the opening to *Absalom, Absalom!*, whose very first sentence puns on the temporal and kinetic meaning of the word "still": "From a little after two oclock until almost sundown of the long still hot weary dead September afternoon they sat in what Miss Coldfield still called the office because her father had called it that" (3). The stillness of Rosa's room—the description carrying faint echoes of Keats, Yeats, and Eliot—offers the perfect setting for her first description of Sutpen, frozen in midstride crossing Jefferson town square. True to Faulkner's definition of art, however, this image quickly comes to life: "Then in the long unamaze Quentin seemed to watch [Sutpen and his men] overrun suddenly the hundred square miles of tranquil and astonished earth and drag house and formal gardens violently out of the soundless Nothing and clap them down like cards upon a table beneath the up-palm immobile and pontific, creating the Sutpen's Hundred, the *Be Sutpen's Hundred* like the oldentime *Be Light*" (4).[32] The seemingly cinematic injunction "*Be Light*" might be read as a tagline for *Absalom, Absalom!* as a whole, which repeatedly puts its still characters into motion in the manner of early cinema. Just as often, however, the novel freezes its characters in place: the description of Sutpen's Hundred being built with the terrific energy of a silent movie is immediately followed by a description of Sutpen falling into a "completely static" state, "as if he were run by electricity and someone had come along and removed, dismantled the wiring or the dynamo" (31–32).[33] Sutpen's purported grandson, Charles Etienne, suffers much the same fate, experiencing life as "a succession of periods of utter immobility like a broken cinema film . . . broken by other periods, intervals, of furious and incomprehensible and apparently reasonless moving" (167). What attracts Faulkner to metaphors such as "a broken cinema film" is that they make visible the fact that a medium defined by movement depends for its existence on the still image. Indeed for Jean Epstein, writing in 1921, what made the cinema such a "striking and prodigious" form was the fact that "it permits the synthesis of discontinuous and static elements into a continuous, mobile whole."[34]

This synthesis is particularly crucial to *Light in August*, a novel whose governing mode has been famously defined by Alfred Kazin as the "stillness" of pastoral: "Its stillness is rooted in the peaceful and timeless world which Lena Grove personifies and in which she has her being. It is the stillness of the personal darkness inside which Joe Christmas lives. But this stillness is also the sickly, after-dark silence of the Reverend Gail Hightower sitting in his study."[35] Kazin's account of Christmas's stillness would seem to be contradicted by the fact that Joe is described as being "doomed with motion."[36] But although Joe spends almost the entire novel in flight, he ends up running in exactly the same place, along a "street which ran for thirty years" (339). His running is thus a form of standing still: "Though Joe had not moved . . . he was still running" (215). This image of Joe running from himself takes on literal form after he is believed to have killed Joanna Burden, not just in the sense that he is now on the run from the police, but in the sense that he no longer seems to inhabit his own consciousness. Joe finds himself no longer able to know the things that the subject cannot not know—his own desires, emotions, and bodily needs: "He is not sleepy or hungry or even tired. He is somewhere between and among them, suspended" (339). This state of suspension extends even to the gap between waking and sleeping: Joe passes from one condition to the other "seemingly at an instant, between two movements of the eyelids, without warning" (333–34).[37] His condition can obviously be read as a physical manifestation of the radical uncertainty of his legal status under the one-drop rule, an uncertainty that at one point is explicitly rendered in photographic terms when Joe, caught in a car's headlights, "watches his body grow white out of the darkness like a kodak print emerging from the liquid" (108).[38] The comparison of Joe to a developing photograph gives a sense of how much his body seems not to be his own, to belong to the outside community—since it is their interpretation of his actions according to racial stereotypes that "fix" him in place. This explains why so much of Joe's story is reported by others; why Jefferson's district attorney, Gavin Stevens, can speak of Joe's "white blood" and "black blood" (449) determining his every move; why, finally, Joe can be so detached from his own life that he experiences it in much the same way as the watching community—as if, in the words of one of that community, "he never even knew he was a murderer, let alone a nigger too" (350).

Light in August is thus a novel about a man on the run yet "suspended" in time. But if Joe cannot catch up to himself, the problem faced by the other characters in the novel is that they cannot catch up with someone else: Lena hoping to find the man who made her pregnant, Lucas Burch, so that, as one character sarcastically tells her, "your name will be Burch in time" (18); Burch himself trying to catch Christmas to prove that he is not guilty of Joanna's murder, a situation described as being "like a murderer trying to catch himself to get his own reward" (101); Byron Bunch attempting to "catch up" (411) with Lena. These pursuits function as mirror images of Joe's endless running in the same place. Indeed the novel persistently depicts identity in terms of being out-of-step, in the sense that characters are repeatedly described as knowing something they do not know they know: Byron "already in love, though he does not yet know it" (55); Hightower's face displaying an emotion of which "Hightower himself is unaware" (81); Lena "betrayed and deserted and not even aware that she has been deserted" (52). The character most obviously out of step is Hightower, who every day at dusk looks out of his study window onto the very street where his Confederate grandfather was shot in order to make believe that he sees the very "instant" of his grandfather's death. What Hightower believes he sees at this moment is not simply his grandfather but himself: "I am my dead grandfather on the instant of his death" (491). There is something obviously cinematic about Hightower's vision, but also something photographic, since it only arrives "[i]n the lambent suspension of August" (492), at the exact moment when "it would be night save for that faint light which daygranaried leaf and grass blade reluctant suspire" (60). It is fitting, then, that the minister has at one time attempted to make a living developing photographs. For what Hightower wants is to fix his vision and have it continue at the same time; he wants, as Barthes says of his desire to understand film by examining the photogram, to see "*inside*" the film that unrolls every night before him.[39]

These descriptions of lives caught between stillness and motion become a means for Faulkner to rethink ekphrasis, a trope, needless to say, defined by stillness—a quality critics have frequently associated with Faulkner's work. Michael Millgate, for example, suggests that the crucial moments in *Absalom, Absalom!* are "presented in a kind of tableau arrested at a particular point of time and held in suspension while looked at, approached from all sides, inspected as if [they] were an artifact, like [a] Grecian urn."[40] It seems more accurate to say, however, that people and things in Faulkner's work are held suspended not in a tableau but *between* the stillness of a tableau and the ceaseless movement of film. This is the effect of the famous opening to *Light in August*, which, in describing a heavily pregnant Lena sitting by the side of the road waiting for a ride into Jefferson, explicitly references Keats's ode and prepares us for the opening of *Absalom, Absalom!*: "backrolling now behind her a long monotonous succession of peaceful and undeviating changes from day to dark to day again, through which she advanced in identical and anonymous and deliberate wagons as though through a succession of creakwheeled and limpeared avatars, like something moving forever and without progress across an urn" (7). The passage anticipates the description of Christmas watching "numberless avatars" (226) of himself endlessly running in the same place. Paradoxically, it is the very iteration of Lena's and Joe's experience of movement that allows Faulkner to think of it as a form of stasis.

The excruciatingly slow progress of Lena toward town offers the illusion of stasis while actually moving; the endless running of Christmas, by contrast, offers the illusion of movement while remaining in the same place. Even on horseback Joe resembles "a moving picture in slow motion" (210), but as his "horse slowed . . . stopped," Joe continues to "lean forward in the arrested saddle, in the attitude of terrific speed" (210).[41] The image of Joe on the horse represents the *idea* of movement rather than movement itself. Whereas the train Ike watches cross the wilderness creates, like a film, the visual illusion of a "point between immobility and absolute motion," Joe's monument-like "attitude" functions like the photogram—an image that can be seen only by destroying the very medium that it makes possible yet is itself destroyed in the operation of that form.[42] Joe's endless movement is not only a form of stillness but also, ultimately, a form of self-obliteration, a disappearing from sight the way a photogram disappears *into* a film: "running on up the stairs, vanishing as he ran, vanishing upward from the head down as if he were running headfirst and laughing into something that was obliterating him like a picture in chalk being erased from the blackboard" (208).

The Shadow of the Negro

Light in August depicts identity as emerging, like the photogram, in the place between motion and stillness. This emergence is also, however, an erasure—as it was in *Sanctuary* and in "The Bear." *Light in August*'s depiction of history follows many of the same principles as its depiction of identity, offering a view of the past not unlike that of Faulkner's contemporary, Benjamin, for whom "the *true* picture of the past is the one that is always in a state of passing away."[43] Hightower's belief that the air in the street outside his house retains the marks left by his grandfather's horse "because the same air will be there even if the dust, the mud, is gone" (483) imagines history being preserved *in* its vanishing, as it were—as if every moment of the past were retained by a kind of invisible photography. Fascinatingly, at the same moment that Hightower's grandfather was fighting for the Confederates, Oliver Wendell Holmes was imagining the sky functioning as "one great concave mirror, which reflects the picture of all our doings, and photographs every act on which it looks upon dead and living surfaces." Holmes imagined this invisible photographic record being read by "celestial eyes," for whom "the leaves of the forest are but undeveloped negatives."[44] In Faulkner's fiction about the Civil War, however, this record is read not just by the celestial but by the grieving: the protagonist of the story "Pantaloon in Black" imagines that the footprints of his dead wife are "vanished but not gone, fixed and held in the annealing dust" (*Moses*, 133), while Rosa in *Absalom, Absalom!* insists that Jefferson bears a record of her lover Bon's existence, his body having left behind it an "*invisible imprint*" (*Absalom, Absalom!*, 119).

The prevalence of such images in Faulkner's work suggests that he imagines the world of Yoknapatawpha as an enormous recording device, preserving history in invisible yet perceptible form. From the heated stillness of Rosa's room in Jefferson to the frigidity of Quentin and Shreve's Cambridge dormitory, *Absalom, Absalom!* seems to convert the very air in which it is told into a repository of the past. In one moment in the novel Rosa imagines the traces left by Judith and Bon from their walks in the garden of Sutpen's Hundred: "*[I] would walk those raked and sanded garden paths and think 'This print was his save for this obliterating rake, that even despite the rake it is still there and hers beside it . . . the obliterating sand, the million finger-nerves of frond and leaf, the very sun and moony constellations which had looked down at him, the circumambient air, held somewhere yet his foot, his passing shape, his face, his speaking voice, his name . . .*'" (119). Rosa is able to see the traces of Bon's body despite the "*obliterating rake*," indeed almost because of it. Yet in the context of the novel such a belief is not as absurd as it might seem. Faulkner—like James before him—deliberately confuses metaphorical and actual vision by giving literal form to his characters' memories and imaginings. Hence Bon can literally be described as possessing a "*passing shape*," since he appears to be—the novel never allows us to be certain—a legally black man passing as a white one.

This sense that Bon's very existence breaches the barrier between the metaphorical and the literal is compounded by Rosa's insistence that he leaves behind him "*no more trace than . . . [if] he had been but a shape, a shadow*" (120), for black identity is so persistently spoken of as a "shadow" in Faulkner's fiction that it almost comes to seem like a literal designation.[45]

Rosa's repeated references to Bon's shadow suggest that what remains of the man she loved, paradoxically, is the record of his own absence. It is fitting, therefore, that the only tangible physical record of Bon is a photograph, an image Rosa apparently has in her possession.[46] She tells Quentin that she first hears of Bon as "*that shadow with a name emerging from Ellen's vain and garrulous folly, that shape without even a face yet because I had not even seen the photograph then*" (117). Indeed she has never seen Bon in the flesh: "*I never saw him. I never even saw him dead. I heard a name, I saw a photograph, I helped to make a grave: and that was all*" (117). Her image of Bon is thus a projection based first upon his name and then upon the framed photograph of him she sees on her niece Judith's bedside table. Like the photograph carried by the protagonist of "Beyond," the shadowy Bon—seen only in a photograph—is a figure for loss itself. It is surely no coincidence, then, that the two subjects in *Absalom, Absalom!* who fall under what we might call "the shadow of the Negro"—Bon and his mother, Eulalia—are described either in terms of their photographic image or in terms borrowed from photographic discourse.[47] Like her son, Eulalia first appears in the novel as "a shadow that almost emerged for a moment and then faded again" (199).[48] But whereas Bon is first seen in a photograph, Bon's mother is first seen *as* a photograph, "just emerging for a second of the telling," Quentin tells Shreve, "in a single word almost, so that Grandfather said it was like he had just seen her too for a second by the flash of one of the muskets" (201). If Rosa forms her photographic-like image of Bon's character as good simply from hearing his name—Quentin's father describes her as having "got the picture from the first word" (59)—Grandfather Compson develops his picture of Eulalia out of the handful of words Sutpen uses to describe her shadow cast against the wall of the cabin on the Haitian plantation.

Bon and Eulalia remain shadowy figures despite—or perhaps because of—the fact that they are repeatedly depicted in photographic terms. The novel constantly resorts to ekphrasis and photographic imagery to describe a history that seems to become more obscure the more it emerges. This crisis of vision is exemplified by the fate of the four actual photographs referred to in the course of the novel: those of Bon, of Bon's wife and child, of Judith, and of the Sutpen family. In order to understand both the importance and the instability of these four images, we first need briefly to return to the story that anticipates *Absalom, Absalom!* "Evangeline." The story's plot centers on the discovery of a photograph in the burnt ruins of the Sutpen estate; this picture, sealed inside a metal case, is handed to the unnamed first-person narrator by the old black woman who stands guard over the Sutpen home. The woman tells the narrator that the photograph formerly belonged to a young man named Bon, who was shot in front of the Sutpen mansion by Henry, the brother of Bon's fiancée, Judith. Bon, we are told, first learns of Judith's existence through seeing her photograph, just as in *Absalom, Absalom!* Rosa first learns of Bon through seeing *his* photograph. In "Evangeline" Bon goes off to the war carrying with him "Judith's picture in a metal case that closed like a book" (588). Not surprisingly, then, this is the picture that the narrator expects to find inside the metal case: "I looked at the face and thought quietly, stupidly . . . 'Why, I thought she was blonde . . .' Then I came awake, alive. I looked quietly at the face: the smooth, oval, unblemished face, the mouth rich, full, a little loose, the hot, slumbrous, secretive eyes, the inklike hair with its faint but unmistakable wiriness—all the ineradicable and tragic stamp of negro blood" (608). The photograph reveals that Bon is already married and that his wife is black. But the narrator immediately contains the threat posed by this woman's racial identity by impressing a fatal historical certainty upon her features, which are said to possess the "ineradicable and tragic stamp of negro blood." His reading of Bon's wife's portrait transfers the responsibility for slavery onto the fact of race itself, the tragic ineradicability of which can be confirmed through an appeal to photographic evidence. The picture thus operates as an alibi for both the narrator and the history he is determined to recover, the woman's blackness neatly explaining the ruin of the Sutpen family while absolving the narrator from any responsibility for his story.

The difference between the careful demarcation of black from white in "Evangeline" and the refusal of such distinctions in *Absalom, Absalom!* is encapsulated by what happens to this photograph of Bon's wife in the novel. Rosa tells Quentin that the photograph "in its metal case" (114) that she sees Judith clasping moments after the shooting of Bon is precisely the image that the narrator of "Evangeline" had expected to find: the picture of Judith that her niece had given Bon. Quentin, Shreve, and Mr. Compson, however, all insist that Judith's photograph, as in "Evangeline," has been replaced by a picture of Bon's wife and child. Judith thus opens the metal case to be confronted with a "photograph which was not her face, not her child" (73). Yet what shocks Judith is not the race of the woman who stares back at her—in the novel, unlike in the story, the racial status of Bon's wife cannot be read from her face, which looks "like a tragic magnolia" (91)—but the fact that the face Judith sees is not her own.

The fact that the novel's narrators confuse the image of Judith with the image of Bon's first wife and child points not just to the insufficiency of photographic proof as a guarantor of identity in *Absalom, Absalom!* but also to the general instability of the visual world in Faulkner's fiction. This can be seen most clearly in what happens to the fourth and last of the novel's photographic images: that of Sutpen's family. As I noted above, *Absalom, Absalom!* opens with Quentin listening to Rosa tell her story in Mr. Coldfield's study. As Rosa's story unfolds Quentin begins to see Sutpen's body constituting itself out of the dust trapped in the stillness of the late afternoon air, an "ogre-shape"

> which, as Miss Coldfield's voice went on, resolved out of itself before Quentin's eyes the two half-ogre children, the three of them forming a shadowy background for the fourth one. This was the mother, the dead sister Ellen . . . Quentin seemed to see them, the four of them arranged into the conventional family group of the period, with formal and lifeless decorum, and seen now as the fading and ancient photograph would have been seen enlarged and hung on the wall behind and above the voice and of whose presence there the voice's owner was not even aware, as if she (Miss Coldfield) had never seen this room before. (8–9)

Quentin's extraordinary image narrates an alternative photographic—or, better, ekphrastic—space of reproduction. Sutpen's body is described as "resolv[ing] out of itself" his two children and his wife, a kind of cellular-like reproduction that is explicitly compared to a photographic one. Faulkner's unusual choice of the verb "resolve" offers a clue to the centrality of photography to Rosa's story. To resolve means to cause something to separate into its constituent elements, often in order to distinguish things similar in magnitude or close together in time; its most familiar use is in photography, which uses the term to gauge the level of reproduction in an image.[49] Two related processes appear to be happening here: first, the Sutpens emerge out of Rosa's extraordinarily heightened language in a manner comparable to the resolution of a photographic image; second, this metaphorical image is then compared to one that actually exists within the story, "enlarged and hung on the wall behind and above the voice." It is impossible to be certain as to the status of this second photograph, though this does not stop Faulkner from chiding Rosa for remaining unaware of the portrait hanging behind her, "as if she (Miss Coldfield) had never seen this room before." As if this were not confusing enough, this image later resurfaces in a slightly different form in the library of Sutpen's Hundred, which Quentin describes as containing "the photograph, the group—mother and two children—on the desk behind" (236) Sutpen. Although Sutpen has moved from being in the image of his family to sitting in front of it, Quentin's reference to "*the* photograph" (italics mine) suggests that this image is the same as the one he describes at the beginning of the novel.

To recap: the image of Sutpen that Quentin imagines forming in the air in front of him while listening to Rosa's story serves to remind him of a photograph that might be located in Rosa's father's study, or, in a slightly altered form, in Sutpen's library. In "The Leg," a photograph convinces its subject that he was in two places at once; in *Sanctuary*, a photograph forces two people to share the same experience; in "The Bear," a photograph literally merges two different spaces and times into one; and in *Light in August*, a photographic-like space comes into being between two separate places. The logical endpoint to this sequence, it would seem, is for a photograph to take two different forms. Faulkner uses the trope of photographic ekphrasis to draw attention to the impossible relation between referentiality and fiction—a question that is central to identity in the age of Jim Crow. Nothing else can explain the following extraordinary passage from Rosa's narrative, in which she expresses a desire not only for something that already exists—the camera—but for something that will produce the very thing she already possesses: a picture of Bon's face.

> *And I know this: if I were God I would invent out of this seething turmoil we call progress something (a machine perhaps) which would adorn the barren mirror altars of every plain girl who breathes with such as this . . . this pictured face. It would not even need a skull behind it; almost anonymous, it would need only vague inference of some walking flesh and blood desired by someone else even if only in some shadow-realm of make-believe.—A picture seen by stealth, by creeping . . . into the deserted midday room to look at it.* (118)

What Rosa wants, it seems, is to reproduce her own experience of falling in love with Bon's photograph, since this is all "*every plain girl*" needs. Her language—"*such as this . . . this pictured face*"—seems to suggest that she is showing Bon's photograph to Quentin at the very moment that she wishes for a device that could produce just such an image. It is in fact impossible to know whether Rosa is actually pointing to the photograph of Bon at this moment, since Quentin never suggests that he has seen the image; her assertion as to the mesmeric potency of this image only underlines her failure to describe it. Yet, as we have seen, Rosa punctiliously tells Quentin that all she knows about Bon has come from seeing his photograph.

As much as she insists upon the authenticity of her eyewitness account—Cleanth Brooks notes her tendency to preface every remark with "I saw," "I saw,"—Rosa recognizes that basing her account of Bon's existence upon only a photograph throws into question the very notion of what seeing is: "*I never saw* [his face]. *I do not even know of my own knowledge that Ellen ever saw it, that Judith ever loved it, that Henry slew it; so who will dispute me when I say, Why did I not invent, create it?*" (118). Rosa seems to be suggesting that seeing a photograph of Bon is not only not the same—obviously enough—as seeing him for herself but that it actually seems to be a different kind of seeing altogether, one that invents rather than records its subjects. In the endlessly repeated and reimagined world of Yoknapatawpha photography is not, then, the sign of the real but its opposite—the collapse of reference, the vanishing of the visible world, the impossibility of establishing not only who someone is but what he or she looks like.

Face to Face

For all of Rosa's protestations, what is really at stake in *Absalom, Absalom!* is not whether she "invent[ed]" Bon's face but what this face looks like. Yet, despite the fact that the crucial question in the novel is whether Bon is Sutpen's son by his first wife Eulalia—and thus possibly black—none of Faulkner's four narrators ever describe his physical appearance. Ironically, although Bon only appears in the novel in the form of what Rosa calls his "pictured face," this face is never pictured. One reason for this could be that Rosa *does* actually show Quentin a picture of Bon; another is that Bon's face is so familiar to her—and even perhaps to Quentin—that she feels no need to describe it, which might be why she tells Quentin that "*even before I saw the photograph I could have recognised, nay described, his very face*" (118). The picture of Bon offered in Faulkner's novel is a faceless one. Yet what—or, better, who—Bon looks like is absolutely crucial to establishing who Bon is.

There is, however, one way of working out what Bon looks like—by working backwards from what Sutpen looks like, since the question of Bon's appearance is intimately connected to that of his father's. What Bon wants from his father, we are told, is a sign that Sutpen recognizes him as his son. Bon imagines the various forms this recognition might take, perhaps the most telling of which is a physical token: "*a lock of his hair or a paring from his finger nail and I would know them because I believe now that I have known what his hair and finger nails would look like all my life*" (262). The reason that Bon believes he has known what Sutpen's hair and nails would look like all his life is because he believes that Sutpen has "*[m]y brow my skull my jaw my hands*" (251). Recognition, as Bon imagines it, would not so much be a matter of Sutpen seeing himself in Bon as Bon seeing himself in Sutpen. Yet Bon goes against the entire logic of the novel in his certainty that seeing equals knowing, that all he need do is see "the man who made him and then he would know" (255). Bon assumes that because Sutpen is his father—because they share, in the language of Jim Crow, the same blood—they must therefore share the same features. Furthermore, he believes that his father cannot not see this—cannot, that is, not recognize his own face in Bon's: "He [Bon] knew it was in his [Sutpen's] face because he [Bon] knew that the other [Sutpen] had seen it there" (257).

Shreve imagines this encounter in explicitly photographic terms, suggesting that Bon believes that seeing his father "would reveal to him at once, like a flash of light, the meaning of his whole life" (250). Yet Sutpen's impassive reaction to his son reveals nothing; Bon sees his father "face to face" (256) and nothing happens; the sign of recognition he has longed for is absent.[50] When Quentin retells this story, however, Bon is described as believing that he *has* seen recognition on his father's face: "*[F]or the second time he looked at the expressionless and rocklike face, at the pale boring eyes in which there was no flicker, nothing, the face in which he saw his own features, in which he saw recognition, and that was all*" (278). Denied the legal recognition he wants—the father acknowledging the son—Bon substitutes a very different form of recognition—that of seeing his own face mirrored in another's.[51] What allows for this substitution is the fact that Sutpen's failure to acknowledge Bon—signaled by his lack of expression—is itself the sign *of* recognition—what identifies Sutpen as Sutpen is his "*expressionless and rock-like face.*" By refusing to acknowledge that he recognizes his son, Sutpen allows Bon to recognize his father—and because Bon believes that the two of them share the same face, recognizing his father is the same as his father recognizing him.

Bon cannot have Sutpen's face or he would, of course, be recognized—by Sutpen, by Henry, even by Rosa when she looks at his photograph. Yet believing that Bon does *not* have his father's face is to ignore Faulkner's insistence that the one thing family members—indeed entire ethnic communities—have in common is the cast of their face.[52] In the rather strange story "Lo!" for example, the president of the United States is besieged by a group of petitioning Indians whose faces exactly resemble one another: "He did not know the faces, though he knew the Face, since he had looked upon it by day and dreamed upon it by night for three weeks now. It was a squat face, dark, a little flat, a little Mongol; secret, decorous, impenetrable, and grave. He had seen it repeated until he had given up trying to count it or even estimate it" (382). The "Face" expresses a racial difference so absolute that even the biracial descendants of Native Americans—such as Sam Fathers in *Go Down, Moses*—retain its "impenetrable" features. This belief that the Indian race survives in the form of an "Indian face" resurfaces in Faulkner's essay "Mississippi," which depicts the disappearance of Native American life from his home state in physiognomic terms: "Except for looking occasionally out from behind the face of a white man or a Negro, the Chickasaws and Choctaws and Natchez and Yazoos [are] . . . gone."[53] The Indian race, which Faulkner's fiction consistently reduces to a blank, impenetrable face, survives only "behind" other faces, an image that converts the face from the record of an individual's experience to the sign of a shared lineage. According to Faulkner's racialist logic, Native American identity is inseparable from the "*rocklike and firm*" face to be found on all Indians, no matter their age or sex. And what the blankness of the Native American face testifies to is a shared experience of loss. The "Face" thus signifies for Faulkner in exactly the same way photography does.

It is the very notion of shared experience that seems to be at stake in *Absalom, Absalom!* Like the Native Americans in "Lo!," the Sutpens possess a collective blank face, a face "smoothed of all experience" (59). Quentin describes how Sutpen's "*expressionless and rocklike face*" (278) is repeated across generations—on the "absolutely impenetrable" (100) face of his daughter Judith and on the "wasted yellow face" (298) of his son Henry; across races—on the "*sphinx face*" (109) of his black daughter Clytie; and even across families—on the "unblemished" face of his wife, Ellen, which becomes blank only after her marriage. Mr. Compson describes Sutpen's face as "like the mask in Greek tragedy interchangeable not only from scene to scene but from actor to actor and behind which the events and occasions took place without chronology or sequence" (48–49). In refusing to show—or even, in Ellen's case, actually erasing—the marks of experience, this face disrupts both the distinctions between people and the distinctions between periods, robbing those who look upon it of the means of marking time. It can thus be seen as responsible for the temporal inversions and impossibilities of Rosa's narrative. Ellen's sister insists that she "seemed already to know" how Sutpen's face was going to look "just as I seemed to know how Ellen and Judith and Henry would look before I saw them" (18). The reason Rosa already knows what Sutpen's face looks like—just as she knows exactly what Bon's face will look like—is because she is unable to locate the first time she sees it; never changing, yet interchangeable, the Sutpen face represents the limit point of Rosa's sense of the world as retaining the imprints of all that has happened, even when those prints cannot be seen.

No wonder, then, that Rosa says of Sutpen, "It was in his face; that was where his power lay" (35). Her ingenuous account of what attracts her to Sutpen cannot be squared with the fact that his face is most often described as being "on" both him and his family like a mask, as if it were separate from his body. Mr. Compson's comparison of a face to a mask necessarily raises the question of the minstrel mask, a subject I examine in my next chapter. Faulkner, however, turns the stereotypical association of the mask with blackness inside out, as it were. Although Sutpen's daughter Clytie is visibly black, Rosa's description of the "impenetrable mask which she used for face" (163) functions as a sign of Clytie's lineage rather than of her race. Like Judith, Henry, and Bon, Clytie's face duplicates Sutpen's; it is a "*replica of his own which he had created*" (110). The resemblance between Clytie and her father is important to note because critics have repeatedly argued that Quentin works out that Bon is Sutpen's son by seeing Clytie; if she has her father's face, so this logic runs, then so must Bon. And though this still does not prove that Bon is black, several critics have suggested that the reproduction of Sutpen's face on Clytie offers a clue to that question too. Peter Brooks, for one, argues that the novel clearly specifies that Quentin begins to entertain "the possibility of other part-Negro Sutpen children" after seeing Clytie.[54] Hershel Parker, meanwhile, proposes that Quentin sees three "Sutpen" faces on the night he visits Sutpen's Hundred with Rosa: those of Clytie, Henry, and Bon's idiot grandchild, Jim Bond. "The book turns on the fact of there being a 'Sutpen face,'" Parker contends, and thus "Bon ought to bear it, however disguised, and transmit it."[55] That there *is* a Sutpen face is by this stage, I hope, incontrovertible, but to insist that this face must be "on" Bon simply wishes away the fact that the only proof we have that Bon's face resembles Sutpen's is Bon's insistence that it must.

Richard Godden has recently challenged Brooks's and Parker's reading, arguing that "[n]either Clytie's expression nor her bone structure tells Rosa anything about Bon." As he points out, Rosa describes Clytie's face "as '*rocklike and firm*,' insisting that the face that faces her has neither '*sex [nor] age*' and has from birth remained that of a '*sphinx*' with '*no change, no alteration in it at all*.' Signals, there are none. And because Rosa reiterates that she never saw Bon, Clytie's features are similarly mute. Rosa simply cannot have read the Sutpen connection from Clytie's face."[56] Godden is right to suggest that Rosa cannot work out who Bon is from looking at Clytie but wrong about why this is. After all, the very characteristics which make Clytie's face supposedly unreadable—Rosa describes Clytie's face as being "*without sex or age*"—are the very characteristics which actually identify her as a Sutpen. Clytie's features might be mute on the subject of her own life—she possesses "*the same sphinx face which she had been born with*" (109)—but they are eloquent on the subject of her ancestry. Godden's mistake is to assume that the faces of Faulkner's characters reveal who they are by bearing the traces either of their experiences or their relatives. As we have seen throughout this book, however, the faces described in photographic fiction are typically blank, so they need to be read according to a model of resemblance rather than reference. This model confuses the metaphorical with the literal in much the same way that physiognomy itself does. Hence Clytie's face is like Bon's in a way that is neither exactly metaphorical nor exactly literal: Clytie's face is blank in the sense that it is without features; Bon's face is blank in the sense that it is never described. Both can be said to bear the blank Sutpen face but only by erasing the divide between the literal and the figurative in a manner that calls into question the entire project of fictional description, let alone the entire project of identification.

There is another, infinitely more disturbing, example in the novel of a face without features, a face that is definitively *not* a Sutpen face—the one belonging to the black butler who turns Sutpen away from the plantation house. Bearing a "balloon face . . . slick with paper-thin distension" (187), the butler is reduced to a screen upon which the white men of Sutpen's class project fantasies of revenge upon the black race they believe has disenfranchised them. Yet Sutpen can also imagine himself as looking out from within this face. After the butler refuses to deliver

Sutpen's message to the owner of the plantation, the young boy tries to picture how he must look to the servant, an identification that takes a literal form: "[S]omething in him had escaped, and was looking out from within the balloon face" (189). The moment is then compounded by another act of transference, Sutpen imagining the plantation owner looking "through and beyond the boy, he himself seeing his own father and sisters and brothers as the owner, the rich man (not the nigger) must have been seeing them all the time" (189–90). Unable to bear seeing himself as the black butler would see him, Sutpen must invent another face—the face of the unseen white plantation owner—in order to establish a racially correct origin for the birth of self-consciousness.

We have seen this substitution of a white face for a black one before, in the varying descriptions of the photograph "in its metal case" found on Bon's dead body. What "Evangeline" pictured as an image of Bon's visibly black wife becomes in Rosa's account an image of Bon's fiancée Judith, and in Quentin and Shreve's retelling of the story reverts back to being a photograph of Bon's wife. But because in *Absalom, Absalom!* Bon's octoroon wife is legally black but not visibly so—as we have seen, she has "a face like a tragic magnolia" (91)—the only way of working out her race is through her son, whose skin bears a "faint olive tinge" (161)—a tinge that could also be inherited, of course, from Bon himself. The absurdity of this kind of detective work is evident enough. Yet it is exactly what Sutpen bases his "design" upon. Sutpen's attempt to establish a white lineage depends upon his having a white ancestry, something that—because definitive proof of racial identity cannot be established under the one-drop rule—he must shape, paradoxically, for himself. Here again we see Faulkner turning a metaphor—the American self-made man—into literal fact: Sutpen literally makes himself by seeing himself through the eyes of a subject he is forced to imagine because he is not allowed to see him—the plantation owner. And just as he must project his face onto the world so as to be able to see himself for the first time, so he almost seems to will his face onto his family in order to prove that he has succeeded in reproducing himself.

The Face of a Generation

The fact that the face Sutpen makes is perfectly blank is appropriate in the sense that its emptiness accurately records Sutpen family history, which, as we have seen, Faulkner imagines as a perpetual vanishing act. Sutpen's masklike face is another manifestation of the crisis of resemblance I have been tracing throughout this book, a crisis in which—thanks to the invention of photography, which allows everyone to have their picture taken—everyone begins to look the same. It is also, however, a figure for the crisis of vision generated by Jim Crow. Sutpen's face differs from Bon's in that it is not only repeatedly described but also seemingly endlessly reproducible. Yet because this face is like a mask, it is in a sense no different from having no face at all. Sutpen's condition is thus a kind of mirror image of Bon's, just as Bon's was a mirror image of Joe Christmas, who, as Kazin notes in "The Stillness of *Light in August*," "is never seen full face, but always as a silhouette, a dark shadow."[57] Kazin neglects the fact that Joe's face *does* emerge, however, at the end of the novel, as the final picture in Hightower's vision of what can only be called the wheel of time at the moment of his grandfather's death:

> In the lambent suspension of August into which night is about to fully come, it seems to engender and surround itself with a faint glow like a halo. The halo is full of faces. . . . they all look a little alike, composite of all the faces which he has ever seen. But he can distinguish them one from another: his wife's, townspeople . . . Byron Bunch's; the woman with the child; and that of the man called Christmas. This face alone is not clear. It is confused more than any other, as though in the now peaceful throes of a more recent, a more inextricable compositeness. (492)

Like the fictional photograph, the stereopticon, and the film still, the composite image Hightower sees from his study window brings together past and present and black and white and locates them in a kind of impossible, nonreferential, ekphrastic space between the metaphorical and the literal.

Faulkner's description of Joe's confused, composite face inevitably recalls Francis Galton's composite photographs—the idea for which came to Galton, appropriately enough, after he had seen the stereopticon.[58] Even more suggestively, Galton contended that composite photography worked in the same way that "blended inheritance" worked in evolution, in which the "children of the white and negro" possess "a skin of blended tint."[59] Faulkner had in fact a rather more recent example to draw upon for his metaphor of a composite face—August Sander's proposed twenty volume set of photographs of German society, *Face of Our Time*. Although Sander's portraits are not composites in Galton's sense, his pictures of laborers, soldiers, bureaucrats, and politicians are meant to convey the sense of society as a whole in much the same way; as he put it in 1934, his aim was "to arrive at a physiognomic definition of the German people of the period." But by "physiognomic definition" he meant not the tautological reduction of a person to a racial or social type—in which a person's face simply reflects who he or she is—but the rendering of that person's place within society as a whole. "All things that happen have their appearance, or 'face,'" Sander declares, extending the logic of physiognomy to history itself. "An event's total appearance is its physiognomy. It is possible to record the historical physiognomic image of a whole generation and . . . to make that image speak in photographs."[60]

Faulkner's obsession with faces and photography suggest that he shared Sander's belief that it was possible even in language to render "the historical physiognomic image of a whole generation." Indeed the phrase, or one remarkably similar, appears in his story "The Fire and the Hearth." Lucas Beauchamp, the great-grandson of Ike's grandfather, Carothers McCaslin, is described as possessing a face that is "a composite of a whole generation . . . reproduc[ing] with absolute and shocking fidelity the old ancestor's entire generation and thought" (114). What accounts for the extraordinary communicability of Lucas's face—its ability to function as a "physiognomic image of a whole generation"—is the fact that, somewhat tautologically, it is "shaped even in expression in the pattern of his great-grandfather McCaslin's face" (69). Lucas, that is, has Carothers McCaslin's face. Yet *this* face is itself "the face of the generation which had just preceded them: the composite tintype face of ten thousand undefeated Confederate soldiers" (104–5). Lucas's face reproduces Carothers McCaslin's face, which is itself a composite of ten thousand photographs. Faulkner thus turns Sander's belief that a face can make visible a composite picture of its time on its head, by having faces express periods that are not their own—periods that we think we know only because we have seen photographs of them. We recognize what Lucas's face looks like because we have seen the faces of Confederate soldiers reproduced so many times that their images have blurred together in our minds.[61] Inevitably, then, Lucas's face is described as being "absolutely blank" (69). There is one further twist, however. Lucas is black, the descendant of Carothers McCaslin's rape of "*His own daughter His own daughter*" (259). If the repetitious language and imagery of "The Bear" represent Faulkner's attempt to render Carothers's incest linguistically, the exact resemblance between Lucas's face and that of his great-grandfather in "The Fire and the Hearth" might be said to represent his attempt to render it visually. Yet the result in both cases is the same—a blankness that offers its own eloquent record of a history whose horror cannot be effaced precisely because it resides precisely in the act of effacement itself—the vanishing of people, indeed entire races, into financial ledgers and historical records.

Stephen's problem, like ours, was not actually one of creating the uncreated conscience of his race, but of creating the *uncreated features of his face.*
RALPH ELLISON, *Invisible Man*

CHAPTER FOUR

"Seeing Myself like Somebody Else"

Hurston's Similarities

I HAVE BEEN arguing that American fiction's debt to the camera takes the form of a fascination with questions of resemblance, driven principally by the sense that in the photographic age everyone begins to look the same. It is time, however, to mark the limits to this uniformity. The representation of American homogeneity in what I call photographic fiction borrows its terms from stereotypes such as the indomitable Mexican, the exuberant Italian, and the impassive Indian. According to Bill Brown, such stereotypes can be understood "as the memorializing disavowal of the sameness effected by universal male suffrage."[1] It is precisely because racial stereotypes obey the same logic of replication and similarity as the American subject that they can function as a means of denying the universality *of* this logic. White middle-class American men project their own similarity to one another—a similarity that is itself the result of the failure to imagine Americans as anything but white—onto the racial other. Generalizing about others is thus the means by which the white American male asserts his own claim to difference.

Robyn Wiegman has called this process America's "visual scripting of identities," a scripting that, it seems reasonable to suggest, typically takes place in front of the camera.[2] Deborah E. McDowell points out that "U.S. culture apprehends black Americans . . . largely through the ubiquitous artifacts and metaphors of photographic technology."[3] Yet, as Ralph Ellison observes in his introduction to *Invisible Man*, the " 'high' visibility" of black life "actually rendered one *un*-visible, whether at high noon in Macy's window or illuminated by flaming torches and flashbulbs."[4] What we might call the photographic erasure of the black subject was noted by Frederick Douglass as early as 1849. Responding to claims that photography showed its subjects as they actually were, Douglass pointed out that the camera's claim to objectivity was undone by the inevitable prejudices of its operators: "Negroes can never have impartial portraits at the hands of white artists. It seems to us next to impossible for white men to take likenesses of black men, without most grossly exaggerating their distinctive features. And the reason is obvious. Artists, like all other white persons, have developed a theory dissecting the distinctive features of Negro physiognomy."[5] Misrepresentation is built into the structure of race relations since, as Douglass points out, physiognomic theory—whose claims that appearance offered an infallible index to character inevitably helped propagate racial stereotypes—determines the choice, content, and form of the photographic image. Even the supposedly impartial camera thus sees black identity through the lens of prejudice.

Douglass returned to this question fourteen years later, in the speech "Pictures and Progress":

> Once fairly in the book and the man may be considered a fixed fact, public property. In nine cases out of ten he so regards himself. The picture may be

> like him or not like him, or like any body else than him. . . . On no account whatever, either in deference to an improved taste or a change of fashion, can he be allowed any liberties with the style of his coat, the shape of his collar, or the cut of his hair. His position is defined, and his whole *personae* must now conform to, and never contradict the immortal likeness or unlikeness in the Book.[6]

As I noted in my introduction, rather than the image copying the subject, the subject, according to Douglass, now copies his image. That this is an explicitly racial question is suggested by Douglass's use of the term "property" to describe the relation of the subject to his image. The modern subject *belongs* to his photographic image, Douglass suggests, whether or not this image looks like him. Photographic identity thus follows the logic of the stereotype, which judges the subject in terms of a preexisting model. The photographed subject's protest that his public image bears no resemblance to what he actually looks like proves as ineffectual as the minority subject's protest against racist and ethnic stereotypes, since, in order to be recognized as himself, the photographed subject must resemble his own likeness.[7]

This vicious circle is the subject of Henry Louis Gates's examination of early twentieth-century attempts to escape racist stereotyping, "The Trope of a New Negro." The problem African Americans faced was an enormous one, Gates proposes, because "[e]verywhere a white American saw a black image, that image would be negative."[8] The sheer proliferation of derogatory illustrations—on toaster and teapot covers, magazine advertisements, popular postcards, and billboard posters—created a pressing need for "a full facelift." "Black Americans sought to re-present their public selves in order to reconstruct their public, reproducible images," Gates suggests, because black writers were acutely aware that "to manipulate the image of the black was, in a sense, to manipulate reality."[9] Gates points out that photographic attempts to combat racism had their origins in the practice of upper-middle-class African Americans commissioning first paintings and then photographs "so that they could metaphorically enshrine and quite literally perpetuate the example of their own identities."[10] Believing that there was "a correlation between the specific *characteristics* of the individuals depicted and the larger *character* of the race," black magazines reproduced images of ideal New Negro men and women so that their readers "might pattern themselves after the prototype."[11]

The difficulties involved in such a project lead Gates to conclude that the rise of the New Negro was a discursive rather than a visual phenomenon. Gates notes that it was to be "the precise structure of the black *voice* by which the very *face* of the race would be known and fundamentally reconstructed." Voices are easier to find, of course, than faces are to change, and scholars of African American literature have tended to follow Gates's lead, insisting that "[t]he key to blackness . . . is not visual but *auditory*."[12] Critics as different as Robert B. Stepto (*From Behind the Veil*), John Callahan (*In the African-American Grain*), and Susan Willis (*Specifying*) have read black literature according to this model, one in which the slave narrative—which narrates the struggle to find a voice—is seen as emblematic. This focus on voice has recently been challenged by bell hooks, who contends that "[t]he history of black liberation movements in the United States could be characterized as a struggle over images as much as it has been a struggle for rights." hooks points out that the walls of black homes tend to be covered in family photographs: "When the psychohistory of a people is marked by ongoing loss, when entire histories are denied, hidden, erased, documentation may become an obsession." These images give African Americans "a way to see ourselves, a sense of how we looked when we were not 'wearing the mask.'"[13] hooks thus finds a space for photographic particularity, but only in the private noncirculating realm of the family, where the subject need no longer present themselves as an idealized type to be imitated in accordance with white stereotypes—the "mask."

This chapter examines the work of a writer who has been repeatedly read in terms of voice despite her fascination with the relation between visual images and racial stereotypes—Zora Neale Hurston. Even though Hurston's most famous work, *Their Eyes Were Watching God*, declares an investment in vision in its very title, critics have tended to agree with Gates's assertion that the novel is an example of what he calls a "speakerly text."[14] This bias is reflected in the titles of some of the most well-known studies of the novel: "Metaphor, Metonymy and Voice," "The Inaudible Voice of it All," "The Erotics of Talk."[15] Recently, however, critics have begun to pay attention to the fact that vision plays just as important a role as voice in the formation of Janie's identity. Deborah Clarke, for example, sees the novel as outlining "the possibility of reclaiming the visual as a means of black expression and black power," noting that Joe Starks's desire to become a "big voice" offers compelling evidence that the novel is far from regarding speech as an unambiguous good.[16] Karen Jacobs, meanwhile, argues that the scene often regarded as the moment Janie finds her voice—her decision to stand up to her second husband Joe after suffering years of insults about her appearance—"actually signals the conflation of verbal and visual registers."[17] "When you pull down yo' britches," Janie tells her astonished husband in response to yet another jibe, "you look lak de change uh life."[18] Joe's pretence that he has not understood his wife is quickly shattered by his friend Walter's synesthetic taunt "[y]ou heard her, you ain't blind," a taunt Jacobs reads as proof that the novel insists on a fundamental equivalence between the visual and the verbal, as if hearing and seeing were inextricable.

The most obvious example of the central role played by visuality in *Their Eyes* is the fact that Janie finds out that she is black not from looking at herself but from looking at her photographic image. Early in the novel, a six-year-old Janie asks "Where is me? Ah don't see me" (9) while looking at a group photograph of herself and the white children of the Washburn family with whom she lives. Hurston's heroine cannot recognize the black girl in the photograph as herself for the simple reason that she believes herself to be white. The identity Janie discovers in her photographic image is thus her own difference; as she puts it to her friend Pheoby Watson, "[B]efore Ah seen de picture Ah thought Ah wuz just like de rest" (9). The moment would seem to mark an end to the photographic crisis of resemblance I have been tracing throughout this book. Indeed Janie's discovery can be read as a kind of literal enactment of what Frantz Fanon describes as the photographic-like fixing of black identity by the white gaze: "Sealed into [a] crushing objecthood . . . the glances of the other fixed me there, in the sense in which a chemical solution is fixed by a dye."[19]

Paradoxically, however, rather than securing Janie's status as black, the photograph actually inaugurates a series of moments in which Janie is mistaken—first by herself, and then by others—for someone else. These misrecognitions always take the same form: reversing Janie's discovery of herself in the photograph, they show the visibly black Janie being identified as someone who "looks white." As we will see, relations of racial difference in Hurston's novel are repeatedly expressed through relations of likeness. This explains why Janie is represented at one point in the novel as a figure for metaphor itself, as "a familiar strangeness." It makes perfect sense, then, that her story takes the rich figurative form it does, and that her story ends with her retreating to her house and turning her back on the community in order, in her words, to "live by comparisons" (191). For, as we shall see, Janie has lived her whole life not only *by* comparisons but as a figure *for* comparison itself. *Their Eyes* does not simply reproduce the visual scripting of racial identity in the photographic age, then, it also imagines this script being written by the subject herself, who in the age of photography is able to step outside of herself and see herself as if she were someone else.

A Familiar Strangeness

Their Eyes is punctuated by moments in which Janie expressly compares herself to her own image, whether in the form of a photograph, her reflection, or simply her own ideal of herself. That this comparison of the self with itself is for Hurston the very structure of subjectivity is suggested by a story from her 1942 autobiography, *Dust Tracks on a Road*. Hurston recounts how her first patron, Fannie Hurst, used to ring her own doorbell, answer it, and invite herself in to tea—a fantasy the novelist reads as a physical enactment of a fundamental truth about identity. As Hurston sees it, we judge ourselves according to a general image of ourselves; we typify *ourselves*, as it were: "[P]eople are prone to build a statue of the kind of person that it pleases them to be. And few people want to be forced to ask themselves, 'What if there is no one like my statue?'"[20] If for Douglass the modern subject continually struggles to turn herself into a copy of her own photographed image, for Hurston the modern subject imagines herself as a copy of her own idea of herself, even if there is in fact little resemblance between the two.[21]

We might read Janie's strange and seemingly inexplicable moment of photographic self-identification at the beginning of *Their Eyes* as a means of staging just such a confrontation between the subject and her self-image. Despite the fact that Janie is undeniably black, she is constantly compared to white people, believes herself to be white until she is six years old, and, most important, takes her own notion of what she looks like not from looking at her own body but from the judgments passed upon her by others. Janie's great complaint in the novel is that the various communities in which she lives keep, as she puts it, "mixin' up mah doings wid mah looks" (79). Yet, as I argue in this chapter, Janie is herself guilty of determining who she is from what she looks like. This model is apparent from the opening of the novel, when the Eatonville community first gaze upon and then offer an inventory of Janie's body. Indeed because the question of what Janie looks like in the novel is ultimately as much a metaphorical issue as it is a visual one, this question is inseparable from the telling of Janie's story. As Barbara Johnson has famously pointed out, Janie's great discovery in the novel is of "the necessity of figurative language." Johnson argues that "Janie's increasing ability to speak" is the result of her learning to mask her true feelings in order to survive her disappointing marriage to Joe. This explains the unlikely image Hurston uses to describe Janie's reaction after she comes to understand that Joe is far from the man she believed him to be: "[S]he had an inside and an outside now and suddenly knew how not to mix them" (72). Johnson reads this formula as a description of metaphor itself, in which "inside and outside are never the same."[22] Yet it is important to note the *visual* nature of this discovery. Learning to speak in *Their Eyes* is learning to see; learning to see is itself a matter of learning how others see you and matching that to the ways in which you see yourself—of matching, that is, inside and outside.

Johnson's suggestion that in discovering metaphor Janie discovers her own voice depends upon a distinction between the literal and the metaphorical that Johnson's definition of metaphor drawn from the novel—in which "inside and outside are never the same"—itself confuses, in the sense that Janie is speaking about a literal as well as a metaphorical divide between inside and outside. Johnson's approach could be said to be vindicated, however, by the fact that Hurston herself repeatedly confuses the two. Consider, for example, the following observation made by a character in Hurston's 1935 anthropological study of Floridian black life, *Mules and Men*: "Words got a hidden meaning. Most people is thin-brained. They's born wid they feet under the moon. Some folks is born wid they feet on the sun and they kin seek out de inside meanin' of words."[23] The metaphor imagines language having an inside and an outside, suggesting that if Janie's ability to put on a front for her husband is the recognition of the difference *between* inside and outside, then what Janie discovers, in keeping with Johnson's model, is language itself.

Indeed this discovery is even larger still, for according to the terms set out by Hurston in the essay "Characteristics of Negro Expression," black language *is* metaphor, and thus to discover metaphor is to discover language, and to discover language is to discover blackness. We might say then that Janie *becomes* black more than once, in the sense that her discovery of black language comes many years after her recognition of her blackness in the photograph. Hurston herself provides a bridge between the two moments in her observation that the black subject's "interpretation of the English language is in terms of pictures. One act described in terms of another. Hence the rich metaphor and simile." This is because, she suggests,

> The stark, trimmed phrases of the Occident seem too bare for the voluptuous child of the sun, hence the adornment. It arises out of the same impulse as the wearing of jewelry and the making of sculpture—the will to adorn.
>
> On the walls of the average Negro one always finds a glut of gaudy calendars, wall packets and advertising lithographs. The sophisticated white man or Negro would tolerate none of these, even if they bore a likeness to the Mona Lisa.[24]

Metaphor is here explicitly identified with visuality. Black speech changes the meaning of words by treating them as pictures, a transformation similar, Hurston's analogy suggests, to the way African Americans change the meaning of pictures by treating them as ornamentation. The calendars and posters on black walls are there not as quotes from the outside (white) world, but as manifestations of a specifically black language. What interests Hurston about images is not whether they are "like" their subject so much as how subjects use images to define their relation to the world.

Hurston's own model of figurative language thus seems to be opposed to Johnson's in that it reduces metaphor to the role of adornment rather than seeing it as a mode of transformation. Yet the metaphorical terms in which Hurston lays out this model—through a comparison with pictures—itself gives the lie to her insistence that metaphor is simply ornamentation. The surprisingly high stakes of this seemingly arcane question become clearer if we briefly examine the image that gives this book its title, that used by the women of Eatonville to describe what they see as the "whiteness" of the middle-class life Joe has given Janie. The women express their contempt for this life not simply *in* metaphor but through a comparison *to* metaphor: "It was bad enough for white people, but when one of your own color could be so different it put you on a wonder. It was like seeing your sister turn into a 'gator. A familiar strangeness. You keep seeing your sister in the 'gator and the 'gator in your sister, and you'd rather not" (48). The image marks Janie as different from the women around her yet also as different from the white people she is accused of imitating. Janie is a black woman accused of looking white, a view that defines racial identity as dependent on actions rather than looks. Such a definition obviously muddies the division between the races expressed in Hurston's characterization of a specifically African American attitude toward language and image. Hence Janie's condition is itself a comment *upon* language and image. The women do not compare Janie to a 'gator, they compare Janie to the act of comparing someone to a 'gator, to seeing something familiar in something foreign. As Hurston puts it, in a term seemingly borrowed from the philosophical discourse on metaphor, the women are confronted with "a familiar strangeness."

Hurston's use of the term "a familiar strangeness" marks the moment when her own highly metaphorical text—in keeping with what I argue is the text's reflexive mode—steps outside metaphor in order to comment upon it. The threat to identity in *Their Eyes* posed by metaphor's unveiling of the familiarity of strangeness and the strangeness of familiarity has been well detailed by Samira Kawash, who proposes that figurative language in the novel confuses inside and outside rather than—as Johnson contends—keeping the two separate. Kawash notes that the storm that ends the novel washes away not only the boundaries between humans and animals but seemingly the boundary between the literal and the figurative as well. After the rabid dog who surfaces during the storm bites Tea Cake, for example, Janie's lover is soon compared *to* a mad dog, the circle of exchange only being broken when Tea Cake's attempt to bite Janie—and thus turn *her* into a mad dog—fails to break the skin.[25] Indeed, even the moment offered by Johnson as evidence of Janie's ability to maintain a distance between her inner thoughts and outward behavior can equally be read as proof of their inevitable amalgamation: "Then one day she sat and watched the shadow of herself going about tending store and prostrating herself before Jody, while all the time she herself sat under a shady tree with the wind blowing through her hair and her clothes" (77). Rather than Janie's body being in one place and her mind in another, both seem to be in two places at once—which is why the wind can blow through her hair and clothes while she watches herself tend store. Janie's inside, in other words, has its own outside, as it were.

Thus not only do the residents of Eatonville continue to confuse Janie's inside with her outside even after Janie supposedly learns to keep them separate—so that they judge her "doings" in terms of her "looks"—Janie herself repeatedly mixes them up even after she learns her mistake in marrying Joe, a strategy reflected in the text's deliberate confusing of the third-person frame with Janie's first-person account.[26] Rather than rendering uncertain the question of whether Janie really does win her own voice—a question that has frequently bedeviled critics of the novel—this confusion actually signals precisely the manner in which that question is answered. For it is only by seeing herself from the outside—as if from the perspective of a third-person narrator—that Janie is able to find herself, as it were, a process that begins with the viewing of the photograph and continues until the highly intimate final scene of the novel, which depicts Janie communing with herself, calling in her soul to view her own story. It is tempting to see this structure as Hurston's staging of W. E. B. Du Bois's theory of double consciousness, his contention that the black subject is beset by the "sense of always looking at one's self through the eyes of others."[27] As I see it, though, Janie's repeated experience of seeing herself from the outside is not so much the experience of discovering what she looks like to those around her but that of discovering the gap between what she looks like and who she imagines herself to be. The experience is not, then, a Fanon-like fixing in place—in which the black subject understands that her identity is, in part at least, a result of how others see her—but in a sense quite the opposite, a withdrawal from the social into a private space of self-reflection.

Unnatural History

Kawash's reading of the metaphorical confusions both enacted and emblematized by the storm suggests the insufficiency of Johnson's ultimately binary account of identity in *Their Eyes*. Another more fluid model is required, one true to the reflexive structure of the novel. In order to begin the task of supplying one, I want briefly to return to *Mules and Men*, and specifically to its famous opening lines: "From the earliest rocking of my cradle, I had known about the capers Brer Rabbit is apt to cut and what the Squinch Owl says from the house top. But it was fitting me like a tight chemise. I couldn't see for wearing it. It was only when I was away in college, away from my native surroundings, that I could see myself like somebody else and look at my garment. Then I had to have the spy-glass of Anthropology to look through at that."[28] Reading strictly grammatically, the "that" which is seen through "the spy-glass of Anthropology" refers not to the stories Hurston heard as a girl—which she imagines in the form of a tight-fitting chemise—but to the act of "seeing myself like somebody else." This is metaphorical vision turned in upon the self, the subject seeing herself in terms of a "familiar strangeness." And it is *this* vision that is the key to *Their Eyes*, a vision that does not separate inside and outside but confounds them, a vision that does not so much double the self as imagine identity as something that can be understood only by seeing oneself in terms of someone or something else.

The fact that Janie is constantly compared to someone else can be understood as a kind of literalization of Hurston's belief—recorded in *Dust Tracks*—that vision is radically subjective: "There is no single face in nature, because every eye that looks upon it, sees it from its own angle."[29] Insisting on the dissimilarity of the human face would seem to put Hurston at odds with the other writers in this study. Indeed, not only does Hurston see every face as different from every other, she notes that an individual face is different from moment to moment. After Joe's death, for example, Janie "starched and ironed her face, forming it into just what people wanted to see . . . sent her face to Jody's funeral, and herself went rollicking with the springtime" (88). Janie treats her face as if it were as changeable as an article of clothing. Yet her ability to separate what her face shows from what she is feeling, to separate inside from outside, is itself a function, paradoxically, of her rediscovery of her face. In the moments following Joe's death Janie remembers that "[y]ears ago, she had told her girl self to wait for her in the looking glass. It had been a long time since she had remembered. Perhaps she'd better look. She went over to the dresser and looked hard at her skin and features. The young girl was gone, but a handsome woman had taken her place" (87). Just as with her earlier experience with the photograph, Janie is confronted with the difference between her sense of what she looks like—the composite image of ourselves we all carry round in our heads—and her actual likeness.[30]

This depiction of Janie finding out what she looks like—and thus who she is—from looking at herself (whether in the form of a photographic image or a reflection in a mirror) is repeated several times throughout the course of the novel. Yet rather than being a sign of the novel's skepticism about the physiognomic equivalence between inside and outside—Janie can, after all, form her face into the shape people want to see—this topos actually works to guarantee it, as if who the subject is is not reflected on her face but something the subject discovers by looking *at* her own face—and even at the faces of others. After Joe dies, for example, Janie is described as "stud[ying] his dead face for a long time. Poor Joe! Maybe if she had known some other way to try, she might have made his face different" (87). Janie later stares into the dead face of her third husband, Tea Cake, after he dies inches from her own face, a face-to-face encounter that constitutes the "meanest moment of eternity" (184). Tea Cake is, in fact, the one person who is able to read Janie's face—he tells her "Yo' face jus' left here and went off somewhere else" (104) when he realizes that she is lying to him. He criticizes what he sees as Janie's ability to separate her face from herself, advising her that she should "go tuh de lookin' glass and enjoy yo' eyes yo'self. You lets other folks git all de enjoyment out of 'em 'thout takin' in any of it yo'self" (104).

Tea Cake's suggestion renders what I am offering as the model of identity in the novel—the subject looking at herself "like somebody else"—in the form of an injunction, as a command to look at and enjoy oneself in the way that others do. The command raises the possibility that physiognomic logic operates in the novel most effectively when applied to oneself, so that the subject works out not just what she looks like but who she *is* from seeing her own image. The subject thus applies to herself the same model of judgment rendered by the community around her, which repeatedly bases its views of people on what they look like. The clearest example of this judgment by appearance occurs after Janie is found innocent in court of killing Tea Cake. The black community dismisses the verdict by announcing, "you know dem white mens wuzn't gointuh do nothin' tuh no woman dat look like her" (189), the racist judgment repeating Joe's mistake of mixing up Janie's "doings" with Janie's "looks."

Mixing up people's doings with their looks is one way of defining the method—if it can be called that—of physiognomy, the application of which Hurston repeatedly resisted in her work as an anthropologist. Hurston became familiar with physiognomic thinking during her studies under Franz Boas at Barnard. As Valerie Boyd points out, Hurston's first fieldwork, undertaken in 1926, consisted of "measuring the skulls of Harlemites to disprove claims of racial inferiority."[31] The same year Hurston declared in a letter to her patron Annie Nathan Meyer that she was "being trained for Anthropometry," and she remained interested in measuring and classifying the human body through the 1930s. In December 1933, for example, Hurston wrote to Ruth Benedict wondering whether "the Museum of Nat. Hist. would loan me a sliding caliper and a pair of spreading calipers too. I am working on my Negro ear placement and getting in fine."[32] Studying anthropometry under Boas did not, however, entail subscribing to a nineteenth-century hierarchy of racial types. As Stephen Jay Gould points out in *The Mismeasure of Man*, Boas made "short work of the fabled cranial index by showing that it varied widely both among adults of a single group and within the life of an individual."[33] Boas thus overturns the physiognomic model we have encountered in previous chapters, in which the face supposedly determines the subject.

Hurston's measuring of the ears, noses, and foreheads of her fellow

Harlem residents was a continuation of Boas's attempt to undermine belief in the correlation of physical characteristics and racial identity—to show the differences between people rather than differences between "types." Hurston's own opposition to racial typology is evident from her essay "What White Publishers Won't Print," which describes the existence of what the essay calls "THE AMERICAN MUSEUM OF UNNATURAL HISTORY": "The whole museum is dedicated to the convenient 'typical.' In there is the 'typical' Oriental, Jew, Yankee, Westerner, Southerner, Latin, and even out-of-favor Nordics like the German." Despite the fact that minorities are "just like everybody else . . . the majority cannot conceive of a Negro or a Jew feeling and reacting inside just as they do," producing a society in which "It is assumed that all non-Anglo-Saxons are uncomplicated stereotypes. Everybody knows all about them. They are lay figures mounted in the museum where all may take them in at a glance. They are made of bent wires without insides at all. So how could anybody write a book about the non-existent?"[34] Anticipating Ellison's theory of black invisibility, Hurston contends that the African American subject's every act is interpreted according to a simple and stultifying binary: laughing banjo-player or humorless complainer. Reduced to the color of their skin, robbed of interiority, African Americans are forced into a relationship of absolute resemblance—"they are all like that." They are thus excised from the field of representation itself, since they can be understood "at a glance."

Hurston's account of the stereotyping of black life as either joyful or joyless makes use of the very terms deployed against her thirteen years before by Richard Wright in his infamous 1937 attack on *Their Eyes*. In a brief but influential *New Masses* review Wright declared that Hurston's characters "swing like a pendulum eternally in that safe and narrow orbit in which America likes to see the Negro live: between laughter and tears."[35] Wright's criticism of Hurston—echoed at various times by Alain Locke and Sterling Brown—is approvingly cited in Hazel Carby's prejudicial account of Hurston's "nostalgic" depiction of African American life. According to Carby, the rural settings and paucity of references to real events in *Their Eyes* result in the representation of "a folk outside of history," and thus rather than challenging stereotypes of the black subject the novel actually contributes to them, since Hurston ultimately views African American life as "an unchanging, essential entity."[36]

Carby's condemnation of *Their Eyes* has been echoed by a number of critics, most notably Cheryl Wall, Paul Gilroy, and Susan Willis.[37] Yet such accounts of Hurston's supposed racial essentialism overlook, perhaps deliberately, the writer's repeated rejection of typological thinking.[38] Hurston addresses the damage done by African American stereotypes in a 1944 newspaper article detailing the reduction of black life to the same two categories Wright had criticized *Their Eyes* for blithely accepting: "There is over-simplification of the Negro. He is either pictured by conservatives as happy, picking his banjo, or by the so-called liberals as low, miserable and crying. The Negro's life is neither of these. Rather, it is in-between and above and below these pictures."[39] *Dust Tracks* repeatedly insists on its own freedom from such debilitating pictures. "If you have received no clear cut impression of what the Negro in America is like," Hurston assures her readers, "then you are in the same place with me. There is no *The Negro* here."[40] The reason that "there is no *The Negro*" in *Dust Tracks* is because Hurston, despite Carby's belief in the novelist's supposed essentialism, at times seems to regard black identity as a social construct. Such a belief is obviously incompatible with Hurston's insistence on the intrinsic properties of black language in "Characteristics of Negro Expression." In a sense, however, the one view might be said to produce the other. For if black language is pictorial, a matter of "one act described in terms of another," then it cannot help *but* describe black identity in terms of something else—as, that is, not essentially one thing or another, but always relational, contextual. As Hurston puts it in the appendix to *Dust Tracks*, perhaps there is no such thing as an African American at all but simply "the shade patterns of something else thrown on the ground—other folks, seen in shadow."[41]

Seen this way, blackness becomes something that can be acquired, since it depends on a certain relation to language and visuality. And this is precisely how Hurston represents black identity in her essay "How It Feels to Be Colored Me." As she memorably puts it, "I remember the day I became colored. I left Eatonville, the town of the oleanders, as Zora. When I disembarked from the river-boat at Jacksonville, she was no more. It seemed that I had suffered a sea-change. I was not Zora of Orange County any more, I was now a little colored girl. I found it out in certain ways. In my heart as well as in the mirror, I became a fast brown—warranted not to rub or run."[42] Becoming black is identified with the loss of recognition that inevitably accompanies leaving home; whereas in Eatonville everyone knows her as Zora, in Jacksonville Hurston is transformed into an anonymous "colored girl." The loss of Hurston's name coincides with her entry into a visual economy—an entry signaled by the fact that she becomes "a fast brown" in both heart and mirror—and her embrace of this color represents a way of negotiating the alienating experience of being identified solely by her looks. In the process, identity becomes something that, because it is projected onto the subject by others rather than being coterminous with the subject, can be erased—at least temporarily. "I do not always feel colored," Hurston asserts. "Even now I often achieve the unconscious Zora of Eatonville . . . I feel most colored against a sharp white background" (154). According to Priscilla Wald, Hurston's "sea-change" anticipates Janie's photographic "discovery" of her blackness in *Their Eyes*.[43] And there certainly does seem to be something photographic about the scene—the "sharp white background" against which Hurston feels most black, for example, sounds uncannily like the backdrop to a photographic portrait. Identity is thus something projected from the outside onto the subject *and* something the subject projects onto the outside world.

The Same Thing Over and Over Again

In light of his bitter critique of *Their Eyes* for "over-simplification of the Negro," we might expect to find a more complex representation of black life in Wright's own work. Yet, needless to say, the hero of Wright's 1940 novel *Native Son*, Bigger Thomas, embodies rather than contradicts racist stereotypes: killing a white woman and raping and murdering a black one. What accounts for this contradiction is that Wright's novel, in a similar manner to Hurston's, depicts the ways in which the emergence into visibility of the black subject is also the process by which he is rendered invisible—the narrative that will provide the subject matter for Ellison's *Invisible Man* a decade later. In *Their Eyes*, as we have seen, this process takes place around the question of resemblance, so that Janie comes to understand who she is by understanding the ways in which she is like others—both literally and metaphorically; in *Native Son*, by contrast, this process takes place around the question of plot, so that Bigger Thomas comes to understand who he is by understanding the ways in which his story has already been told. I outlined in chapter one my sense that photography's impact on American fiction can be found not in what Nathaniel Hawthorne thinks of as the camera's "minute fidelity" to the world but in what Leo Bersani calls the realist's novel's "parade of sameness."[44] And it is this parade that we find in *Native Son*. For just as in *The House of the Seven Gables*, the shocking and bloody events that provide the plot for *Native Son* are repeated over and over again, thereby forming the repetitive or redundant narrative endemic to photographic fiction.

I am not the first critic to suggest that the second half of the text—which relates Bigger's trial for the murder and rape of Mary Dalton, the daughter of the wealthy white family for whom he works as a chauffeur—mostly retells the first half. As Michael Bérubé observes, Wright's reader is entitled to ask whether "the function of the entire legal apparatus in *Native Son* is to retell *Native Son*."[45] During Bigger's trial, for example,

> The brick he [Bigger] had used to strike Bessie with was shown; then came the flashlight, the Communist pamphlets, the gun, the blackened earring, the hatchet blade, the signed confession, the kidnap note, Bessie's bloody clothes,

> the stained pillows and quilts, the trunk and the empty rum bottle which had been found in the snow near a curb. Mary's bones were brought in and women in the court room began to sob. Then a group of twelve workmen brought in the furnace piece by piece from the Dalton basement and mounted it upon a giant wooden platform.[46]

As Bigger comes to realize as he first listens to the evidence in court and then reads descriptions of this evidence in the press, "it was the same thing over and over again" (366).

Bérubé attempts to account for the repetitive structure of *Native Son* by suggesting that "the novel enacts its concerns with representation partly by representing itself in its own machinery."[47] And what accounts for the reflexive form of Wright's novel is its attempt to depict the extent to which black identity is shaped by technologies of reproduction. *Native Son*, that is, struggles with the fact that, in the words of Bigger's lawyer, Max, "a thousand newspaper and magazine artists have already drawn [Bigger's story] in lurid ink upon a million sheets of public print" (384). Bigger himself comes to realize that there is no escaping the reach of the mass media when he sees a photograph of Mr. and Mrs. Dalton in the newspaper he buys soon after fleeing the Dalton house after the discovery of Mary's remains: "That the image of Mr. and Mrs. Dalton which he had seen but two hours ago should be seen again so soon made him feel that this whole vague white world which could do things so quickly was more than a match for him, that soon it would track him down" (224).[48] Needless to say, Bigger soon *is* tracked down, a hunt Wright's protagonist follows in the papers themselves, which print an up-to-the-minute map showing which areas of Chicago have already been searched: "He was there on that map, in that white spot, standing in a room waiting for them to come" (256). Bigger might be said to fulfill the desire of a character in Henry James's *The Bostonians* not just to find out what was "going in" the paper but "to go in himself, bodily."[49] Bigger is not, however, the only character in the novel to go in the papers. The discovery of Mary's remains by the newspapermen provides a literal counterpart to the image of Mary's decapitated head that continually "hover[s] before [Bigger's] eyes" (113), an image he always sees lying on the newspapers he used to soak up the blood. Bigger will later see Mary's head reproduced in the newspapers in the form of her photograph, an image "so lifelike . . . it reminded him of how she had looked the first time he had seen her; he blinked his eyes. He was looking again in sweaty fear at her head lying upon the sticky newspapers" (207). Bigger's image literalizes the fact that the Daltons are always *in* the news: he first sees Mary in a newsreel, an experience that prompts Bigger to wonder whether "she'd like to come to the South Side and see the sights sometime" (34)—which is, of course, precisely what happens.

It seems appropriate then that Bigger's eventual capture is a media event: "[A] huge, sharp beam of yellow light shot into the sky. Another came, crossing it like a knife. Then another. Soon the sky was full of them. They circled slowly, hemming him in; bars of light forming a prison" (258). Bigger spends Book Two of *Native Son* in this lighted prison, his every act and word chronicled by the mass media. Ellison criticized *Native Son* for just this reason in his 1945 essay "Richard Wright's Blues," complaining that Wright had chosen to focus on the way black life was represented in the media rather than on that life itself, as if "what whites think of the Negro's reality is more important than what Negroes themselves knew it to be."[50] If anything, however, Ellison's critique of *Native Son*, like Bérubé's, does not go far enough. For if Book Two focuses on how the trial and the media tell the story of Book One over and over again, Book One is itself the story of the same thing over and over again. This story is simply the coming-true of Bigger's sense that "something awful's going to happen to me" (20), a sense that renders the awful things that *do* happen to him not only inevitable but not qualitatively different from his everyday life. This sense of redundancy is a result not simply of Wright's adherence to the determinist model of identity typical of the naturalist novel, nor even of realism's "parade of sameness," but of what we might call the novel's photographic or media determinism: *Native Son* reflects the fact that the press tell the same story every day. Yet so closely does the portrayal of black identity in *Native Son* follow the script laid down by the mass media that it might be said to expose that script precisely by repeating it. In the process, the novel narrates the breakdown of the gap between representation and reality, a gap dramatized in *Native Son* as the one between the media and the society on which it reports.

Book One begins by describing a lighted prison just as confining as the actual prison of Book Two: "Light flooded the room and revealed a black boy standing in a narrow space between two iron beds, rubbing his eyes" (3). Wright's desire to expose the prison in which his hero lives is mirrored by Mary's desire to see it, as she tells Bigger during her evening with him on the South Side:

> "You know, Bigger, I've long wanted to go into these houses," she said, pointing to the tall, dark apartment buildings looming to either side of them, "and just *see* how your people live. You know what I mean? I've been to England, France and Mexico, but I don't know how people live ten blocks from me. We know so *little* about each other. I just want to *see*. I want to *know* these people. Never in my life have I been inside of a Negro home. Yet they *must* live like we live. They're *human*. . . . There are twelve million of them." (69–70)

Mary's desire, despite its inanity, anticipates to some extent Wright's own in writing *Native Son*. As he outlines in his account of the genesis of the novel, "How Bigger Was Born," he wanted to make "the reader . . . feel that there was nothing between him and Bigger; that the story was a special *première* given in his own private theater" (458). Inevitably, then, Bigger has the constant sense of being in a lighted prison. Wright's hero feels "naked, transparent" (67), "as if he were acting upon a stage in front of a crowd of people" (84); even the friendly attentions of Mr. Dalton make him "conscious of every square inch of skin on his black body" (46).

It would be easy enough to characterize the novel's fascination with visuality as photographic, to suggest that *Native Son* follows the naturalist rubric of "scrutiny and surveillance" outlined by Mark Seltzer that

I discussed in my introduction.[51] Indeed, Wright makes clear his debt to Émile Zola in "How Bigger Was Born": "Why should I not, like a scientist in a laboratory, use my imagination and invent test-tube situations, [and] place Bigger in them?" (447). Yet what the rhetoric of visibility produces in *Native Son*, as in all the fiction I am discussing, is not a sense of the subject's transparency but of its opacity. Mary's inability to see the lives of twelve million people constitutes, after all, a quite remarkable form of blindness, a condition crudely symbolized in the novel by the literal blindness of Mary's mother. Mrs. Dalton's condition serves the obvious role of panicking Bigger into suffocating Mary in the young girl's bedroom while her mother stands just feet away. But the point of Mrs. Dalton's condition is in fact precisely its obviousness, since in locating the metaphorical blindness of society in an actual person Wright draws attention to the redundancy not just of the events depicted in the text but to the whole project of exposing a life visible almost every place one can look.

Jonathan Elmer has recently read the scene in which Mrs. Dalton witnesses Bigger's killing of Mary as a kind of dramatization of the Lacanian gaze. In Elmer's account, it is Mrs. Dalton's unseeing gaze that begins the process whereby Bigger comes to see himself; put into Lacanian terms, "[T]he gaze creates the field of visibility while remaining external to it."[52] Lacan explicitly compares the gaze, interestingly enough, to photography: "What determines me, at the most profound level, in the visible, is the gaze that is outside. It is through the gaze that I enter light and it is from the gaze that I receive its effects. Hence it comes about that the gaze is the instrument through which light is embodied and through which . . . I am photo-graphed."[53] According to the terms of this model Mrs. Dalton's sightless gaze operates as a photographic camera, allowing Bigger to see himself in much the same way as Janie comes to see herself in *Their Eyes*. Yet to read Mrs. Dalton's blindness as a literal instantiation of the Lacanian gaze is to overlook the importance of what Elmer himself calls her "overdetermined symbolic and narrative presence." As I see it, the obviousness of the symbolism is precisely the point. For as Elmer himself notes, *Native Son* is preoccupied with "following out Bigger's compulsive repetitions," a redundancy reflected in Bigger's developing sense that in killing Mary he is merely conforming to an identity already supplied him by the society in which he lives.[54] Bigger comes to this realization after the mutilated body of the other woman he kills, his girlfriend Bessie, is brought into the court, an experience that leads Wright's hero to realize that "the black girl was merely 'evidence'" (331). Yet what the prosecution's strategy of repeatedly "proving" the same thing over and over again demonstrates is that black skin itself is "evidence." Hence the failure to make Bigger reenact his purported crime in the actual location—Mary's bedroom—in which it supposedly took place does not harm the prosecution's case, since Bigger's crime is simply, as he comes to recognize, "the crime of being black" (296). The only evidence needed to be produced in court to prove this crime is Bigger himself; the only witness needed is someone who cannot see.[55]

The task of announcing Bigger's crime belongs, of course, to the press. Yet the media do not simply report on Bigger's trial, they are a crucial element in it. The state prosecutor calls fifteen newspapermen as witnesses, all of whom say the same thing, "that Bigger acted 'just like all other colored boys'" (379). The fact that the journalists think of Bigger as no different from every other black male explains why Bigger is not surprised to discover that the newspapers are "full of him" while he is on the run from the police: "It did not seem strange that they should be, for all his life he had felt that things had been happening to him that should have gone into them" (222). If Bigger is just like every other colored boy, after all, the newspapers are indeed full of him every day. No wonder, then, that Bigger, like Hurstwood in Theodore Dreiser's *Sister Carrie*, becomes an obsessive reader of the newspapers, and particularly of himself *in* the newspapers, to the extent that his appearances in court seem more real to him when he reads about them in the press than when they actually take place.

The fact that Bigger is both the subject of and the reader of the news mirrors the fact that the press is both the subject of and the producer of the news. The reason the media are called as witnesses, after all, is not simply because they have met Bigger, but because they solved the crime on which they were reporting. The newspapermen and photographers who gather to record Mary's disappearance—lighting up the Dalton basement "with the white flash of a dozen silver bulbs" (201)—end up cracking the case themselves, since it is they who discover the girl's bones in the family furnace. Wright's decision to make the press both observers and actors can be seen as one more example of the familiar truth that the media shape as well as report events. The most devoted observer of events, however, is not a member of the media but Bigger himself. Bigger reflects on the irony that the press "were looking for the girl and the girl was ten feet from them, burning" (208), yet he himself is also present, anxious "to be back on the spot to see what would happen" (121). This leads to the odd redundancy of Bigger delivering his fake ransom note through the front door of the Dalton house and then slipping in through the back in order to see the note read, so as to find out what will happen next. Indeed, even when the police arrive and Bigger feels that his life is in danger he cannot bring himself to flee the Dalton house, being "tensely eager to stay and see how it would all end" (189).

Cathy Jurca has recently pointed out that Bigger's tiny apartment and the Daltons' mansion are only ten blocks apart, a surprising proximity emblematic not just of the intimacy of racial relations in prewar Chicago but of the novel's fascination with depicting life crowded into smaller and smaller spaces: Bigger squeezed between Mary and her boyfriend Jan in the front seat of the Dalton car; Mary's body crammed into the furnace; Bigger's family and friends, his lawyer, the police, and the state attorney all jammed into Bigger's cell in the famous "unrealistic" scene Wright justified as "symbolically" true even if not literally possible.[56] Yet Wright's decision to place all the protagonists of the novel in one small space is justified not simply as a literalization of Bigger's mental space but as a physical enactment of the form of the novel. The collapse of the actual distance between people's bodies in the text is mirrored, that is, by the collapse of the distance between actor and observer: Bigger makes the news at the same time as he reads the news, just as the media make the news as the same time as they report it.

Bigger's dual role as actor and observer could simply be read as a sign of the extent to which the mass media determine his existence, were it not for the fact that his position contravenes the very principle of the media as outlined by Niklas Luhmann "*that no interaction can take place between sender and receivers.* Interaction is ruled out by the interposition of technology."[57] In *Native Son*, however, technology does not rule out all interaction between sender and receiver; it facilitates it. Indeed, watching the press report on and finally solve the mystery of Mary's disappearance in the Daltons' basement is for Bigger just a more immediate way of reading about this story. The fact that Bigger knows how this story will end—"[h]e was black and he had been alone in a room where a white girl was killed; therefore he had killed her" (106)—has as little bearing on his anxiety to see what will happen as it does on the reader—who knows that Bigger will be captured but still reads on to see what will happen nonetheless. In *True Crime* Seltzer notes the link between popular interest in crime reenactment—in the form of "true crime" books and television programs—and "the popular, and dubious, presumption of the return to the scene of the crime."[58] Bigger does not so much return to the scene of the crime, however, as refuse to leave it. This is true even during his flight, since although Bigger knows—because he reads the papers—exactly where the police are searching, he does the very thing that will bring him to the attention of the police—escaping to the criminal's traditional location: the roof. Indeed, in a very real sense Bigger has never left the scene of the crime, since Chicago, like the novel itself, is one entire crime scene, a place where anything and everything is evidence for "the crime of being black." And in a world where the mass media is as inescapable as the police—indeed in Wright's novel they basically do the work of the police, first solving the crime then finding the criminal—the crime of being black is announced on every page.

The reason Wright is so willing to examine the crime of being black in

Native Son—despite the risk that doing so means reproducing the racist stereotypes he deplored in *Their Eyes*—has to do not just with his sense of the inescapability of the mass media but with his determination to have Bigger emblematize this inescapability. According to Luhmann, the staple product dispensed by the media is something he calls the "topic": "[T]he success of the mass media throughout society is based on making sure that topics are accepted. . . . Once having been made public, topics can be dealt with on the basis of being known about."[59] Topics are recursive, since in order to be recognized as news they must already be "known to be known about." But the problem is not simply that the information dispensed by the mass media comes in the form of the stereotype, but that, because the mass media turns everything into a topic of mass media communication, the only thing the mass media have to report on, ultimately, is the world they themselves create. This reflexive structure sheds some light on Bigger's disturbing sense at the end of *Native Son* that in acting exactly in the way the white world expects him to he has finally become himself. "Whatever we know about our society, or indeed about the world in which we live, we know through the mass media," Luhmann points out at the beginning of *The Reality of the Mass Media*.[60] Bigger's triumph is the fact that he comes to understand this. Narrating this triumph both turns the novel into another form of the mass media and also exposes the way the media turns everything into itself—the same thing over and over again. The newspapers are in *Native Son*, and *Native Son*, like Bigger and Mary, is in the newspapers.

Ellison's criticism that Wright depicts black life in terms of how it was already seen by the white public thus misses the fact that African American life—like everything else—cannot be separated from the mass media. Wright suggests as much by adopting the language of this media—photography—in his account of the writing of *Native Son*, "How Bigger Was Born." He describes how what he calls "Bigger Thomas conditioning" is present in every African American, "not . . . as blatant or extreme as in the originals, but . . . there, nevertheless, like an undeveloped negative" (439–40). Wright's task in writing *Native Son* was thus to "develop the dim negative which had been implanted in my mind in the South" (442). The metaphor suggests not that the novel will possess the "minute fidelity" of the photograph but that, like the photograph, it will show "the same thing over and over again." This is, after all, the lesson of photography in the novel. Despite possessing "enough pictures of him now to know him by sight in a crowd," for example, the police conduct their search for Bigger by rounding up "[s]everal hundred Negroes resembling Bigger Thomas . . . from South Side 'hot spots'" (244). Photography does not make Bigger more visible since he is already all too visible—he can be seen at any South Side hot spot since he is "just like all other colored boys." The fear uttered by the black community in the novel—a fear also held by some of Wright's black readers—that Bigger will make "the white folks think we's *all* jus' like him!" (251) is, Wright wants to demonstrate, ultimately redundant, since white folks already do.

Max's insistence during his plea for Bigger's life that the public should "multiply Bigger Thomas twelve million times" (463) is the most fatuous statement of this fact, since it is precisely the fact that whatever Bigger does is multiplied twelve million times that is responsible for his being in court in the first place. Max's comment echoes Mary's desire to "just see" the "twelve million" black lives that surround her and anticipates the title of Wright's next project, his 1941 phototext *12 Million Black Voices*. Wright's fascination for drawing the reader's attention to the number of black people living in America has to do with his sense of the redundancy of exposing black life to a world that only sees things in terms of color. This is why Bigger's actions, as shocking as they might be, are in strict conformity to the identity already supplied him by the media. And this is why it makes sense to think of Bigger in emblematic terms, as, to borrow from Seltzer, a "*particularized type*." As we have seen, Seltzer's formulation updates Francis Galton's notion of real generalizations—the composite photograph.[61] The formulation seems particularly appropriate in light of the fact that "How 'Bigger' Was Born" reveals that Bigger Thomas—like Harriet Beecher Stowe's Uncle Tom—

was actually a composite of a number of different men. I referred in my introduction to Stowe's declaration to the readers of *Uncle Tom's Cabin* that her task was to "daguerreotype" her hero—a promise that has been noted by almost every critic who writes on the intersection of literature and photography. But what these critics have repeatedly overlooked is that Stowe's afterword makes it clear that Uncle Tom is actually more akin to a composite photograph: "The incorruptible fidelity, piety and honesty, of Uncle Tom, had more than one development, to her personal knowledge."[62] This is why appearing in the newspapers allows Bigger to finally feel as if he has become himself, since, like every black subject, he has always been in the newspapers. What he wants, Bigger tells himself, is "that his black face and the image of his smothering Mary and cutting off her head and burning her could hover before their eyes as a terrible picture of reality" (130). Bigger's triumph at the end of the novel, as I see it, is his recognition that this has always been the case.

We Wear the Mask

The absurdity of the fact that "several hundred" men supposedly resembling Bigger are rounded up by the Chicago police during the manhunt is the counterpart to the fact that, as Wright notes in "How Bigger Was Born," any African American subject, when placed in certain "stereotyped situations"—such as being picked up by the police to assuage public outcry in the wake of the murder of a white person—will inevitably develop into the image of Bigger Thomas. The black subject is thus a creation of the camera, shaped by and in response to the stereotyped images reproduced in the mass media. Wright here confronts a familiar question: how to depict the particular lives of people whose existence has been shaped by and in response to general categories. Photography—that is, photographic imagery—offers American fiction a compelling means of exploring this paradox, since the camera appears to reproduce a generalized view of a literal thing. Martin Heidegger comes to this verdict in *Kant and the Problem of Metaphysics*, where he attempts to account for the fact that photography seems to show us both the particular thing and what that thing typically looks like:

> The photograph of the death mask, as copy of a likeness, is itself an image—but this is only because it gives the "image" of the dead person, shows how the dead person appears, or rather how it appeared. . . . Now the photograph, however, can also show how something like a death mask appears in general. In turn, the death mask can show in general how something like the face of a dead human being appears. But an individual corpse itself can also show this. And similarly, the mask itself can show how a death mask in general appears, just as the photograph shows not only how what is photographed, but how a photograph in general appears. But what do these "looks" (images in the broadest sense) of this corpse, this mask, the photograph etc., now show? . . . [T]hey show how something appears "in general"[63]

Heidegger's example of a photograph of a death mask itself brilliantly exemplifies the redundant logic of the type, in the sense that the camera has often been defined as functioning in much the same manner *as* a mask—most famously by André Bazin, who compared the way photography "take[s] an impression" of its subject to the molding of a death mask.[64]

The problem Wright confronts in *Native Son* is the fact that the black subject is viewed as an example of a type rather than as an particular individual. Indeed, this could well be said to be the problem all African American fiction faces, a problem often represented, fittingly enough, by the minstrel mask. The task black writers face cannot exactly be described as representing what lies behind the mask because the black face has repeatedly been represented *as* a mask—a representational equivalent, we might say, to being denied a face altogether. This very situation is dramatized in Stephen Crane's 1898 story "The Monster," in which the black servant Henry Johnson's face is burnt off while saving his employer's son from a fire. Bill Brown compellingly argues that the story "arrest[s] the realist imperative to make things visible."[65] It does so, however, not, as Brown contends, by making Henry Johnson different from all the rest—that is, by making him a monster, a man without a face. For Johnson's monstrosity can be read simply as a literalization of the predicament of black identity, in the sense that the eradication of the black face precisely signals the triumph of physiognomy's reduction of people *to* their face.[66] Since to be black is by definition to be without interiority, the black subject's face can *only* be a mask, and hence not a face at all.[67]

Wright specifically addresses the question of the relation between physiognomy and power in *12 Million Black Voices*, where he suggests that the sequestration of African Americans from society is written on the black face: "Our outward guise still carries the old familiar aspect, which three hundred years of oppression in America has given us. . . . For years we watch the timid faces of poor white peasants—Turks, Czechs, Croats, Finns, and Greeks—pass through this curtain of smoke and emerge with the sensitive features of modern man. But our faces do not change. Our cheek-bones remain as unaltered as the stony countenance of the Sphinx."[68] The reason black faces do not change is not because African Americans are actually all the same, needless to say, but because they are perceived to be all the same. And the reason African Americans are perceived to be all the same is because America continues to be governed by the racist logic of Jim Crow: "We black folk, our history and our present being, are a mirror of all the manifold experiences of America . . . If America has forgotten her past, then let her look into the mirror of our consciousness and she will see the *living* past in the present, for our memories go back . . . Look at us and know us and you will know yourselves, for *we* are *you*, looking back at you from the dark mirror of our lives!"[69] Operating as a kind of mirror with a memory, the black face records American history so perfectly that, were white America only to open its eyes, it would see its own history reflected back at it. Wright's black Americans bear witness to a shared history from which his readers are warned not to turn away. Rather than seeing black physiognomy as a product of photography, Wright sees it as a form *of* photography.

We have encountered this somewhat redundant structure throughout this book, in which the faces of photographed subjects are themselves depicted as acting photographically. Wright imagines that the faces of his photographed African American subjects had all pretty much the same story to tell, and therefore that—accounting for obvious differences in age and gender—they all looked the same. Inevitably, then, *12 Million Black Voices* has been criticized for reproducing the very stereotypes it was intended to challenge—and that he accused Hurston of perpetuating. William Stott observes that "Wright's use of the first person plural conflates the present with the past so that all American Negroes of all time are made to share his opinions," and there is something of a typological insistence in Wright's invocation of what he calls "America's . . . black maid, her black industrial worker, her black stevedore, her black dancer."[70]

James Baldwin, in his 1955 response to Wright, *Notes of a Native Son*, directly challenges Wright's homogenizing vision by imagining the "Negro face" as endlessly different. Here is how he imagines a white observer would describe the black face:

> Time has made some changes in the Negro face. Nothing has succeeded in making it exactly like our own, though the general desire seems to be to make it blank if one cannot make it white. When it has become blank, the past as thoroughly washed from the black face *as it has been from ours*, our guilt will be finished—at least it will have ceased to be visible, which we imagine to be much the same thing. But, paradoxically, it is we who prevent this from happening; since it is we, who, every hour that we live, reinvest the black face with our guilt; and we do this—by a further paradox, no less ferocious—helplessly, passionately, out of an unrealized need to suffer absolution. (italics mine)[71]

Like Wright, Baldwin pictures the black face as a record of American history. But whereas for Wright this history writes itself in the unchanging lineaments of African American physiognomy, for Baldwin this history is one of unceasing change. The white spectator's desire to eradicate all expression from the black face is precisely what gives this face its features, since it records the guilt of those who look upon it. For Wright it is the black face that is blank, for Baldwin it is the white face.

Baldwin invokes the tradition I have been tracing in this book so as to exempt African American life from it. Americans have always assumed, he contends, "that the black man, to be truly human and acceptable, must first become like us. This assumption once accepted, the Negro in America can only acquiesce in the obliteration of his own personality, the distortion and debasement of his own experience, surrendering to those forces which reduce the person to anonymity."[72] As we have seen, the blankness of the reproducible American face can stand in for many different things: the redundancy of representation in the photographic age (in Hawthorne); the homogeneity of American society (in James); even the impossibility of distinguishing between white and black subjects (in Faulkner). Baldwin, by contrast, depicts the black American face not as blank but as formed by the very desire *for* blankness. His account of the features of the black face being literally formed by white guilt exposes the circular logic of physiognomy, which projects onto the face the very features it then reads as proof of the validity of its conclusions. This is the imposition of the mask that reduces all African American faces either to blank unreadable surfaces—as in Joseph Conrad's highly disturbing description of the "tormented and flattened face . . . the repulsive mask of the nigger's soul"—or to joyful expressions of servitude—the minstrel mask donned by performers in blackface.[73]

The dual status of the mask—its double duty as both literal thing and metaphorical designation—emblematizes the paradox of racial identity under Jim Crow. In Kawash's elegant formulation, according to the logic of the one-drop rule "the visible marks of the racialized body are only the signs of a deeper, interior difference, and yet those visible marks are the only difference that can be observed. The body is the sign of a racial difference that exceeds the body."[74] Racial difference under the rule of Jim Crow is both announced by bodies and indifferent to them, since it takes place at the level of the general and the particular simultaneously. The minstrel mask operates as the ideal technology for imposing a regime of similarity upon the black subject in that it obscures that subject's actual face while insisting that what it shows *is* his or her face.[75] The racial subject thus remains subject to the rule of physiognomy even under what Kawash succinctly identifies as one-drop rule's "separation of *looked like* from *was*."[76] Wright's and Baldwin's opposing accounts of the black face—one seeing it as a blank mask, the other as formed by the *desire* to see it as a blank mask—demonstrate that the belief in racial difference insistently confounds the very notion of a separation between the literal and the metaphorical.

Looking White

If the one-drop rule separates "*looked like* from *was*," Hurston, we might say, attempts to put them back together. She does this not by reclaiming the logic of physiognomy, in which people supposedly are how they appear, but by casting the relationship between "looked like" and "was" as a relationship between the metaphorical and the literal. No better emblem of this relationship can be imagined than the minstrel mask. This mask is not only something forced on the black subject by Jim Crow racism, of course, but also something black writers have been attacked for deliberately donning. This charge is at the core of Wright's condemnation of *Their Eyes*, which accuses Hurston's novel of adopting a "minstrel technique."[77] Hurston, in turn, felt that Wright grossly misrepresented black life in *Native Son* by portraying it as unending misery. Yet Wright and Hurston are both invested in exploring the relationship between lived black identity and the ceaseless reproduction of racial stereotypes. The obvious stylistic and political differences between Wright and Hurston should not blind us to this shared project, which, though it runs the danger of being seen as perpetuating racial stereotypes, is actually the product of the realization that any realistic depiction of African American life is impossible without them. Carby's critique of Hurston for depicting black life as "an unchanging, essential entity" thus represents a failure of reading, since it fails to acknowledge the fact that Hurston takes this structure—the structure of the stereotype—as her very subject.

One reason for the difference between Hurston and Wright has to do with their markedly different backgrounds. Eatonville, the all-black town in which Hurston grew up, was described by one journalist as "like a four-walled room" in comparison to the kind of world inhabited by Bigger Thomas, a place where black people are forced to live in "rooms with one wall missing, exposing their lives to the white man's intentions and inspection."[78] Hence it seems appropriate that Hurston remembered her childhood in terms of looking at others rather than being looked at herself. As she puts it in her 1928 essay "How It Feels to Be Colored Me," "The front porch might seem a daring place for the rest of the town, but it was a gallery seat for me. My favorite place was atop the gate-post. Proscenium box for a born first nighter."[79] Yet, although Janie spends much of her time looking at the world in *Their Eyes*, her most important moments of vision concern herself. It is time now to return to what I see as the central moment of the novel, the moment Janie discovers that she is black through seeing a group photograph of herself and the white children with whom she grows up, as if she had never looked at her own body before. As she explains to Pheoby:

> Ah was wid dem white chillun so much till Ah didn't know Ah wuzn't white till Ah was round six years old. Wouldn't have found it out then, but a man come long takin' pictures and without askin' anybody, Shelby, dat was de oldest boy, he told him to take us. Round a week later de man brought de picture for Mis' Washburn to see and pay him which she did, then give us all a good lickin'.
>
> So when we looked at de picture and everybody got pointed out there wasn't nobody left except a real dark little girl with long hair standing by Eleanor. Dat's where Ah wuz s'posed to be, but Ah couldn't recognize dat dark chile as me. So Ah ast, "where is me? Ah don't see me."
>
> Everybody laughed, even Mr. Washburn. Miss Nellie, de mama of de chillun who come back home after her husband dead, she pointed to de dark one

> and said, "Dat's you, Alphabet, don't you know yo' ownself?"
>
> Dey all useter call me Alphabet 'cause so many people had done named me different names. Ah looked at de picture a long time and seen it was mah dress and mah hair so Ah said:
>
> "Aw, aw! Ah'm colored!"
>
> Den dey all laughed real hard. But before Ah seen de picture Ah thought Ah wuz just like de rest. (9)

According to Wald, Janie's experience is an example of "the stock scene of racial discovery" familiar from the passing novel.[80] In this scene, enacted in texts as different as Johnson's *The Autobiography of an Ex-Colored Man* and Nella Larsen's *Passing*, a visibly white but legally black subject minutely examines his or her own features in front of a mirror, finding in the process no physical trace of blackness. Yet Janie's examination of the photograph seems to represent precisely the reverse process: whereas the ex-colored man sees a white face where he believes he should see a black one, Janie sees a black face where she expects to see a white one. The ex-colored man cannot recognize society's notion of who he is from looking at himself in the mirror, while Janie cannot recognize her own notion of who she is from looking at herself in the photograph. One fails to resemble society's image of himself, the other fails to resemble her own image of herself.

Janie's failure to recognize herself in the photograph is described as her inability to know her "ownself," a term that takes us back to Douglass's notion that the photographed subject *belongs* to her image as if she were "public property."[81] What ties the question of physical likeness to that of property is, needless to say, the treatment of human beings as if they *were* property. The following story from Harriet Jacobs's *Incidents in the Life of a Slave Girl* exposes how questions of physical resemblance become matters of life or death under slavery:

> One day I saw a slave pass our gate, muttering, "It's his own, and he can kill it if he will." My grandmother told me that woman's history. Her mistress

> had that day seen her baby for the first time, and in the lineaments of its fair face she saw a likeness to her husband. She turned the bondwoman and her child out of doors, and forbade her ever to return. The slave went to her master, and told him what had happened. He promised to talk with her mistress, and make it all right. The next day she and her baby were sold to a Georgia trader.[82]

Unable to bear the sight of her husband's features reproduced on his property, the master's wife forces him to sell his slave children. The story underscores the fact that to note the physical resemblances between black and white children is to acknowledge the systematic rape of black women, a knowledge so unbearable it threatens to land its owners in the madhouse of Ellison's Golden Day, where even white millionaires can be mistaken for black.[83] *Their Eyes* willingly enters into this madhouse, indeed even locates Janie's origins there.[84] In a manner eerily similar to the story recounted by Jacobs, Nanny tells Janie that her master's wife accosts her moments after she gives birth, repeatedly "astin me how come mah baby look white" (17) before demanding that she leave the plantation.

In one sense the question of physical resemblance appears to have little to do with Janie's story, since Hurston never reveals whether her heroine looks like her parents. Indeed Janie does not know what her parents look like: she tells Pheoby that "[a]h ain't never seen mah papa. And Ah didn't know 'im if I did. Mah mama neither" (8).[85] Yet despite the fact that she has never seen her parents, Janie's identity is intimately related to the question of family resemblance. The first thing Pheoby says to her friend when Janie returns to Eatonville after Tea Cake's death is that she "looks like youse yo' own daughter" (4). Phoeby's unlikely comparison of Janie not with her parents (whom she does not know) or her children (whom she does not have) but with herself takes us back to Hurston's notion in *Dust Tracks* that people judge themselves and others according to a generalized notion of what they and others look like: "[P]eople are prone to build a statue of the kind of person that it pleases them to be.

And few people want to be forced to ask themselves, 'What if there is no one like my statue?'"[86] Here, however, it is Pheoby who confronts the question of the difference between her idea of Janie and her friend's actual appearance. But rather than simply change her notion of what Janie looks like, Pheoby suggests that her friend no longer looks like herself.

The fact that Janie looks younger to Pheoby than she did when she left Eatonville is somewhat remarkable considering that she has just lived through a flood, shot her lover Tea Cake in self-defense after he was driven mad by rabies, and been tried for murder. Janie's extraordinary history cannot be read, it seems, from her body. Yet this conflicts with the fact that the narrator says that the storm leaves an indelible impression on Tea Cake and Janie: "It was next day by the sun and the clock when they reached Palm Beach. It was years later by their bodies" (166). Janie's body bears the marks of the storm one day yet is seemingly unmarked the next, suggesting a certain crisis of vision within the novel. Such a conclusion is hard to reconcile, however, with the moral Janie proffers at the beginning of *Their Eyes*, where she promises to give Pheoby "de understandin' to go long wid'" her story: "Unless you see de fur," she tells her friend, "a mink skin ain't no different from a coon hide" (7). The lessons of Janie's own body seems to be that even if you *can* see the fur, you do not always know what you are looking at. Nanny's belief that "we don't know nothin' but what we see" (14) is thus as suspect as Janie's advice to Pheoby that "you got to *go* there tuh *know* there" (192)—Janie's insistence that "[y]o' papa and yo' mama and nobody else can't tell yuh and show yuh" (192) is, after all, contradicted by the fact that her friend learns a valuable lesson about independence from listening to Janie's story.

Contradictions such as these are the result, I want to suggest, of the novel's Jamesian-like confounding of metaphorical and literal vision. *Their Eyes* famously opens with a parable of metaphorical *and* literal sight: men watching the horizon, waiting for their ships to come in; women acting to bring about what they want, ensuring that "the dream is the truth" (1). This vision is matched by examples of metaphorical and literal blindness: the eyes of the people Tea Cake is forced to bury after the storm "flung wide in sudden judgment" (1); the blind judgment of Janie's behavior offered by the porch dwellers of Eatonville. Hurston's insistent conflation of metaphorical and literal vision explains how Janie can be repeatedly judged by her looks rather than by her actions, despite the fact that what Hurston's heroine looks like depends upon the viewpoint of the observer (every eye that looks upon her, we might say, sees her from its own angle).

The novel's repeated confusion of metaphorical and literal, inside and outside, is closely connected to its deliberate confounding of the boundary between blackness and whiteness. The one thing upon which every observer in the novel agrees is that, as Jacobs has pointed out, both Janie's actions and her looks are comparable to "white folks."[87] The problem of "looking white" is central to Janie's story from the very beginning of the novel. When she first arrives in Eatonville, for example, the men of the town mistake her for Joe's daughter—a man who they, like Janie herself, respect because he acts "like rich white folks" (34).[88] The Eatonville women, meanwhile, see Janie in precisely the same terms, as a black person who behaves like a white one. If the camera proves to Janie that she is black, the community attempts to prove to her that she is white. The racist Mrs. Turner goes so far as to extol what she thinks of as "Janie's Caucasian characteristics" (145), the effect of which is to make herself feel less black: "[W]hen she was with Janie she had a feeling of transmutation, as if she herself had become whiter and with straighter hair" (145). Whiteness, according to this formulation, is transmissible (just as blackness, according to "How It Feels to Be Colored Me," is acquirable).

That Mrs. Turner associates whiteness with straight hair is particularly revealing, since Janie is repeatedly reduced to what the narrator calls "the weight, the length, the glory" (87) of her hair. All three of her husbands fall in love with her partly because of this hair; indeed after Janie spurns Hicks, he sourly comments that there "[t]ain't nothin' to her 'ceptin' dat long hair" (38). Janie's hair continues to enrage Eatonville years later: when she returns to the town after Tea Cake's death the porch dwellers gleefully ask, "What dat ole forty year ole 'oman doin' wid her hair swingin' down her back lak some young gal?" (2). That this is an explicitly racial question is demonstrated by the fact that the only way of telling the white bodies apart from the black ones after the storm—at least according to the authorities who demand that Tea Cake bury only the white bodies—is by their hair. Janie's hair identifies her, according to this twisted logic, as white. Yet her hair comes not from her white father and grandfather but from her grandmother, who tells Janie that the reason she gave birth to Janie's mother was because the slave owner could not resist "the weight, the length, the glory" of her (Nanny's) hair. The implication is that Janie's grandmother is herself of mixed heritage. To complicate things still further, Wald points out that Janie identifies herself as black in the photograph not by noting her skin color but by recognizing "my dress, my hair."[89] Janie's hair, in other words, is a signifier of *both* blackness and whiteness. It is a sign of her likeness to her mother—whose features recall the white slave owner—*and* a sign of Janie's resemblance to her grandmother, whose features attract the white slave owner.

This confusion about what Janie's body signifies reflects the fact that racial identity in the novel ultimately has to do with the question of resemblance, in both a physical and a metaphorical sense. This is why acting "white" is expressed in terms of looking white—"like seeing your sister turn into a 'gator" (48). Indeed, it is precisely because he acts like "rich white folks" (34) that Joe has the Sutpen-like "bow-down command in his face" (47) that subdues Eatonville. Mrs. Turner lays claim to a literal version of this in her description of herself as "uh featured woman. Ah got white folks' features in mah face" (142).[90] What makes the connection between Eatonville's scorn for Janie's supposedly white behavior and Mrs. Turner's pride in her friend's supposedly white appearance so revealing is that even after Janie stops "acting white" in the eyes of the community—at the moment, that is, she begins a new life with Tea Cake, who both looks black and, by the logic of the novel, acts black—she continued to be identified as white. Once again Janie's looks—the fact that she supposedly "looks white"—are seen as more important than her doings. Even worse, Janie's looks are themselves subject to someone else's doings: Tea Cake's beating of Janie in order to send a message to the community on the Muck. "'Ah didn't whup Janie 'cause *she* done nothing,'" he tells his friend Sop-de-Bottom, "'Ah beat her tuh show dem Turners who is boss'" (148). And what allows him to demonstrate that he bosses his wife is Janie's light skin; Tea Cake is a "lucky man," according to Sop-de-Bottom, because "'uh person can see every place you hit her. Dat's de reason Ah done quit beatin' mah woman. You can't make no mark on 'em at all. Lawd! Wouldn't Ah love tuh whip uh tender woman lak Janie!'" (147–48). Janie's looks do, finally, allow her to be read—but only in relation to her husband's character, as if physiognomic logic were transferable (in much the same way that faces in Hawthorne, James, and Faulkner reflect the subject's relation to others rather than who that subject is). Even Tea Cake's death leaves an impression on Janie's body, the marks left by his teeth on her skin leaving her with an indexical record of her late husband.[91] Janie's looks are endlessly subject to the determination of others—whether in the metaphorical form of the voice of the community, or in the literal form of her husband's abuse. Her body, we might say, is never her own. The question of seeing yourself like someone else is thus intimately connected to being seen *as* someone else, a metaphorical structure that, in the case of the bruises left by Tea Cake's beating, takes a surprisingly literal form.

Just like the Rest

In *Roland Barthes by Roland Barthes*, the French critic reminds us that whenever we look at ourselves we look at an image: "*'But I never looked like that!'—How do you know? What is the 'you' you might or might not look like? Where do you find it—by which morphological or expressive calibration? Where is your authentic body? You are the only one who can never see yourself except as an image: you never see your eyes unless they are dulled by the gaze that rests upon the mirror or the lens . . . even and especially for your own body, you are condemned to the repertoire of its images.*"[92] Barthes suggests that we are fundamentally unable to judge whether photographs of ourselves look like us since, strictly speaking, we are without a term of comparison: because we only know what we look like through seeing images of ourselves, it makes little sense to speak about images of ourselves as either good or bad likenesses. Photography, it seems, is all we have, since the image provides the very referent to which it is compared.

The consequences for identity of this photographic remaking of the world can be uncovered by focusing on a seemingly minor aspect of *Their Eyes*: the lengthy stories of Mat Bonner's mule related by Sam and Walter that interrupt Janie's narrative. In one of these "crayon enlargements of life" (51), Sam tells Walter that Bonner's mule attacks everyone he sees because he fears that they are his owner come to work him, to which Walter replies: "Dat mule don't think Ah look lak no Matt Bonner. He ain't dat dumb. If Ah thought he didn't know no better Ah'd have mah picture took and give it tuh dat mule so's he could learn better" (53). Walter's objection suggests that photography is a more effective guarantee of identity than bodily presence; rather than showing himself to the mule, Walter will give the animal his photograph so that when the mule sees Walter the animal can compare him to his image. The camera guarantees identity, in Walter's model, in much the same way as Douglass's notion that the photographic subject conforms to his or her own image.

Walter reiterates his belief in the authenticating power of the photographic image during his argument with Sam over whether Eatonville is being menaced by a "great big ole scoundrel-beast." According to Walter, a huge monster has been eating people and houses "up dere at Hall's fillin' station" (66), a claim rejected by Sam, who refuses to believe in a monster he has not seen with his own eyes. As Walter notes, however, the beast must be chained in the backyard of the gas station because "dey got his picture out front dere" (66):

> "Dey got uh great big picture tellin' how many gallons of dat Sinclair high-compression he drink at one time and how he's more'n uh mullion years old."
>
> "Tain't *nothin'* no million years old!"
>
> "De picture is right up dere where anybody kin see it. Dey can't make de picture till dey see de thing, kin dey?" (66)

The picture, of course, is of the famous Sinclair cartoon dinosaur—a crayon enlargement if ever there was one. Walter's insistence that "[d]ey can't make de picture till dey see de thing" assumes a mimetic model of representation, in which images are copies of a preexisting original. Indeed his joke insists that *all* representation is mimetic, since the fact that there is an image operates as ironic proof that there exists an original. The representative crisis I have traced in this book—in which the mimetic hierarchy of original and copy gives way to a photographic equivalence of one copy to another—has thus come full circle. For Walter, the image guarantees the existence of the original of which it is a copy. And this, according to Barthes, is precisely how we are able to speak of photographic likeness in the first place, in the sense that we "speak of 'likeness' [in a photograph] without ever having seen the model." All we are really doing in talking about photographic likeness is judging one image by another; the copy, in other words, provides the very standard by which its likeness to the original is judged.

The "lying" sessions on the porch thus provide a facetious guide to the circular or tautological logic of identity in the photographic age. They make clear the exemplary status of Janie's photographic discovery of what she looks like; indeed, the fact that Janie's grandmother refers to black women as "the mule of the world" (14) suggests that the extended discussion of Matt Bonner's mule is closely related to Janie's sense of herself. Hurston's seemingly fantastical notion that Janie has never seen her own body before she sees it in the photograph explores the implications for identity of Barthes's belief that, when it comes to understanding our own body, we *"are condemned to the repertoire of its images."*

As we have seen, Janie tells Pheoby that she "was wid dem white chillun so much till Ah didn't know Ah wuzn't white till Ah was round six years old." But if we read the passage carefully we see that it is not simply the case that Janie must never have looked at her own body; rather, she says that she is with the white children *until* she does not know that she is not white, suggesting that there was a moment when she did know that she was not white.[93] What has happened, we might surmise, is that Janie has been unable to confirm her knowledge of what her own body looks like by seeing it outside herself—in the form of a photographic image or a reflection in a mirror—and thus she has taken her identity from those bodies she *can* see: the white bodies of the Washburn children.

According to Wald, Janie's photographic identification of herself operates as the trigger for the text's controversial shift from first- to third-person narrative: "As the photograph distances Janie from herself, enabling her to contemplate the self-image she had internalized, consciousness requires the distance of third-person narration."[94] Wald's reading dovetails nicely with the traditional critical insistence that the novel's choice of third- rather than first-person narration proves that Janie, in the words of Robert Stepto, "has not really won her voice and self after all."[95] I have to admit to finding the entire debate surrounding whether Janie wins or loses her voice in *Their Eyes* somewhat baffling, if not entirely futile. For not only can fictional voices—like fictional selves—not really *be* won or lost, the debate ignores the truly important aspect of the text's oscillation between first- and third-person narration: its enactment at the level of narrative of what Hurston thinks of as the structure of subjectivity itself—the subject seeing him- or herself as if he or she were someone else.

As Wald sees it, Janie's unsettling ability to step outside of herself represents the birth of double consciousness. Yet this ignores the fact that the gaze of others in *Their Eyes* is never a white gaze but is instead either a gaze of people just like Janie or of the camera. Du Bois's model was the result, he tells us in the beginning of *The Souls of Black Folk* in a passage so famous it hardly merits quoting, of a formative childhood experience of being singled out as different: "I was a little thing, away up in the hills of New England. . . . In a wee wooden schoolhouse, something put it into the boys' and girls' heads to buy gorgeous visiting-cards—ten cents a package—and exchange. The exchange was merry, till one girl, a tall newcomer, refused my card,—refused it peremptorily, with a glance. Then it dawned upon me with a certain suddenness that I was different from the others."[96] Du Bois's card is refused because the tall newcomer does not admit its likeness to her own; thus removed from the merry exchange, the little boy realizes his difference. The moment obviously anticipates Janie's recognition of her difference in the Washburn family photograph: "[B]efore Ah seen de picture Ah thought Ah wuz just like de rest." Yet the two episodes also possess significant differences. In order to claim her "ownself," Janie must replace the girl in the picture with herself; she must exchange herself for herself. Janie does not, in other words, look at herself through the eyes of others; she looks at herself as if she *were* other. This is not a doubling of the self but a turning of the self into somebody else. Janie, that is, might be said to discover the concept of likeness at this moment just as surely as she discovers the concept of difference.

Ultimately, *Their Eyes Were Watching God* tells a story of becoming similar as much as it tells a story of being different—a story in which what Janie looks like, despite her protests, determines who she is, both for others *and* for herself. This explains why her story is punctuated by a series of moments in which she looks at herself. What she sees is a woman forced into relationships of similarity: with mules, with 'gators, with white women, with her own sense of who she is. Just such a predicament, curiously enough, forms the subject of the most memorable of the porch-dweller debates between Sam and Walter. Arguing the case for nature versus nurture, Sam tells Walter that nurture is a humbug: "He's uh inseck dat nothin' he got belongs to him. He got eyes, lak something' else; wings lak somethin' else—everything! Even his hum is de sound of somebody else" (65). Nurture is like an insect that mimics its environment.[97] By contrast, Hurston suggests in "Characteristics of Negro

Expression" that the African American imitates "for the love of it, and not because he wishes to be like the one imitated."[98] But Janie's predicament suggests that one person can be taken for another even when no imitation is involved—simply because we see the world in terms of likeness and difference. This is why Hurston begins *Their Eyes* with Janie's photographic recognition. What Janie sees is her difference from everyone else. But what this difference consists of, paradoxically, is precisely the fact that because she fails to resemble herself—because what she looks like seemingly changes from moment to moment—she can therefore be compared *to* everything else. What makes Janie different from everyone else, in other words, is that she is so often the same. Ultimately, then, she embodies rather than contradicts the photographic crisis of resemblance I have suggested is constitutive of modern American identity. Moreover, this process, though it erases the differences between one American and another, might be said to be precisely the thing that provides Janie with her own voice. Janie ends her story with the following moral: "Love is lak de sea. It's uh movin' thing, but still and all, it takes its shape from de shore it meets, and it's different with every shore" (191). Always different, because always similar, love is what Janie invites into her house in the form of Tea Cake's memory, the "kiss" of which "made pictures of love and light against the wall" (193). Love is the means by which she is able to reclaim the visible world for herself, a form of photographic memory that takes its shape from Janie's untransmissible images of herself and others. These, then, are the comparisons Janie means to live by, comparisons Hurston refuses to describe in order, in the last resort, to preserve Janie's difference from us.

every one looks like some one else
GERTRUDE STEIN, "The Gradual Making of the Making of Americans"

CONCLUSION

Likeness Has Ceased to Be of Any Help

Fiction and Film

THIS BOOK has argued that photography shaped American fiction not by offering novelists a model of faithful reproduction, but by offering them a language in which to record the increasing homogeneity of modern identity, a homogeneity that is itself the product *of* photography. What American literature's repeated invocations of the camera tell us is not that the two mediums see the world in the same way but that the world American fiction sees is one shaped by photography. Hence it ultimately does not matter whether American writers see photography as signaling either the impossibility of mimesis or its perfection. Christopher Isherwood's proclamation "I am a camera" thus needs to be read alongside rather than against Sherwood Anderson's belief that "[n]o man can quite make himself a camera," William Dean Howells's praise for "the impartial fidelity of the photograph" alongside rather than against Mark Twain's insistence that "[t]he sun never looks through a photographic instrument that does not print a lie."[1] Indeed for Twain it was precisely photography's ability to produce accurate likenesses of its subject that rendered the image a lie: "The piece of glass it prints is well named a 'negative'—a contradiction—a misrepresentation—a falsehood. I speak feelingly of this matter, because by turns the instrument has represented me to be a lunatic, a Solomon, a missionary, a burglar and an abject idiot—and I am neither."[2] By joking that he is "neither" one of five different things, Twain implies that, although he might have looked like a lunatic, a wise man, a missionary, a burglar, and an idiot at the various times he was photographed, these seemingly exclusive states are not who he is. The very particularity of the photographic image, in other words, ends up being read in terms of typicality: Twain *looks like* the way a missionary, burglar, and lunatic are supposed to look—an expectation that is the result, ironically enough, of photographic reproduction.

Twenty years later Twain, one of the most photographed Americans of the nineteenth century, was still facetiously insisting that the camera misrepresented him. He remarked that Napoleon Sarony's famous portrait of him actually depicted a gorilla, though admittedly a gorilla wearing his overcoat: "The result was surprising. I saw that the gorilla, while not looking distinctly like me was exactly what my great grandfather would have looked like if I had one." Although frustrated that this gorilla was being constantly mistaken for him, Twain congratulated Sarony on having "found my great grandfather in the person of the gorilla."[3] Twain displaces the question of the foreignness of his photographic image onto the strangeness of the idea of family resemblance, for in a sense the unlikeliness of a gorilla looking like him is equivalent to the unlikeliness of likeness in general, since exactly where can likeness be said to take place? "In a certain photograph, I have my father's sister's 'look,'" Roland Barthes reflects in *Camera Lucida*.[4] What this "look" consists of, however, remains as unclear to Barthes as it did to Oliver Wendell Holmes a century before. "There is something in the face that corresponds to *tone* in the voice," Holmes declared in 1864, "recognizable, not capable of description; and this kind of resemblance in the faces of kindred we may observe, though the features are unlike."[5] For Barthes the features that unite family members are a matter of "the structure of the face," but what intrigues the French critic about photography is that it occasionally reveals something "more insidious, more penetrating than likeness: the Photograph sometimes makes appear what we never see in a real face (or in a face reflected in a mirror): a genetic feature, the fragment of oneself or of a relative which comes from some ancestor."[6] It is this actual material fragment, this genetic feature, seemingly, that Twain sees in the Sarony photograph, yet for him this likeness is precisely what renders the photograph foreign. No wonder, then, that the photograph does such violence to our sense of likeness.

Barthes's belief that the photograph uncovers a likeness unavailable to the naked eye—a kind of analog to Walter Benjamin's theory of the optical unconscious—runs contrary to most modern accounts of the camera, which tend to insist that photography has made it harder to see the world as it actually is. Benjamin himself famously claimed that, because "photography records practically nothing of the essence of, for example, a modern factory," photographers needed to supply their images with captions so as to prevent them from simply becoming "modish commerce."[7] For Siegfried Kracauer, as for C. S. Peirce, this problem was intimately bound up with the twin issues of iconicity and indexicality, a combination that he believed signaled the end of traditional mimesis. Kracauer's 1927 essay "Photography" maps the Barthesian question of family resemblance onto modernity's ceaseless proliferation of photographic images, the effect of which, for him as for Nathaniel Hawthorne, Henry James, and the rest of the writers in this study, is to make everything and everyone look the same. Here is how the essay begins:

> This is what the film diva looks like. She is twenty-four years old, featured on the cover of an illustrated magazine, standing in front of the Hotel Excelsior. The date is September. If one were to look through a magnifying glass one

> could make out the grain, the millions of little dots that constitute the diva, the waves, and the hotel. The picture, however, refers not to the dot matrix but to the living diva on the Lido. Time: the present. . . . Everyone recognizes her with delight, since everyone has already seen the original on the screen. It is such a good likeness that she cannot be confused with anyone else, even if she is perhaps only one-twelfth of a dozen Tiller girls. Dreamily she stands in front of the Hotel excelsior, which basks in her fame—a being of flesh and blood, our demonic diva, twenty-four years old, on the Lido. The date is September.
>
> Is this what grandmother looked like? The photograph, more than sixty years old and already a photograph in the modern sense, depicts her as a young girl of twenty-four. Since photographs are likenesses, this one must have been a likeness as well.[8] (ellipses in original)

The trick with which the essay opens—comparing two photographs of twenty-four-year-old women that, despite being taken more than sixty years apart, are confused with one another through the simple device of deictically referring to both as "this"—creates an artificial resemblance as a way of staging a series of genuine ones: that between all photographed subjects; that between the photograph *and* its subject; and that between the photograph and our own already preformed image *of* its subject. The resemblances generated by photography thus become the principle of identity, as necessary to our sense of what grandmothers look like as to our sense of what the Tiller girls look like. Kracauer contends that we understand the photograph to refer not to its material form—since this is after all simply the dot matrix—but to the thing that it shows, precisely because it exactly resembles that thing: "Since photographs are likenesses, this one must have been a likeness as well." Reference, in this model, is ultimately subordinated to resemblance.

The trouble with this formulation is that the various resemblances engendered by photography work to cancel one another out. In the absence of the living grandmother the only evidence to prove that she *is* the twenty-four-year-old girl pictured is the fact that she said she was. "It might turn out after all that the photograph depicts not the grandmother but a friend who resembled her," Kracauer mischievously observes. "None of her contemporaries are still alive. And the question of likeness? The ur-image has long decayed." For Barthes subjects of a photograph are unable to judge whether the image is a true likeness because they have no access to what they look like except through images and thus they can only compare one image with another; for Kracauer, conversely, the viewer of a photograph is unable to judge whether the image is a true likeness because the subject who stood before the lens is no longer present—and thus the viewer too can only compare one image with another.

Identifying the subject of the photograph is complicated still further by the fact that all young girls are rendered alike by the hopelessly antiquated fashions of the nineteenth century, as impossible to tell apart as one decayed corpse from another: "All right, so it's grandmother, but in reality it's any young girl in 1864. The girl smiles continuously, always the same smile. The smile is arrested yet no longer refers to the life from which it has been taken. Likeness has ceased to be of any help."[9] The young girl's smile refers not to her character or state of mind, nor even to the moment she faces the camera, but to the genre of photography itself, which demands that all its subjects smile. Here again Kracauer anticipates Barthes. In posing for the camera, Barthes suggests, the photographed subject has already turned herself into something else: the photographic. Before the lens, Barthes admits, "I pose, I know I am posing, I want you to know that I am posing"[10] The twenty-four-year-old girl in Kracauer's photograph is thus inevitably more like a girl being photographed than she is like herself; in Kracauer's terms, "the resemblance between the image and the object effaces the contours of the object's 'history.'" Hence the Tiller girl "cannot be confused with anyone else" because she is *already* a reproduction; in being like herself in the photograph, that is, she is like her fellow Tiller girls.[11]

A Photographic Face

The society depicted in Kracauer's essay lacks both history and meaning since "the flood of photos sweeps away the dams of memory. . . . The blizzard of photographs betrays an indifference to what . . . things mean." Kracauer's fondness for natural metaphors is itself an ironic sign that nature has been reduced to a sign, that, as he memorably puts it, "[T]he world itself has taken on a 'photographic face.'"[12] Kracauer's critique is echoed by a number of his contemporaries. Gertrude Stein, for example, believed that the camera had corrupted vision to the extent that the artist "cannot look at the world any more, it has been photographed too much."[13] Stein's Kracauer-like disdain for the camera offers a compelling insight into the relationship between photography and resemblance I have been tracing throughout this book. The principal aim of her writing, Stein observed in *How Writing Is Written*, was to capture the "sense of immediacy" of the lived moment, a sense she believed could be had by "ma[king] a description of every kind of human being that existed, the rules for resemblances and all the other things."[14] Stein's rather terrifying sense of what was required of a writer was thus based on the question of likeness. From the beginning of her writing career it had been "very important to me to always know it, to always see it which one looks like others" (274); as she disarmingly puts it, "[O]ne always does like a resemblance" (237).

Being able to see who people looked like allowed Stein to believe that she could "describe really describe every kind of human being that ever was or is or would be living" (274). Stein's modernist aesthetic turns out to be modeled on the familiar realist division of the world into types, or "kinds," as she calls them. The problem was that her ability to recognize who people looked like, she came to realize, ultimately prevented her from seeing who they were: "I made charts and charts of everybody who looked like anybody until I got so that I hardly knew which one I knew on the street and which one looked like them. I did this until at last any one looking like any one else had no importance" (297). With typical thoroughness, Stein pursues the taxonomic approach to its logical conclusion, her "charts and charts" of resemblances resulting in her being unable to tell "which one I knew on the street and which one looked like them." In a world where everyone looks like someone else, who people look like is, in a sense, immaterial—one person looks like someone else, who in turn looks like someone else, and so on; resemblance, here, has made the world indistinguishable rather than representable. Stein's attempt to rectify this erasure led her to various visual models for composition—first painting and then film. These models did not include photography, however, since, as she puts it in *Everybody's Autobiography*, "photography is different from painting, painting looks like something and photography does not."[15] Photographed subjects do not look like "something" precisely because they *are* that thing. Whereas painting opens up a gap between the thing and its representation—the gap that, as I outlined in my introduction, is crucial to the existence of mimesis, which operates via a model of original and copy—photography conflates the two, rendering the thing and its image consubstantial.

Stein's account of likeness is in many ways the one offered by the other writers in this book. She defines the problem with typical exactitude in *The Making of Americans*:

> this seeing resemblances between those one is knowing is interesting, defining, confusing, uncertain and certain. You see one, the way of looking at any one in that one that is like some one, the way of listening, a sudden expression, a way of walking, a sound in laughing, a number of expressions that are passing over the face of that one, it is confusing, too many people have pieces in them like pieces in this one, it began as a clear resemblance to some one, it goes on to be a confusing number of resemblances to many.[16]

No wonder, as she wearily remarked in "The Gradual Making of the Making of Americans," that "description is really unending" (283–84). Inevitably, the problem was particularly acute when it came to representing Americans, who, as she noted in her very first work, *Q. E. D.*, "all look alike."[17] This lack of what she called "vital singularity" is reflected in the seemingly endless repetitions that make up *The Making of Americans*, a history of three families chosen precisely because "there have been always many millions made just like them."[18] Stein's method of knowing people by resemblances thus ultimately results in her being unable to distinguish one person from another: "Types of people I could put down but a whole human being felt at one and the same time, in other words while in the act of feeling that person was very difficult to put into words" (276). And the reason putting people into words proved so difficult is that seeing resemblances involves remembering what other people looked like, and "remembering is repetition and confusion" (296). Remembering muddles up "present with past and future time" (301), so that Stein did not know whether the person she was trying to picture was someone she knew or a stranger—someone she might simply have passed on the street. What was needed to make an accurate portrait of somebody, Stein came to realize, was not remembering but perceiving: "[T]he making of a portrait of any one is as they are existing and as they are existing has nothing to do with remembering any one or anything" (293). We initially perceive people according to the ways they resemble others, but this ultimately prevents us from understanding who those people are—their history, their day-to-day existence. This is ultimately a problem of the relation between the typical and the particular.

Stein's turn away from resemblance represents her attempt to make mimesis possible again in a photographic age. The central problem faced by the modern artist, she believed, was how to find a form in which to depict both the inevitable similarities between people and the obvious similarities between each moment without being confused by remembering. Repetition thus begins to take over from resemblance as the key term in Stein's aesthetic precisely because the problem of resemblance *is* a problem of repetition: a person repeats many others in her or his way of being, and repeats the same actions in her or his history; as Stein puts it near the end of *The Making of Americans*: "One is doing something and then doing that thing again and then doing another thing and then doing that thing again and then doing the one thing and then the other thing."[19] Seen from one perspective, Stein's conception of identity based on repetition would seem to demand a photographic model. What the camera failed to give the writer, however, was a sense of how, as she observes in *The Autobiography of Alice B. Toklas*, "everything being the same everything is always different."[20] Stein, in contrast to the other writers in this book, finds a way of escaping the "photography effect." She recognizes, along with Hawthorne, James, Faulkner, and Hurston, that American history in the photographic age is a matter of the same thing over and over again. What makes Stein the exception to the tradition of photographic fiction I have examined, however, is her belief that it is precisely the iterative quality of life in the photographic age that makes each moment different from the last.

Photography is thus unusable as a model, to adopt the language of James's "The Real Thing," not so much because of its ceaseless reproduction of the real thing as because of its ceaseless reproduction of the same thing. The stillness of the photographic image cannot do justice, Stein insists, to her Emerson-like sense that the world was endlessly changing even as it appeared to stand still.[21] Stein came to think of this belief in terms of movement. Wendy Steiner suggests that Stein's move from resemblance to repetition was motivated by a developing sense that "the generation in America had ceased to operate as the stable basis of comparison it once was. Stein thought of America as discontinuous from its past, as caught up in a frantic movement which was constantly changing and recreating it."[22] As Stein noted in "The Gradual Making of the Making of Americans," "[I]t is strictly something American to conceive a space that is filled with moving" (286). Whereas James depicts the ceaseless movement of American life as a process of erasure, continually destroying lived life from moment to moment, for Stein this process is the principle of history itself, which only exists *as* movement.

This principle is given its definitive treatment in Stein's essay "Portraits and Repetition." Stein explains that the differences between generations in America demonstrate that existing is moving, but that, as with a moving train, we can only perceive this movement against a still background. And whereas for Faulkner the viewing of a moving train produces the illusion of a space *between* stillness and motion, for Stein it is the motion itself that matters. The problem with the current generation of Americans, she suggests, is that they have "conceived an intensity of movement so great that it has to be seen against something else to be known, and therefore, this generation does not connect itself with anything, this is what makes this generation what it is and that is why it is American" (287–88). Linear modes of representation—which Stein disparaged as mere "successivity"—seemed to her utterly inadequate for depicting this new postwar generation. What was needed was not the nineteenth-century English model of beginning, middle, and ending, but a "twentieth century American mode of simultaneity," in which, to quote Marianne DeKoven, "a thing [is] not accreted through time but composed instantaneously of its various, interchangeable, equally important parts."[23] What matters is not, as in James, the ways in which something was like something else, nor even, as in Hurston, the ways in which something is like itself, but how a thing might be said to differ from itself from moment to moment.

Stein was to find this model of difference in the cinema, a technology that allowed her to reconceive her work in terms of a "continuous present," in which writing recreates itself anew in each successive moment. She would call this method "insistence," a model in which her trademark style of repetition "reinvents itself anew in each moment of narrative, is unaware of its past and therefore free to repeat it."[24] As she triumphantly declared in "Portraits and Repetition," "By a continuously moving picture of any one there is no memory of any other thing and there is that thing existing, it is in a way if you like one portrait of anything not a number of them" (293–94). Film abolishes memory and thus does away with repetition and confusion, resulting in one portrait rather than many—a picture of the person as she actually is rather than of the people she is like. And this, Stein declares, is the form taken by her own portraits, which, like the cinema (and like modern painting), offer "a continuous succession of the statement of what that person was" (294). What looks like an absolute commitment to repetition is actually a commitment to singularity. Because the same word means different things in different contexts, Stein's strategy of constructing portraits out of repeated words and phrases eliminates resemblance word by word, just as film eliminates resemblance frame by frame. As Stein puts it, "In a cinema picture no two pictures are exactly alike each one is just that different from the one before" (294). Rather than looking like someone else, the cinematic subject—because he or she is different from moment to moment—looks like who he or she is.[25]

Put Yourself in My Place

Stein's adoption of the cinema as a representational model for her work takes us back to a question I raised in my introduction: whether the relation between technology and American fiction is one of likeness or of causality. Stein's answer to this question in her essay "Portraits and Repetition" conforms to Mark Seltzer's insistence that "the tension between likeness and determination is irreducible":[26]

> I was doing what the cinema was doing, I was making a continuous succession of the statement of what that person was . . . I of course did not think of it in terms of the cinema, in fact I doubt whether I had ever seen a cinema but, and I cannot repeat this too often any one is of one's period and this our period was undoubtedly the period of the cinema and series production. And each of us in our own way are bound to express what the world in which we are living is doing. (294)

Stein's reasoning follows the same circular model I noted in my introduction: she writes like the cinema because her work has been formed by it, yet the evidence that she has been formed by the cinema is that she writes like it. The model leaves open the question of determinism by proposing that "each of us in our own way" express the time in which we live; Stein leaves open the question of likeness by doubting whether she "had ever seen a cinema."

According to Stein's model, to write like the cinema is to leave behind, ironically enough, the question of likeness, and thus the question of the relation between literature and the visual arts—at least in the terms that I have been posing it. Stein disables the analogy between literature and the visual arts—the analogy that ever since Stein's portraits of Picasso and Matisse has provided the model for understanding her work—by simply sidestepping the question of analogy altogether; her work is not like the cinema, it is simply a product of the same world that produced the cinema—the world of serial production. But since the world of serial production is a world in which everything is the same, her work is inevitably like the cinema even as it renders moot the whole question of resemblance.

The irrelevance of whether the relation between literature and the visual arts is one of likeness or causality is also the lesson of one of the writers most influenced by Stein's trademark plain repetitious style, Theodore Dreiser. Although the camera is crucial to the plot of Dreiser's 1925 *An American Tragedy*, for example, and although this novel turns on the striking physical resemblance between Dreiser's hero, Clyde Griffith, and Clyde's cousin, Gilbert, the entire role of the camera—and the entire topos of resemblance—seems somehow irrelevant to the novel. Philip Fisher points out that "[i]t is only because he can so easily be 'taken for' someone else that Clyde can exist in Lycurgus as 'himself,'" yet the text never examines this question in any detail. Fisher notes that Clyde, together with other more famous American fictional protagonists such as Leatherstocking, Uncle Tom, and Gatsby, is characterized by "a puzzling blankness or passivity."[27] This blankness is reflected in Claude's bewildering inability to understand why the various things that happen to him happen to him. Arriving in the upstate New York town where his uncle owns a shirt factory, for example, Claude is frustrated by his resemblance to his cousin Gilbert, despite the fact that this resemblance is the very reason why he was offered a job by his uncle in the first place: "It was just his luck that on arriving here he should find this same Gilbert looking almost like him and being so opposed to him for obviously no reason at all" (236).

The seeming irrelevance of Clyde's family likeness is reflected in the seeming irrelevance of the central role Dreiser allocates to photography. Clyde both kills with and is convicted by a camera, yet in the end this fact seems not to matter either to Clyde or to the novel. For some "strange, equivocal, frivolous" reason Clyde decides to bring a camera and tripod with him on his trip to the lake with his pregnant girlfriend, Roberta.[28] He ends up using the camera, however, to knock Roberta into the lake—accidentally perhaps, yet in conformity with his plan to murder her. And it is the camera that secures Clyde's guilt, partly because it proves that he was at the lake with Roberta, and partly because it matches the wound on Roberta's face.

Dreiser might be said to invert the camera's traditional role in the murder mystery. At least since Dion Boucicault's 1859 play *The Octoroon*, photography has been a staple of the genre, its untiring all-seeing eye helping solve endless numbers of crimes. In Dreiser's novel, however, a detective has to take things into his own hands—twining two strands of Roberta's hair inside the lid of the camera to "prove" that it was indeed the murder weapon that it actually was. In *An American Tragedy*, the real is not real enough, it seems. Indeed, the pictures Clyde takes of Roberta on their trip barely even identify their subject, consisting of "four views which showed a person looking more like Roberta than any one else" (708). The fact that Roberta's photographs picture her as only just distinguishable from anyone else *does*, however, provide one clue to her murder, since it is precisely because she seems just like everyone else that Clyde kills her. What Dreiser's hero wants is a supposedly one-in-a-million girl like Sondra Finchley—the wealthy and smart daughter of a successful businessman—not a girl like Roberta, who is similar in almost every respect to himself. For it is Clyde himself who is more like anyone else than anyone else is, so to speak. Described as "true to the standard of the American youth" (26), what makes Clyde "different" (80)—a term Dreiser repeatedly uses to describe him—is that he is so much the same. This explains why imitation is so central to Dreiser's hero: Fisher points out that Clyde "murders by imitation (after reading of a drowning in the newspaper) as he loves by imitation (his being mistaken for Gilbert)."[29]

Clyde's inability to live his own life is most vividly demonstrated during his trial. Unable to say whether he is guilty or not—he intended to kill Roberta but not at the moment he did kill her, although he then proceeded to ignore her cries for help—Clyde has to be told by his lawyers to remember that he is not guilty. Indeed, such is Clyde's separation from anything that could be thought of as a life of his own that he has to be provided with "a dummy or substitute" (681) story for what happened on the lake; the truth, his lawyers assure Clyde, would fail to convince anyone. Clyde displaces his failure to see his own life with any clarity onto the outside world: "[I]f only somebody could only know how it had all come about! If Sondra, his mother, any one, could truly see!" (617). The truth, of course, is that everyone *can* truly see—during his murder trial every detail is recalled with what Clyde thinks of as astonishing precision: "How people seemed to remember things—more than ever he would have dreamed they would have" (687). Clyde discovers that, although he had "imagined himself fully unobserved" (703), every event of his life in Lycurgus had been recorded by someone.

An American Tragedy thus seems to fit the surveillance model of American realism to perfection, a model Clyde himself imagines in cinematic terms: "Were not the eyes of all the citizens of the United States upon him? He believed so. It was as if some one had suddenly exclaimed: 'Lights! Camera!'" (689). And, as in *Native Son*, this leads to the entire story of the novel being repeated in court; just as Bigger Thomas must endure seeing the actual furnace in which he burned Mary's body rebuilt in court, so too must Clyde endure seeing the actual boat in which he took Roberta out onto the lake. Unlike in Wright's novel, however, Dreiser's hero fails to gain a sense of who he is by seeing his life reenacted in public, remaining a stranger to us and to himself even at the moment of his death: "But his voice sounding so strange and weak, even to himself, so far distant as though it emanated from another being walking alongside of him, and not from himself" (870). If Dreiser's novel can be said to follow what Seltzer identifies as the realist "imperative of making everything, including interior states, visible, legible, and governable," the result, curiously enough, is to make the modern subject harder rather than easier to see.[30]

An American Tragedy is ultimately the story of what Dreiser describes as "that old mass yearning for a likeness in all things" (18). What Clyde wants is a life like that of his cousin, Gilbert; what he *has* is a life like everyone else. The only alternative is the life given to him in the final section of the novel—a life on the front pages of the newspapers. Yet in a world wearing a photographic face, even the life of the celebrity is just like that of everyone else, since all the celebrity does—whether that celebrity is a New England politician, a much-photographed lady and gentleman, or a quasi-accidental murderer—is make manifest the reflexive logic of identity in the photographic age.

That this logic is common both to photography *and* film is the lesson of a novel concerned solely with the cinema—F. Scott Fitzgerald's unfinished exploration of the Hollywood studio system, *The Love of the Last Tycoon*. People in Fitzgerald's novel look so alike that the text's narrator—the daughter of a successful Hollywood director—even mistakes her own father for a stranger: "What did Father look like? I couldn't describe him except for once in New York when I met him where I didn't expect to; I was aware of a bulky, middle-aged man who looked a little ashamed of himself and I wished he'd move on—and then I saw he was Father."[31] Cecilia Brady's inability to recognize her father is the product, the text suggests, of a culture in which anyone can be impersonated by anyone else; indeed, it is only by noting that anyone can look like anyone else that anyone can be described at all. The representational crisis this provokes is made clear by the bewilderment suffered by a European visitor to a studio lot at seeing an actor playing Abraham Lincoln eating his lunch in the cafeteria: "He had been told Lincoln was a great man. . . . But now seeing him sitting here, his legs crossed, his kindly face fixed on a forty cent dinner, including dessert, his shawl wrapped around him as if to protect himself from the erratic air-cooling . . . This then, he thought, was what they all meant to be" (48–49). Rather than wanting to be Lincoln, Prince Agee reflects, all Americans now want to be actors playing people like Lincoln. If in James the photographic subject can begin to generate types and identities for her- or himself, in Fitzgerald the cinematic subject sees her- or himself as impersonating types she or he already knows to be products of the camera.

The plot of *The Love of the Last Tycoon* does not focus on impersonation, however, but on something closer to reincarnation. The novel's hero, the director Monroe Stahr, finds himself confronted on the studio lot one day with "the face of his dead wife [Minna], identical even to the expression" (26–27). The face belongs to an extra, Kathleen Moore, but no one else at the studio notices the similarity; as Stahr ruefully reflects, "Even on the lot here Minna was forgotten. In three years" (30). Film, it seems, destroys the very resemblances it creates as effectively as does the blizzard of photographs described by Kracauer. The forgetting of Stahr's dead wife—who had been the greatest film star of her day—exposes the amnesia of modern life. But then, as Stahr notes, people seem capable of forgetting even their own lives, since they fall in and out of love with astonishing frequency. "I wonder how they manage it," he says to Cecilia,

> "they look so convinced every time. And then suddenly they don't look convinced. But they get convinced all over."
>
> "You've been making too many movies."
>
> "I wonder if they're as convinced the second time or the third time or the fourth time," he persisted. (120)

The very repetitiveness of modern life accounts, paradoxically, for Stahr's Gatsby-like desire to repeat the past by dating Kathleen, since he thinks of dating her as the only way to avoid betraying his dead wife. Only by falling in love with the same woman, that is, can Stahr avoid falling in love with another woman and thus avoid repeating experiences he believed to be unique. Hence the solace Stahr finds in the repetitiveness of the movies he edits: "[T]wo men met endlessly in a door, recognized each other and went on. They met, they started, they went on. They did it wrong. Again they met, they started, they went on" (56). Because each take repeats the same scene exactly, movies are the ideal form for a man who—in contradistinction to Stein—wants life to stand perfectly still.

Both Stein and Fitzgerald depict the cinema as a technology without a memory. But whereas for Stein this renders every frame different from every other, for Fitzgerald, conversely, this renders every frame like every other. This allows Stahr to mistake a woman no different from any "Smith or Brown or Jones" (44) for his dead wife. He thinks of Kathleen as "[n]ot Minna and yet Minna" (59), a description that could apply to Minna herself. Because a film star like Minna owes her success to being seen as everyone's stand-in, on- and even off-screen she is both herself and not herself at the same time. Like Sister Carrie, Minna has a face that is "representative of all desire"; she has our face for us, as it were.[32] It is not simply that everyone looks like everyone else, then, but that people can actually have other people's faces, as it were, in the sense that this is a world structured around substitution—vicarious desire. For Theodor Adorno and Max Horkheimer this "insatiable uniformity," as we saw in my introduction, was something to be fought against; for Stahr, however, it is actually a solace, since it entails that nothing is ultimately lost.[33]

A world where nothing is ultimately lost is obviously Gatsby's world—one where the past can be repeated, since everyone and everything is the same. It is also, however, as we saw in Stephen Crane's "The Five White Mice," a world where nothing happens. The contours of this world emerge in the following scene from *The Love of the Last Tycoon* in which the hack writer Boxley—a fictional double of Aldous Huxley—suggests a number of changes to the plot of one of the many movies in Stahr's production line: "'Let each character see himself in the other's place,' he said. 'The policeman is about to arrest the thief when he sees that the thief actually has his face. I mean show it that way. You could almost call the thing "Put Yourself in My Place"'" (108). Boxley's inspiration that the thief has the policeman's face mirrors Stahr's realization that Kathleen has Minna's face.[34] For in the modern age everyone has everyone else's face, both in the sense that everyone looks like everyone else, and in the sense that the very things we think of as our own—our desires, emotions, and experiences—are to be found on the faces of others, onscreen and off.

I have argued that the photographic effect in modern fiction is a matter not of representation doubling the self but of the self being made up of its representations. The difference between photography and film, as *The Love of the Last Tycoon* makes clear, is the difference between seeing the self as made up of representations of itself—"I don't know which Walt Whitman I am"—and seeing the self as made up of the representation of others—those whose faces are "representative of all desire." Either way, what is at stake is the erasure of any and all prephotographic notions of who and what the subject is. This erasure is nicely demonstrated by the fact that Boxley's name echoes that of a minor character from *The Great Gatsby*, "Blocks" Biloxi, a cousin of someone Nick Carraway used to know and a man whose family, inevitably, made boxes. Biloxi pretends to have been president of Tom and Nick's class at Yale, which in Tom's eyes makes him a double for Gatsby, who must have gone to Oxford, Daisy's husband sardonically notes, "about the time Biloxi went to New Haven."[35] Yet Gatsby, of course, *did* go to Oxford, a fact that allows Nick to go on believing in him and that binds him to the mimicry of Biloxi.

As critics have often noted, Fitzgerald's novel details both a series of doublings—East Egg and West Egg, Daisy smoking two cigarettes—and a series of mistaken identities—Myrtle thinking that Jordan is Daisy, Wilson thinking that Gatsby is Tom. *The Great Gatsby* could in this respect just as easily have been called *Simon Called Peter*, the name of a magazine Nick flicks through in Myrtle's apartment. Nick is himself mistaken for Wilson at Myrtle's party, just as he is mistaken for an associate of Gatsby's by Wolfsheim, who explains his conclusion with the disarming phrase, "I had a wrong man" (75). In a sense, however, there is no such thing in *The Great Gatsby* as a right man. The endless similarities noted by Fitzgerald's narrator are as meaningless as the "charts and charts" of resemblances compiled by Stein: a man selling dogs on the street bears "an absurd resemblance to John D. Rockefeller" (32); Benny McClenahan arrives at Gatsby's parties with four girls who "were never quite the same ones in physical person but they were so identical one with another that it inevitably seemed they had been there before" (67). The impersonality of the girls suggests a family resemblance to the inconsequential Biloxi, a man remembered for having fainted at Daisy's wedding—though no one knows why he was invited in the first place. Biloxi recovers at Jordan Baker's house and ends up staying three weeks until he is finally kicked out. The day after Biloxi left, Jordan tells Nick, her father died, although, needless to say, "there wasn't any connection" (134). *The Great Gatsby* depicts a world in which, to return to Kracauer's formulation, the "blizzard of photographs betrays an indifference to what things mean": Mr. McKee's 127 photographs of his wife, his pointless studies of Montauk Point, the photograph of Gatsby at Oxford that renews Nick's faith in his friend, the image of Gatsby's mansion that Nick believes is more real to Gatsby's father than the house itself. In a world wearing a "photographic face," Biloxi's anonymity makes him the perfect counterpart to the great Gatsby. Like the New York Kid and the Mexican youth, Biloxi and Gatsby share an "equality of emotion": Biloxi has no personal life and thus every story about him is the same; Gatsby dismisses the personal lives of others as "just personal" (160) and believes that the past can be repeated. For both, as for all of us who live in the age of photography, nothing has happened.

Notes

Introduction. "Likeness Men"

1. Crane, *Prose and Poetry*, 766–67. Future references in parentheses.

2. Although I use the term *crisis* to describe a situation the consequences of which I largely restrict to the operations of a dozen or so novels, the following admonishment from Richard Poirier is worth bearing in mind: "It would be nice indeed if cultural and social crises could be solved or ameliorated by more and closer readings of the 'elder writers.' . . . Most writers, most readers even more so, want to believe in such magnifications of literary method and literary meaning. The belief is essential to the notion that the writing and reading of literature have a culturally redemptive power . . . [but it] cannot be sustained by the operations of language in literary texts" (*Renewal of Literature*, 9). I am not so sure that this *is* what "most readers" want these days, but I take the point.

3. Crane, *Red Badge of Courage*, 88, 193.

4. The quote is from the 1898 short story "The Blue Hotel" (Crane, *Prose and Poetry*, 816).

5. Howells, *London Films*, 33; London, *Martin Eden*, 3.

6. As Richard Pearce tells the story in *The Novel in Motion*, whereas eighteenth century "realists" rarely provide visual descriptions, the invention of photography produces a world alive with visual vitality, culminating in Émile Zola's introduction of what is popularly known as "the camera eye." Michael North has recently made the important observation that "the literary prestige of photography often depended as much on its status as index—on its necessary connection to the real—as on its iconic qualities, which, even when they were not in question, often seemed to give the photograph a disorienting hyperreality" (25). As he rightly observes, "Camera vision, in short, was essentially modern precisely because it was not perfectly mimetic" (30). What makes the idea of a close relationship between the camera and mimetic detail so popular, however, is that this is the story realist novelists tell of themselves. Crane himself, for example, defined *The Red Badge of Courage* as a series of "sharply outlined pictures, which pass before the reader like a panorama, leaving each its own definite impression," while Frank Norris said of Crane's *Maggie* that "[t]he picture he makes is not a single carefully composed painting, serious, finished, scrupulously studied, but rather scores and scores of tiny flashlight photographs" (Orvell, *Real Thing*, 128, 126). Bill Brown, to offer the most interesting recent example of this tradition, speaks in *The Material Unconscious* of the "photographic epistemology" (133) of Crane's work. Brown makes a powerful case that *The Red Badge of Courage* "rewrites the problematic of impressionism as a question about the impressions of the camera" (127). He is careful to note, however, that "it is precisely the power of such photographic epistemology to explain 'everything' that [the novel] everywhere contests" (143). Hence after the battle Fleming finds that the actual distances of the fight, "as compared with the brilliant measurings of his mind, were trivial and ridiculous" (Crane, *Red Badge of Courage*, 193). It is worth bearing in mind that Willa Cather provided a salutary warning against the tendency to characterize Crane's work as photographic in her essay "When I Knew Stephen Crane": "Other men, he said, could sit down and write up an experience while the physical effect of it, so to speak, was still upon them, and yesterday's impressions made to-day's 'copy.' But when he came in from the streets to write up what he had seen there, his faculties were benumbed, and he sat twirling his pencil and hunting for words like a schoolboy" (*Stories, Poems, and Other Writings*, 937).

7. Happily for my purposes, the year in which the New York Kid last saw the barber, 1888, also saw the invention of the Kodak instamatic camera. To read "The Five White Mice" as a drama about resemblance and reproducibility is of course to put to one side more familiar critical questions concerning chance, fate, and free will. In *The Gold Standard and the Logic of Naturalism*, however, Walter Benn Michaels makes the case that the role played by chance in "The Five White Mice" is precisely what constitutes the story's link to photography, in the sense that not even the photographer knows what will happen once the camera button is pressed.

8. Benjamin, "On Some Motifs in Baudelaire," *Illuminations*, 174. Crane's reversal of the relationship between present impressions and past experiences can be productively equated with Freud's proposal that traumatic events are first experienced by the subject at a later date, the model that forms the basis for Benjamin's reading of Baudelaire. Benjamin depicts modern society as a kind of traumatized subject, arguing that this trauma is partly produced by the camera, which "gave the moment a posthumous shock, as it were" (274–75). Modern society is characterized by a series of such shocks, a process that inevitably dulls the responses of its subjects. The result is a homogenized and desensitized society, the contours of which are most visible in Poe's crowd. Benjamin's account is anticipated by Ralph Waldo Emerson, who complains in his essay "History" that the modern faces of the crowd present "a confused blur of features" (*Essays and Poems*, 248).

9. Seltzer, *Bodies and Machines*, 95. The paradigm is given perhaps its clearest articulation in another work of Seltzer's, *Henry James and the Art of Power*; Entin offers a thoughtful critique of Seltzer's model in "'Unhuman Humanity.'"

10. Important studies of the relation between photography and fiction include Williams, *Confounding Images*; Sweet, *Poetry, Photography, and the Crisis of the Union*; Folsom, *Walt Whitman's Native Representations*; Lewis-Green, *Framing the Victorians*; Dijikstra, *Cubism, Stieglitz, and the Early Poetry of William Carlos Williams*; North, *Camera Works*; and Jacobs, *The Eye's Mind*. Schloss's *In Visible Light* offers a comprehensive account of the relationship between fiction and photography similar in scope to the present project.

11. Paul Klee offers the most concise account of this crisis: "Formerly we used to represent things visible on earth" (Bradbury and McFarlane, *Modernism*, 48).

12. Seltzer, *Bodies and Machines*, 95; Jacobs, *Eye's Mind*, 19. The stubbornness of critics' belief in an absolute break between American realism and

modernism owes much to the modernists' own sense of their difference from what they saw as the photographic fiction that preceded them. Cather's repudiation of Balzac's aesthetic aims in her 1922 essay "The Novel Démeublé," for example, is not unlike Ezra Pound's habit of writing "photography" next to what he saw as overly realistic passages in early versions of *The Waste Land*: "To reproduce on paper the actual city of Paris; the houses, the upholstery, the food, the wine, the game of pleasure, the game of business, the game of finance: a stupendous ambition—but, after all, unworthy of an artist" (*On Writing*, 38).

13. Valéry, "The Centenary of Photography," 194.

14. Kaplan, *Social Construction of American Realism*, 7.

15. Ibid., 9.

16. Daniel Boorstin, *The Americans: The Democratic Experience*, quoted in Bill Brown, *Sense of Things*, 36.

17. Norris, *McTeague*, 126. Future references in parentheses.

18. Barthes, *Rustle of Language*, 148.

19. Bourdieu, *Photography*, 20.

20. de Tocqueville, *Democracy in America*, 228.

21. Dickens, *Martin Chuzzlewit*, 415.

22. Adorno and Horkheimer, *Dialectic of Enlightenment*, 117.

23. Ibid., 134, 112, 97, 119. A very different view is offered by Hungarian film critic Béla Balázs, who suggests in his 1924 *Theory of the Film* that the cinema would lead to the establishment of "encyclopedias of facial expression, movement and gesture, such as have long existed for words in the shape of dictionaries" (39–40). What these encyclopedias would show, he predicted, was something he called "microphysiognomics," the science of revealing "how much of what is in our faces is our own and how much of it is the common property of our family, nation or class" (42). This composite face was revealed by film because only the camera could get close enough to reveal how the face was actually composed of two countenances: one belonging to the individual, the other to the race: "In the mingling of the individual and racial character two expressions are superimposed on each other like translucent masks" (45). Balázs's use of the term mask provides a clue to the typological underpinnings of microphysiognomics, suggesting that the method is less opposed to the process I am describing than otherwise might appear. Fascinatingly, Benjamin clearly borrowed his belief in "the physiognomic aspects which dwell in the smallest of things" ("Little History of Photography," 519–20) from Balázs. As Benjamin

saw it, photographic portraits would eventually provide the critic with an invaluable physiognomic "training manual": "Sudden shifts of power such as are now overdue in our society can make the ability to read facial types a matter of vital importance. Whether one is of the Left or the Right, one will have to get used to being looked at in terms of one's provenance. And one will have to look at others in the same way" (520).

24. "Are We a Good-Looking People?" 312. Thanks to Brian Sweeney for alerting me to the existence of this article.

25. Turner, *History,* 75, 76.

26. Elliott, *Culture Concept*, 17.

27. Simms, *Physiognomy Illustrated*, 343.

28. "Are We a Good-Looking People?" 313.

29. Seltzer, *Bodies and Machines*, 55, 49.

30. A number of recent studies have offered compelling accounts of photography's role in the formation of modern American identity, most notably Trachtenberg, *Reading American Photographs*; Strange, *Symbols of Ideal Life*; Wexler, *Tender Violence*; and Smith, *American Archives.*

31. Douglass, "Pictures and Progress," 455.

32. Douglass's use of the term "property" to describe the relation between the subject and his or her photographic image points to the fact that representations of Americans as "all alike" simply erases women, African Americans, Latinos, Jewish Americans, Asian Americans, and other minorities from view. Yet when Henry Louis Gates notes that African Americans have been typically viewed as "'imitative' rather than 'creative'" (*The Signifying Monkey*, 66), or when Lisa Lowe questions why "the status of Asian racial formation [is] one of analogue, duplicate, counterfeit?" ("The International within the National," 77), they are—at least according to Douglass's photographic model—asking the prototypical question of American identity.

33. Barthes, *Camera Lucida*, 13.

34. Norris, *The Pit*, 217.

35. Galton, *Inquiries*, 4

36. Seltzer, *Bodies and Machines*, 115. I am thinking here of Nancy Armstrong's comparison of photographic and literary reference to Galton's composites (see note 38 below) as well as Daniel Novak's superb recent account of photographic identity in *Daniel Deronda*, "A Model Jew."

37. Barthes, *Camera Lucida*, 4.

38. Sekula, "Body and the Archive," 17, 7. Sekula's model provides the template for two of the most persuasive accounts of the photographic making of modern identity—Nancy Armstrong's and Deborah Poole's. Armstrong argues that after having been exposed to "a sufficient number of similar mug shots," the viewer of photographic portraits "will perform synthesizing procedures resembling those Galton developed to produce his combination portraits" (*Fiction in the Age of Photography*, 21). Poole, meanwhile, contends that the making of racial types was propelled by the *carte de visites* of foreign races that circulated throughout Europe and America from about 1850: "Because the reality of the person portrayed in the carte was so distant from the familiar world of the photograph's viewer and owner . . . [it did not make any difference] to a viewer in Paris if the Indian portrayed in his carte was North or South American, Bolivian or Peruvian, Quechua or Aymara, a mule driver or domestic servant. . . . As a *carte-de-visite* the Indian's likeness acquired its meaning as part of an archive made up of all the other equivalent images of types" (*Vision*, 111). The most powerful objections to these somewhat analogous models are supplied by Tom Gunning, who contends that "with the advent of photography the human face became less a realm described in generalities . . . than a zone of intense scrutiny on an individual basis" ("In Your Face," 6), and Robert Ray, who suggests that "by showing that every Spaniard was not dark, every banker not dull . . . [photography] effectively criticized all classification systems" ("Snapshots," 298–300).

39. Sekula, "Body and the Archive," 11.

40. See Cowling, *Artist as Anthropologist.*

41. Rudisill, *Mirror Image*, 236.

42. Simms, *Physiognomy Illustrated*, 19.

43. Trachtenberg, *Reading American Photographs*, 48.

44. Crary, *Techniques*, 13.

45. Ibid., 91.

46. Ibid., 129.

47. Seltzer, *Bodies and Machines*, 51; Brown, *Sense of Things*, 45.

48. Poe, "The Daguerreotype," 5.

49. Trachtenberg, "Lincoln's Smile," 13.

50. Barthes, *Camera Lucida*, 80.

51. Quoted in Kittler, *Gramophone*, 188.

52. I borrow these terms, needless to say, from C. S Peirce, who found photographs to be "very instructive" since "[they] are in certain respects exactly like

the objects they represent. But this resemblance is due to the photographs having been produced under such circumstances that they were physically forced to correspond point by point to nature. In that aspect, then, they belong to the second class of signs, those by physical connection" (Hartshorne, *Collected Papers*, 2:159). Joel Snyder notes that the photograph is in this regard somewhat unusual, since indexicality offers no guarantee of resemblance: "I can smash a hole in the wall with a hammer, but that does not mean that the hole will look like the hammer" ("Picturing Vision," 225).

53. Prendergast, *Order of Mimesis*, 58.

54. Bazin, *What Is Cinema?* 241.

55. Cavell, *World Viewed*, 17, 18.

56. Baudrillard, *Transparency of Evil*, 7–8.

57. Orvell, *Real Thing*, 126; Welty, *One Writer's Beginnings*, 84.

58. Kittler, *Discourse Networks*, 184, 185.

59. Kittler, *Gramophone, Film, Typewriter*, xxxix.

60. Seltzer, *True Crime*, 124.

61. Seltzer, *Serial Killers*, 61.

62. Armstrong, *Fiction*, 28.

63. As a character in Cather's *O Pioneers!* despairingly observes of modern American life, "We are all alike. . . . We live in the streets, the parks, in the theatres. We sit in restaurants and concert halls and look about at the hundreds of our own kind and shudder" (123). Cather explicitly identified this photographically produced homogeneity as American in character, complaining in 1924 that immigrants to the United States were immediately turned "into stupid replicas of smug American citizens. This passion for Americanizing everything and everybody is a deadly disease with us" (Bohlke, *Willa Cather in Person*, 71–72).

64. Jakobsen, "Two Aspects," 111.

65. Horwitz, "*Maggie*," 617.

66. The cost of this photographic erasure for both the modern subject and narrative itself is clearly demonstrated in Herman Melville's short story "The Paradise of Bachelors and the Tartarus of Maids." The story ends with an appalled account of the workings of a paper mill in western Massachusetts, in which the narrator is transfixed by the following sight: "At rows of blank-looking counters sat rows of blank-looking girls, with blank, white folders in their blank hands, all blankly folding blank paper" (Melville, *Billy Budd*, 277). That the narrator's vision of the blankness of the mass-produced paper repro-

ducing itself on the blankness of the girls' faces is photographic is made clear by the dreamlike imaginings with which Melville ends his tale: "Before my eyes—there, passing in slow procession along the wheeling cylinders, I seemed to see, glued to the pallid incipience of the pulp, the yet more pallid faces of all the pallid girls I had eyed that heavy day. Slowly, mournfully, beseechingly, yet unresistingly, they gleamed along, their agony dimly outlined on the imperfect paper, like the print of the tormented face on the handkerchief of Saint Veronica" (285). What robs the girls' "tormented face" of its features is the fact that it is reproduced, in the manner of a photographic image, on the paper itself. Indeed, the girls leave a photographic impression not just on the paper they make but on the narrator who uses that paper to help make them, who finds himself unable to blot out the dim outline of the girls' identical faces. Melville thus describes a remarkably circular process, in which the paper impresses itself on the girls' faces, the girls impress their tormented faces on the paper, and both impress themselves on the narrator. "The Paradise of Bachelors and the Tartarus of Maids" can be read as an allegory for modern fiction's reproduction of the photographic subject. For what better model for the process by which the modern subject conforms to her own photographic reproduction could be imagined than a story in which the inexorable workings of mass reproduction turns its laboring subjects into blank surfaces unable to record that violence? The girls are not only identical to one another—as identical, we might say, as the New York Kid, the Boston barber, and the Mexican youth—they are identical to the very process that has produced them. And since the mark of this identicalness is a shared blankness, all fiction can do is point to the absence of the historical record.

Chapter One. Nature Herself

1. Newhall, *Daguerreotype in America*, 30, 83. Film was to be described in exactly the same terms almost a century later. In his 1933 essay "Film and Radio," Rudolf Arnheim asks, "What is the peculiarity of this reproductive art? That it represents *reality itself.* It is as though the model were taking the brush from the painter's hand when the light rays draw dark and light on the silver bromide" (16).

2. Batchen, *Burning with Desire*, 68.

3. Daguerre, "Daguerreotype," 13.

4. Morris, *Time Pieces*, 57. No wonder that New York critic Philip Hone's reaction to the first exhibition of French daguerreotypes in America in December

1839 was to call the daguerreotype "a confusion of the very elements of nature" (Bayard Tuckerman, *Diary of Philip Hone*, 391).

5. Batchen, *Burning with Desire,* 175. Daguerre's foremost American patron, Samuel Morse, for example, declared photographs both "portions of nature herself" and "*fac-simile* sketches of nature" (Schloss, *In Visible Light*, 33). The most memorable of photography's pleonasms was provided by J. H. Fitzgibbon, who described photographs as "*Nature, copying nature by nature's hand*" (Cohen, "What's Wrong with This Picture?" 55).

6. Fox-Talbot, "Some Account," 39.

7. Williams, *Confounding Images*, 224.

8. Barthes, *Camera Lucida*, 5.

9. I borrow the term *ekphrastic emblem* from Mark McGurl's *Novel Art*, 31.

10. Quoted in Seltzer, *Henry James and the Art of Power*, 53.

11. Seltzer, *Bodies and Machines*, 112.

12. This is why Seltzer identifies these images as "apparently gratuitous but structurally determinate . . . photography for photography's sake" (*True Crime*, 135).

13. As Balzac saw it, fiction simply skimmed the surface of a subject and transferred it to the page, a prephotographic aesthetic model that, almost inevitably, drew upon the tautological logic of physiognomy. "The external life is a kind of organized system," Balzac contended, "which represents a man as exactly as the colors by which the snail reproduces itself on the shell" (Krauss, "Tracing Nadar," 35.)

14. Hawthorne, *House of the Seven Gables*, 1. Future references in parentheses.

15. Trachtenberg attempts to square this circle by suggesting that the preface does not so much oppose Romance to Novel as posit its own hybrid genre, a kind of mimetic Romance. See his "Seeing and Believing," especially 30–32.

16. Schloss, *In Visible Light*, 38; Henry Tuckerman, "Review," 41. The comparison of Hawthorne's work to photography dates back as far as an 1842 review of *Twice-Told Tales*, which observed that Hawthorne's "mind reflects [Nature] like the plate of the Daguerreotype" (Williams, *Confounding Images*, 237). For an extended examination of contemporary comparisons of Hawthorne's work to photography see John Dolis, *Style of Hawthorne's Gaze*, 62–63.

17. Hawthorne's treatment of photography as supernatural phenomenon rather than realistic technology has been the subject of a number of recent

studies, including Cohen, "What's Wrong with this Picture?"; Trachtenberg, "Seeing and Believing"; and Williams, *Confounding Images.* Other important analyses of the role played by the daguerreotype in *The House of the Seven Gables* include Davidson, "Photographs of the Dead"; Gilmore, *Genuine Article*; Sundquist, *Home as Found*; Thomas, "Double Exposures"; Schloss, *In* Visible Light; and Swann, "*House of the Seven Gables.*"

18. Baym, *Shape of Hawthorne's Career*, 154.

19. Pearce, *Nathaniel Hawthorne: The Letters 1813–43*, 384.

20. Michaels, *Gold Standard*, 96. Eric Sundquist, by contrast, anticipates Trachtenberg by characterizing Hawthorne's counterintuitive account of photography as a conflation of realism and romance, arguing that Holgrave's daguerreotypes' "exact mirroring [of their subjects] is an uncanny perfection of mimesis in the speculative world of romance" (*Home as Found*, 99).

21. Michaels, *Gold Standard*, 96, 88.

22. Tucker, *Nature Exposed*, 12.

23. Gilmore draws much the same connection between the redundancy of physiognomic reasoning and the photographs of Judge Pyncheon: "As with Holgrave's daguerreotype of Jaffrey, [physiognomic] distinctions are already known before the daguerreotype is made" (*Genuine Article*, 232).

24. D. A. Miller, *Novel and the Police*, 205.

25. See Hutner's *Secrets and Sympathy.*

26. Davidson, "Photographs of the Dead," 682.

27. Gillian Brown offers a highly suggestive reading of the role Hawthorne's novel allots to the domestic sphere in *Domestic Individualism.*

28. Trachtenberg, *Reading American Photographs*, 27.

29. Dryden, *Form of American Romance*, 36.

30. Williams, *Confounding Images*, 120; Dryden, *Form of American Romance*, 82.

31. Melville, *Pierre*, 13, 259. Future references in parentheses

32. A number of critics have noted the parallels between Pierre's fear of the camera and Melville's own contempt for the practice. See in particular Wald, *Rites of Assent*, 135. Pierre's fear seems reasonable enough in the context of a story told by N. G. Burgess in 1856, four years after the publication of Melville's novel. An inexperienced young man from the country insists that his portrait be taken by a traveling daguerreotypist despite the fact that the photographer had run out of plates: "The Artist was reluctant to comply, but he bethought himself of some old specimens in his plate-box that might answer for a likeness and he

requested the young man to be seated, in front of the camera, when he drew the focus and required him to remain still until he returned which would be at least five or ten minutes. He repaired to his plate box, and found a picture that bore the only resemblance to the young man, in the fact that it was taken for another young man in the city of New York. The likeness was sealed up and put into a case—and then carefully laid in the Camera-box—when five minutes had expired the artist, withdrew the picture from the box, and immediately opened it to the astonished gaze of the sitter. . . . He was quite surprised to learn that he made so good a likeness, and still more so that the artist had given him such a fine suit of clothes; remarking that the coat had more buttons than his, and in fact was a very much better picture than he thought he would make" (Burgess, "Amusing Incidents," 190).

33. Fisher, *Still the New World*, 72.

34. As Emerson was to note four years later in *English Traits*, a "child blends in his face the faces of both parents, and some feature from every ancestor whose face hangs on the wall" (24–25).

35. Dimock, *Empire for Liberty*, 173.

36. Melville, *Moby-Dick*, 212.

37. Folsom, *Walt Whitman's Native Representations*, 161.

38. Holmes, *Soundings from the Atlantic*, 169–70. The situation described by Holmes and Whitman provides the plot for Edward Bellamy's 1884 romance *Miss Ludington's Sister.* The novel is little more than the acting out of a character's observation that human beings are aggregates of "a number of distinct persons, related to one another in a particular way, and having certain features of resemblance" (26). Bellamy tells the story of an aged woman ostensibly brought face-to-face with her seventeen-year-old former self, who returns as a result of a séance conducted in order to contact her. The two women decide to live together—the younger one passing herself off as Miss Ludington's sister—which allows Miss Ludington to "introduce [her younger self] to the rest of the family": "a collection of photographs, one or two for each year, arranged in order. They numbered not less than fifty in all and covered thirty-seven years, from a daguerreotype of Miss Ludington at the age of twenty-five to a photograph taken the last month. Between these two pictures there was not enough resemblance to suggest to a casual observer that they were pictures of the same individual" (145).

39. Kittler, *Gramophone*, 188.

40. Daston and Galison, "Image of Objectivity," 81.

41. Root, *Camera and the Pencil*, 144.

42. Willis, "Pencil of Nature," 71.

43. Rudisill, *Mirror Image*, 185, 213.

44. Newhall, *Daguerreotype in America*, 83.

45. Root, *Camera and the Pencil*, 144, 145.

46. Susan Sontag puts the case with characteristic brio: "Paintings invariably sum up; photographs usually do not" (*On Photography*, 166).

47. Sobieszek and Appeal, *Spirit Of Fact*, 46.

48. Trachtenberg, "Lincoln's Smile," 14; *Reading American Photographs*, 27. In *Photography: A Middle-Brow Art*, Pierre Bourdieu goes so far as to see photography purely in terms of its representative function. "What is photographed and what is perceived by the reader of the photograph," the French sociologist advises, "is not, properly speaking, individuals in their capacity as individuals, but social roles, the husband, first communicant, soldier" (*Photography*, 83). Echoing Root's diagnosis, Bourdieu suggests that the representative function of the photograph is a result of the pose the subject offers to the camera. In front of the camera, he observes, "one presents oneself to be looked at as one seeks to be looked at; one presents one's own image" (83). Photography is therefore "a *technology for . . . reiteration*" (24), in which each person represents who he or she is.

49. "Daguerreotypes," 552.

50. Root, *Camera and the Pencil*, 44.

51. Ibid., 85.

52. Carol Armstrong, *Scenes in a Library*, 49.

53. Ibid., 143. As Rosalind Krauss observes in "A Note on Photography and the Simulacral," "[i]f the photographic image is considered to be objective, that designation occurs within an entirely tautological or circular condition: the societal need to define something as fact leads to the insistence on the utterly objective factuality of the record that is made" (57).

54. Root, *Camera and the Pencil*, 98. Dissatisfaction with the masklike face produced by the photograph was to dissipate in the 1850s, as reduced exposure times and the mass production of albumen prints (of extremely fine detail) resulted in far more accurate portraits.

55. Gilman and Parsons, *Journals and Miscellaneous Notebooks of Ralph Waldo Emerson*, 114–117.

56. Root, *Camera and the Pencil*, 34, 27.

57. The danger that the outward guise of the virtuous might sometimes fail to

correspond to their inner condition was not a problem, Root maintained, when it came to photographing the vicious. "In vain do the profligate, the base, the wicked, and the selfish mimic those outward indications which pertain naturally to the pure, the good, and the generous. The inward unworthiness, despite all effort, *will* glare through the fleshy mask" (Root, *Camera and the Pencil*, 44).

58. Talbot, "Some Account of the Art of Photogenic Drawing," 46.

59. Armstrong, *Scenes in a Library*, 169–70.

60. Evert Augustus Duyckinck, "Review," 27; Pearce, *Nathaniel Hawthorne: The Letters 1843–53*, 382.

61. Melville, "Letter of Herman Melville," 23.

62. James, *American Scene*, 201. Such reactions must have been all too common, for just five years after James's visit the house was remodeled in order to conform to the descriptions in the novel.

63. Pearce, *Nathaniel Hawthorne: The Letters 1843–53*, 308; Hawthorne, *Tales and Sketches*, 1149. Future references in parentheses. Hawthorne stayed true to this conceit all his life. Writing to Fields from Florence in September 1858, for example, Hawthorne told his publisher, "I hire this villa, tower and all, at twenty eight dollars a month; but I mean to take it away bodily and clap it into a Romance, which I have in my head ready to be written out." (Pearce, *Nathaniel Hawthorne: The Letters 1857–64*, 151). The novel was, of course, *The Marble Faun*.

64. Dryden argues that what he calls Hawthorne's peripatetic life leads to "homelessness . . . being the original impulse or basic theme of Hawthornian Romance" ("Hawthorne's Castle in the Air," 295–96).

65. As Sharon Cameron observes, "for Hawthorne . . . houses are not just dwellings, they are bodies of sorts" (*Corporeal Self*, 118). The obvious reason for this, as Richard Poirier noted more than forty years ago, is that "the building of a house is an extension and an expansion of the self" (*World Elsewhere*, 18).

66. Peter Bellis puts it best when he says that "[r]epetition is, in a way, a Pyncheon family trait" ("Mauling Governor Pyncheon," 205).

67. Cameron, *Corporeal Self*, 3, 89.

68. Ibid., 79–80.

69. Hawthorne, *American Notes*, 242–43.

70. That Hawthorne conceived of the birds in cannibalistic terms can be seen from a letter he wrote to his friend Horatio Bridge in October 1850 while "deep

into" the writing of *The House of the Seven Gables*: "Una and Julian grow apace, and so do our chickens, of which we have two broods. There is one difficulty about these chickens, as well as about the old fowls. We have become so intimately acquainted with every individual of them, that it really seems like cannibalism to think of eating them" (Pearce, *Nathaniel Hawthorne: The Letters 1843–53*, 368).

71. Goldberg, *Photography in Print*, 82.

72. Willis, "Pencil of Nature," 71. The image recurs in Paul Valéry's 1939 essay "The Centenary of Photography," which proposes that in the photographic image "the thing speaks for itself without benefit of proxy" (193).

73. Appropriately, Willis was himself one of the first examples of this process. As Glenn Hendler notes in *Public Sentiments*, the essayist pioneered the modern culture of celebrity by continually exposing his private life to the public in his "Editor's Table" articles for *American Monthly* magazine in the 1830s.

74. Barthes, *Camera Lucida*, 98.

75. James, *Complete Stories*, 439.

76. As Batchen puts it, "photography insisted that if one wanted to appear lifelike in a photograph, one first had to act as if dead" (208).

77. Michaels, *Gold Standard*, 100.

78. This is why the account of public life in "The Custom House" announces itself as a text written by a dead man, ending with Hawthorne's complaint that press coverage of his dismissal from the Salem Custom House "kept me for a week or two careering through the public prints, in my decapitated state, like Irving's Headless Horseman, ghastly and grim, and longing to be buried" (*Scarlet Letter*, 41–42). That Hawthorne associates the mask demanded by public life with death is evident from his description of Hester Prynne being forced to hide her feelings in public: "Her face . . . was like a mask; or, rather like the frozen calmness of a dead woman's features" (197).

79. See Trachtenberg, *Reading American Photographs*, 30.

80. Davidson, "Photographs of the Dead," 672. In Eduardo Cadava's elegant formulation, "The image already announces our absence. . . . It announces the death of the photographed. This is why what survives in a photograph is also the survival of the dead" (*Words of Light*, 8).

81. Shamir, "Hawthorne's Romance," 772.

82. Michaels, *Gold Standard*, 88.

83. Brown, *Domestic Individualism*, 70.

84. See in particular Williams's introduction to *Confounding Images*.

85. Pearce, *Nathaniel Hawthorne: The Letters 1843–53*, 606. As Frederick Douglass observed in 1861, "In the making of our Presidents, the political gathering begins the operation, and the picture gallery ends it" ("Pictures and Progress," 457).

86. See Rudisill, *Mirror Image*, 74.

87. Seltzer, *Bodies and Machines*, 95.

88. Haltunnen, *Confidence Men*, 47.

89. This process is imagined by Ralph Waldo Emerson in his essay "Character" as producing a country in which each individual citizen might serve as a model for their fellows. These ideal Americans, both products and producers of American democracy, would then be, Emerson declares, "themselves the country which they represent: nowhere are its emotions or opinions so instant and true as in them . . . The constituency at home hearkens to their words, watches the color of their cheek, and therein, as in a glass, dresses its own" (*Essays and Poems*, 496). America, in Emerson's all-inclusive vision, becomes a country in which the people are represented not only by elected officials but by their fellow citizens, whose exemplary behavior offers a model for imitation. My understanding of Emerson is indebted to Hans von Rautenfeld's recent essay on Emerson, "Thinking for Thousands."

90. Uncle Venner's composite outfit makes visible the fact that fashion, in the words of Franco Moretti, "is *nothing but* time" (*Signs Taken for Wonders*, 114). A patchwork suit can be read as a figure for time itself since every one of its garments indexes a different moment, a fact that is underlined later in the novel when Hawthorne reverses the image and represents time *as* a patchwork suit, describing how the revolutionary Holgrave is mistaken in thinking that the present was "destined to see the tattered garments of Antiquity exchanged for a new suit, instead of gradually renewing themselves by patchwork" (*House of the Seven Gables*, 180).

91. James, *Hawthorne*, 99. James criticized Hawthorne's use of types as the novel's greatest failing, believing that it turned Pyncheon and Maule into "pictures rather than persons."

92. Kermode, *Classic*, 90.

93. Blanchot, *Gaze of Orpheus,* 80, 82–84, 85.

94. Ibid., 84.

95. Such is the unstoppable nature of this process of reproduction that even the Judge himself is able to look upon his own dead body. His ghost forms part of the throng of dead Pyncheons who enter the House of the Seven Gables to

look for the deeds to eastern Maine they (rightly) believe to be hidden behind the Colonel's portrait. Intent on the search, the Judge ignores the fact of his own corpse slumped in a chair underneath the portrait.

96. The clearest example of this is Holgrave's account of his ancestor's hypnotism of Alice Pyncheon, which ends up mesmerizing his listener Phoebe in turn, "the effect, unquestionably, of the mystic gesticulations, by which he had sought to bring bodily before Phoebe's perception the figure of the mesmerizing carpenter" (211).

Chapter Two. Resembling Oneself

1. James, *American Scene*, 363. Future references in parentheses.

2. As Mark Seltzer puts it in his reading of this passage in *Henry James and the Art of Power*, "[I]t is by erasing the traces of power that power 'represents' itself" (133).

3. Sharon Cameron suggests that the constituted blankness of the America depicted in *The American Scene* renders it a "test" of the power of Jamesian consciousness (*Thinking in Henry James*, 29).

4. Saltz, "Henry James's Overexposures," 256. James's well-known fascination with painting—he suggests in "The Art of Fiction" that "the analogy between the art of the painter and the art of the novelist is, so far as I am able to see, complete" (*Literary Criticism*, 46)—has persistently obscured the crucial role in his work afforded photography. Marianna Torgovnick sums up the majority critical position when she declares James "indifferent to the artistic potential of both the cinema and photography" (*Visual Arts*, 29). This position has recently been challenged by Stuart Culver, who points out that in James's late works "images seep into the texts and reconfigure their logic" ("How Photographs Mean," 202).

5. Reading James in this way places him firmly within an American pastoral tradition, a tradition that, according to Annette Kolodny, "took its metaphors as literal truths" (*Lay of the Land*, 6). As she points out, only if we acknowledge the power of the pastoral impulse to shape and structure experience can we reconcile the images of abundance in early Puritan texts with the historical evidence of starvation, poor harvests, and inclement weather.

6. James, *Autobiography*, 231.

7. Salmon, *Henry James and the Culture of Publicity*, 59.

8. Seltzer, *Bodies and Machines*, 55.

9. James, *American*, 35.

10. James, *Bostonians*, 25.

11. As William Righter observes, Americanness in *The American Scene* involves "a strange movement of obliteration" (*American Memory in Henry James*, 25).

12. Ross Posnock notes that James's loss of his own past "implicitly joins him with the very figure he sought relief from—'the ubiquitous alien'" (*Trial of Curiosity*, 147).

13. Seltzer, *Henry James and the Art of Power*, 27.

14. See for example Sara Blair, *Henry James and the Writing of Race and Nation*, and Beverly Haviland, *Henry James's Last Romance*.

15. Baudelaire, "Painter of Modern Life," 417. In this respect the American forms an unlikely companion to Baudelaire's dandy, whose "specific beauty . . . consists particularly in that cold exterior resulting from the unshakeable determination to remain unmoved" (422). Both figures can be read as instances of what Michael Fried calls "hyperbolic forgetting," in which a blank face—he offers the example of Joseph Conrad's Almayer—is the sign of a willed act of forgetting ("Almayer's Face," 209). My next chapter reads Sutpen's face in *Absalom, Absalom!* according to the same logic of erasure.

16. James, *Literary Criticism*, 1316.

17. James, *Literary Criticism*, 58; *Art of the Novel*, 8, 13.

18. Root, *Camera and the Pencil*, 98.

19. Eisinger, *Trace and Transformation*, 34. William M. Murray's 1899 article "Too Well Done!" in the journal *Camera Notes* even claimed that the camera's ability to reproduce the world in all its detail detracted from its ability to produce convincing likenesses. See Smith, *American Archives*, 56.

20. Novak, "A Model Jew," 85.

21. Rudisill, *Mirror Image*, 213.

22. Blair, *Henry James and the Writing of Race and Nation*, 3.

23. Ralph Bogardus's judgment that in "The Real Thing" "James once again exposed his negative attitude toward photography" (*Pictures and Texts*, 120) has remained the standard reading. According to Bogardus, James abandoned this attitude only after collaborating closely with Coburn on the frontispieces to *The New York Edition*. In recent years a few critics have offered a rather more complicated trajectory. For example, though she reads James's extraordinarily detailed instructions to Coburn as evidence "that James never really shook off a conventional understanding of photography as a scenic art devoted to a postal card or tourist aesthetic" ("Pictures for Texts," 24), Wendy Graham does admit

that James was sensitive to photography's relation to nostalgia and memory. Julia Grossman, meanwhile, goes so far as to suggest that "[i]n his late works, James, unwilling to compete with photographic realism, invents new strategies for representing the real that, ironically, appropriate aspects of photography" ("'It's the Real Thing,'" 310).

24. James, *Complete Tales*, 229. Future references in parentheses.

25. As early as 1859 commentator George Sala describes the "poor wretches" of models who haunted photographic studios. See his essay "Since This Old Cap Was New."

26. Edel, *Henry James,* vol. 4, 23. Grossman's conclusion is typical: "The Monarchs represent a vulgar reality—an intractable 'real thing'—that resists the power of the artist to transform that reality into fine images" ("It's the Real Thing," 317).

27. Henriksen, "'The Real Thing,'" 475; Vieilledent, "Representation and Reproduction," 37.

28. According to Alan Thomas, buying photographs of well-known personalities became a "mass craze" (*Time in a Frame*, 82) in the second half of the nineteenth century, the most popular subjects including Abraham Lincoln, Napoleon III, Ludwig II, and Giuseppe Garibaldi. As an 1867 essay notes: "A popular singer or actor or a successful prize-fighter will sometimes have a run entering into tens of thousands of copies; but the demand will suddenly collapse, and their names will be heard no more" ("Photography: Its History and Applications," 209). The fad extended all the way to one of the most photographed icons of all, Queen Victoria, who amassed a substantial collection of celebrity *cartes-de-visites*. By 1866, however, the craze could already be seen as on the wane. Edward Wilson observed in an article in the *Philadelphia Photographer* that "[e]very one is surfeited with them. All the albums are full of them and every body has exchanged with every body" (Taft, *Photography and the American Scene*, 323).

29. As Nancy Armstrong outlines in *Fiction in the Age of Photography*, the celebrity "provides both the original for and the copy of" (256) their own image.

30. Banta, "Artists," 19. Kris Lackey argues that it is precisely the Monarchs' "intransigence of type" ("Art and Class," 190) that renders them unfit for representation.

31. James, of course, was unaware in 1892 that his work would ultimately be collected in the *New York Edition*, but the fact that his narrator confirms

that he works "in black and white" (247) suggests a certain sly self-referentiality—the story first appeared in the magazine *Black and White.*

32. According to James's *Notebooks*, the Monarchs' type is that of "everlasting English amateurishness" (Edel and Powers, *Complete Notebooks*, 55–56).

33. As Shawn Michelle Smith notes, in "The Real Thing," "appearance can be imitated, but interiority is essential and unchanging; Miss Churm can *look* many parts, but she can only *be* [. . .] working-class" (68).

34. Sander Gilman, *Difference and Pathology*, 15; Vance, *Catalogue of Daguerreotype*, 4.

35. See the introduction to Armstrong's *Fiction in the Age of Photography.*

36. James, *Awkward Age*, 22. Future references in parentheses.

37. The blankness of the Brookenhams' faces is noted by David Kurnick in his essay " 'Horrible Impossible,'" 112.

38. Baudelaire notes in "The Painter of Modern Life" that "[i]n a unity we call the nation, the professions, the social classes, the successive centuries, introduce variety not only in gestures and manners, but also in the general outlines of faces. Such and such a nose, mouth, forehead, will be a standard [for painters] for a given interval of time" (404).

39. Roland Barthes outlines the figurative crisis engendered by what he sees as the tautological figure of beauty in ways highly pertinent to *The Awkward Age*: "Beauty (unlike ugliness) cannot really be explained: in each part of the body it stands out, repeats itself, but it does not describe itself. Like a god (and as empty), it can only say *I am what I am*. . . . Every direct predicate is denied it; the only feasible predicates are either tautology (*a perfectly oval face*) or simile (*lovely as a Raphael Madonna, like a dream in stone*, etc); thus, beauty is referred to an infinity of codes: *lovely as Venus*? But Venus lovely as what? As herself? . . . There is one rhetorical figure which fills this blank in the object of comparison whose existence is altogether transferred to the language of the object to which it is compared: catachresis (there is no other possible word to denote the 'wings' of a house, or the 'arms' of a chair, and yet 'wings' and 'arms' are *instantly, already* metaphorical): a basic figure, more basic perhaps than metonymy, since it speaks around an empty object of comparison: the figure of beauty" (*S/Z*, 33–34).

40. "Photography: Its History and Applications," 210. See in this respect David Green, "Veins of Resemblance."

41. Holmes, *Soundings from the Atlantic*, 260.

42. Barthes, *Camera Lucida*, 102.

43. Ibid., 103.

44. An even more striking example of the spectacular character of the modern world is provided by Mrs. Donner, who, like Fanny, is compared to a "new-fashioned bill poster" (72). In Mrs. Donner's case, however, the comparison is the product not of her beauty but of her attempts to make herself beautiful. The narrator cruelly describes her overly made-up face as "retouched, from brow to chin, like a suburban photograph" (71). Even the photograph, then, is no guarantee of likeness, being always open to alteration. Retouching had been common photographic practice since the 1860s—according to photographer Artemus Ward Ryder, the practice "caught like measles and became epidemic" (*Voigtlander*, 113)—and by the late 1890s whole airbrushing factories had come into existence.

45. This reading was first suggested by Michal Ginsburg in *Economies of Change*.

46. J. Hillis Miller points out in *Literature as Conduct* that "*Circle* is a key word in [*The Awkward Age*]" (85).

47. No wonder Van protests to Nanda: "I don't know what you mean by a man 'like me.' I'm not any particular kind of man" (127).

48. Aside from the picture of his mother and of Nanda, Van also has photographs of his sister Mary and of Nanda's Neapolitan friend, Aggie. The latter's image is bordered, memorably, by crimson fur, which Van takes as a license for a dreadful pun, telling Mr. Longdon that "At Naples they develop early" (26).

49. See Todorov, "Verbal Age."

50. Ginsburg, *Economies of Change*, 192–93.

51. Miller, *Literature as Conduct*, 149.

52. Deleuze, *Essays*, 78, 71.

53. James, *Sense of the Past*, 98. Future references in parentheses.

54. James, *Aspern Papers*, 77. Future references in parentheses.

55. Blair, *Henry James and the Writing of Race and Nation*, 50. Indeed the recycling does not end there. James's comment resurfaces in Benjamin's essay "On Some Motifs in Baudelaire," only here it is attributed to Marcel Proust: "Proust, complaining of the barrenness and lack of depth in the images of Venice that his *mémoire volontaire* presented to him, notes that the very word 'Venice' made that wealth of images seem to him as vapid as an exhibition of photographs" (*Illuminations*, 187). The fact that Benjamin was obviously unaware of James's comment only serves to underscore the symbiotic relationship between cultural stereotypes—the photogenic beauty of Venice—and their critique; both, that

is, are the result of the circulation of photographs, a circulation that makes the photographed world *and* the critique of that world somehow inevitable.

56. Luhmann, *Reality of the Mass Media*, 22.

57. Levenson, *Modernism and the Fate of Individuality*, 18.

58. Bersani, *Future for Astyanax*, 138.

59. Quoted in Davis, "'Out of the Medium in Which Books Breathe," 421, 422. I am grateful to Davis's essay for alerting me to the connection between Maggie's knowledge and the miniatures.

60. Armstrong, *Fiction in the Age of Photography*, 130.

61. As Seltzer notes in *Henry James and the Art of Power*, the Ververs' blankness is precisely the means by which they exercise power, just as the blankness of Washington was the sign of American power.

62. Cameron observes that it is not that the Prince and Charlotte do not know that Maggie knows, it is that Maggie refuses to say what she knows, and thereby retains the freedom to act as if she did not know.

63. McKee, *Producing American Races*, 74, 76. Jonathan Freedman points out that this exchange finds its limits in the "resolute failure" ("Poetics of Cultural Decline," 477) of the two Jewish characters in the novel—the shopkeeper who sells Maggie the golden bowl, and the antique dealer who sells her father the Damascene tiles—to be seen as in any way resembling the other characters. Freedman concludes that "the figure of the Jew" in James's work is "thus a figure of the unassimilable, the ineradicable alien" (495). Freedman's groundbreaking reading allows us to see the fundamental centrality of racial stereotypes to James's fiction. Where I differ from Freedman is in reading this centrality as a function of rather than a resistance to the discourse of Americanness outlined in James's work. I see James's stereotypes, in other words, as a product of his sense of the photographic uniformity of modern life. This is reflected in the fact that, as Richard Halpern points out, James's contemporaries tended to depict Jewish identity precisely as a matter of resemblance rather than difference. Werner Sombart's 1911 *The Jews and Modern Capitalism* contends that "the clearest illustration of the way in which Jewish traits manifest themselves is the fact that the Jew in England becomes like an Englishman, in France like a Frenchman, and so forth. And if he does not really become like an Englishman or a Frenchman, he appears to be like one" (Halpern, *Shakespeare among the Moderns*, 171).

64. From Holmes to Susan Sontag, critics of photography have repeatedly compared the act of taking pictures to the hunting of wild game. Here is Ben-

jamin's take in his essay "Little History of Photography": "The amateur who returns home with great piles of artistic shots is in fact no more appealing a figure than the hunter who comes back with quantities of game that is useless to anyone but the merchant" (*Selected Writings*, 523).

65. Edel, *Henry James Letters*, 416–17. James's confusion over whether the photograph offered an image of typicality or particularity leads Miller to wonder whether "[t]he type or idea of a thing . . . is the 'real thing'" (*Ethics of Reading*, 110).

66. Thanks to Craig Dworkin for this irresistible pun.

67. Miller, *Ethics of Reading*, 112.

68. Barbara Johnson, *Critical Difference*, 3. Nancy Armstrong offers a new take on this idea in her essay "City Things": "[t]he photograph confers a new reality on the thing it represents, that of the already seen" (100).

69. I discuss the relationship between James and Stein in my conclusion.

70. As Miller points out, silhouettes are typically of human faces or figures, suggesting that James imagines composition as a matter of physiognomic equivalence.

Chapter Three. Vanishing Race

1. Michaels, "Autobiographies of the Ex-White Men," 235. As Robyn Wiegman puts it, the visible is "the anxiety-producing framework for the one-drop rule's legal articulation" ("Whiteness Studies," 301).

2. See Michaels's recent essay "*Absalom, Absalom*: The Difference between White Men and White Men." Faulkner's heightened sensitivity to racial difference is nicely captured by a description of a character in G. Cabrera Infante's *Three Trapped Tigers*: "[o]ne of those mulattos who aren't mulattos, but so cleverly mixed that only a Cuban or a Brazilian or maybe Faulkner would detect it" (399).

3. Kawash, *Dislocating the Color Line*, 125.

4. Davis, "Signifying Abstraction," 70.

5. Faulkner, *Essays*, 61.

6. Faulkner's prejudice against the camera explains his remark in a press conference during his tour of Japan that same year that he had "never owned a camera and [had] never been too interested in the pictorial, I much prefer to look at faces" (Jelliffe, *Faulkner at Nagano*, 110–11). Yet according to J. R. Cofield, a photographer and longtime companion of the writer, while Faulkner was writing *Absalom, Absalom!* he was also learning how to use "a genuine old Zeiss

camera" ("Many Faces," 109). Indeed Cofield remembered his friend as being "a devout camera fiend" (110). In *William Faulkner: Presentation and Performance*, James Watson argues that Faulkner carefully manipulated the camera in the creation of his public persona in his early years as a writer. Faulkner posed for a series of snapshots in Oxford in 1919, playing the parts of wounded war hero, dandy, and tramp, images that helped him cover up his undistinguished war record when the novelist returned to Mississippi.

7. To date only one critic, Judith Sensibar, has paid attention to Faulkner's preoccupation with the photograph. See her essay "Popular Culture Invades Jefferson."

8. Sartre, "On *The Sound and the Fury*," 89.

9. Barthes, *Camera Lucida*, 77.

10. Krieger, *Ekphrasis*, xv. In *Ordering the Façade* Katherine Henniger makes the compelling point that the force of the fictional photograph comes from our sense that we have been "left with the residue of evidence—our notion that the photograph refers" (9).

11. Faulkner, *Absalom, Absalom!*, 289. Future references in parentheses.

12. Alfred Kazin's *On Native Grounds*, for example, proposes that these novels "photographed . . . [the past] in a succession of glowing scenes" (511).

13. Williamson, *William Faulkner and Southern History*, 244.

14. Armstrong, "City Things," 94.

15. Photography, in this model, can be usefully compared to what Mr. Compson refers to as innocence, a state which he proposes "must be destroyed in order to have existed at all" (77). Innocence can only be known in retrospect, since the innocent do not know that they are innocent; once you know you are innocent, you no longer are. This renders Rosa's and Sutpen's claim that they have remained innocent in the face of their extraordinary experiences all the more revealing. It suggests that what the novel is interested in is less the condition of being innocent than the production of innocence in retrospect, through the stories we tell.

16. Cadava, *Words of Light*, 95.

17. Hortense Spillers notes that the concept of blankness is crucial to understanding *Absalom, Absalom!*, which she reads as preoccupied with "notions of surface and masking" (*Black, White, and in Color*, 333). Spillers offers the example of the "blank wall of black secret faces" (203) that confronts Sutpen on the Haitian plantation.

18. Cadava, *Words of Light*, 22.

19. Faulkner, *Collected Stories*, 790. Future references in parentheses.

20. Barthes, *Camera Lucida*, 106.

21. Matthews, *Play of Faulkner's Language*, 19.

22. Faulkner, "Introduction for *The Sound and the Fury*," 710.

23. Barthes, *Camera Lucida*, 77, 82.

24. David Madden's essay "Photographs in the 1929 Version of *Sanctuary*" is the only critical work to reflect on the central role played by photography in the novel, though his conclusion that "only in *Sanctuary* does Faulkner make significant use of photographs" (96) is, needless to say, one with which I disagree.

25. Faulkner, *Sanctuary*, 149. Future references in parentheses.

26. Melville, *Billy Budd*, 324.

27. Faulkner, *Go Down, Moses*, 284. Future references in parentheses.

28. Crary, *Techniques of the Observer*, 123–4, 127. Rosalind E. Krauss discusses the peculiar depth of the stereoscopic image in *Originality of the Avant-Garde*.

29. Holmes, *Soundings from the Atlantic*, 148. As Beaumont Newhall recounts in *History of Photography*, by the 1850s the collecting of stereoscopes had become something of a craze. "Until the advent of photographically illustrated magazines at the end of the century," Newhall observes, "there was, it seemed, a stereoscope in every home" (115). By 1857 the London Stereoscopic Company had sold five hundred thousand stereoscopes, and its catalog listed more than one hundred thousand different stereo views. An article in *The New-York Weekly Tribune* in 1853 talked of the "impossibility" of describing "the magical and captivating effect of this spontaneous transformation of two images into one solid image. We see the eyes, the lips, the nose, in short, all the striking features of the face and all the projecting parts of the body, coming forward clearly from the background with all their relative proportions. The illusion is complete, and we see the person depicted standing there identically before us" (Photography in the United States," 7).

30. J. Hillis Miller, *Topographies*, 197. Paul de Man calls this "the most demanding of reconciliations, that of motion and stasis, a synthesis that is also at stake in the model of narrative as the diachronic version of a single moment" (*Allegories of Reading*, 68).

31. Meriwether and Millgate, *Lion in the Garden*, 253.

32. Faulkner's characteristic neologism "unamaze" brings to mind Tom Gunning's description of the astonishment felt by viewers of the earliest Lumière exhibitions, an astonishment that was the product not—as has typically been

suggested—of the fear that what they were seeing on screen was actually taking place, but of their amazement at the fact of photography come to life. Gunning notes that the Lumière films began with a still image, which was then set into motion after an agonizing wait of a few seconds, so that "[r]ather than mistaking the image for reality, the spectator is astonished by its transformation through the new illusion of projected motion. . . . The astonishment derives from a magical metamorphosis rather than a seamless reproduction of reality" ("Aesthetic of Astonishment," 118).

33. In *The Mind of the South*, W. J. Cash describes the transformation of the South by men like Sutpen in uncannily similar terms: "Like every aristocrat, . . . [the Southern gentleman] required above all things a fixed background, the sense of absolute security and repose which proceeds from an environment which moves in well-worn grooves, and in which change occurs rarely and never abruptly. The new country, however, was full of the ringing of axes and the acrid smoke of new-grounds. Whirl was its king. From day to day it put on a new face. Landmarks were likely to vanish overnight" (11–12).

34. Epstein, "Magnification," 22. Faulkner's interest in the relationship between film and still suggests how mistaken Cleanth Brooks was to claim that there is "little in Faulkner's narrative treatment that can be certainly attributed to [Henri] Bergson's influence" (Douglass, *Bergson*, 127)—a judgment that explicitly denies Faulkner's claim that he "agree[d] pretty much with Bergson's theory of the fluidity of time," (Meriwether and Millgate, *Lion in the Garden*, 70). According to Bergson, the mind "take[s] snapshots, as it were, of the passing reality," which, once "recomposed . . . artificially" in the manner of a cinema projector yield the illusion of movement. Hence, "the *mechanism of our ordinary knowledge is of a cinematographical kind*" (*Creative Evolution*, 306). Our insistence on thinking in terms of immobile snapshots that we then animate renders us unable, however, to grasp the present, which is characterized by ceaseless movement. "Becoming" is the only reality, but all we have is "its cinematographical imitation" (313).

35. Alfred Kazin, "Stillness of *Light in August*," 528.

36. Faulkner, *Light in August*, 226. Future references in parentheses.

37. The point was first made by Michael Cobb: "Just like the uncertainties of his black or white blood, Joe's black or white place in time corresponds with the uncertain status of his sleeping or waking body" ("Cursing Time," 159–60).

38. Eric Sundquist reads Faulkner's comparison of Christmas to a photographic negative as "a figure of simultaneous concealment and revelation, a

figure that marks with explosive precision, at a point of passing from one to the other, the ambiguity of Joe Christmas who . . . virtually is a *figure* rather than a person" (*Faulkner: The House Divided*, 71).

39. Barthes, *Image Music Text*, 67.

40. Millgate, *Achievement of William Faulkner*, 164.

41. Passages such as this one prompt Laura Doyle to characterize *Light in August* as a "slow-motion world" ("The Body against Itself," 353).

42. As Mary Anne Doane observes, "Film is a series of sequential singularities" (*Emergence of Cinematic Time*, 217). That Faulkner saw film in this way would explain his obsession with early cartoons—arriving in Hollywood in May 1932 he announced to Sam Marx of Metro-Goldwyn-Mayer that he had "an idea for Mickey Mouse," only to be informed that the cartoons were written at the Disney studios (Pearce, *Novel in Motion*, 25). While in Hollywood Faulkner apparently drew a set of animated stills dramatizing his love affair with Meta Carpenter, pictures that, according to his friend Carvel Collins, gave "the illusion of movement if seen in rapid sequence" (Blotner, *Faulkner*, 369). Doug Baldwin has recently argued that Faulkner's interest in early film owed much to the medium's close technical connection to still photography. See his "Putting Images into Words."

43. Cadava, *Words of Light*, 84.

44. Holmes, *Soundings from the Atlantic*, 183. Holmes's belief that the history of the world would eventually reveal itself in the manner of a developing photograph can be traced back to abolitionism's cherished conviction that no act—no matter how obscure—went unseen, and hence that the iniquities of slavery—which were imagined as being at their worst either at sea or in the Deep South, in other words in those places beyond the public eye—would eventually be brought to light. In his *The Ninth Bridgewater Treatise*, mathematician Charles Babbage published a report made by Captain Hayes to the British Admiralty in 1832 detailing life aboard the slave ship. Hayes notes that slaves allowed to go on deck for a breath of air have been witnessed jumping into the sea, despite the fact that the heavy chains around their ankles doomed them to certain death. Confronted with such horrors, Babbage finds solace only in his belief that the slaves' actions will not go unremembered, since "every wave which breaks unimpeded on ten thousand desolate shores . . . will give evidence of the last gurgle of the waters which closed over the head of his dying victim" (108). This was because, he insisted, "[e]arth, air, and ocean, are the eternal witnesses of the acts we have done . . . The track of every canoe, of every vessel

which has yet disturbed the surface of the ocean . . . remains for ever registered in the future movement of all succeeding particles which may occupy its place" (114–15); these tracks would be revealed, Babbage solemnly promised, at the Last Judgment. In *The Religion of Geology and Its Related Sciences,* Edward Hitchcock offered a similarly photographic conception of history, arguing that "*Our words, our actions, and even our thoughts, make an indelible impression on the universe*" (410). This rendered creation, he rather poetically surmised, "Into a vast sounding gallery, into a vast picture gallery, and into a universal telegraph. This photographic influence pervades all nature, nor can we say where it stops. We do not know but it [nature] may imprint upon the world around us our features, as they are modified by various passions, and thus fill nature with daguerreotype impressions of all our actions that are performed in daylight" (456).

45. For *Light in August*'s Joanna Burden, for example, the sheer presence of African Americans constitutes "a shadow in which I lived, we lived, all white people, all other people" (253).

46. The term "shadow" was actually used to describe the first photographic images; as Fox-Talbot put it, photography was "the art of fixing a shadow" (Taft, *Photography and the American Scene*, 3). According to one early photographic subject, "[Y]ou sit in front of [the camera and] your shadow sticks on the plate," while a well-known advertising slogan advised people to "[s]ecure the shadow 'ere the substance fade" (Bogardus, "Lost Art of the Daguerreotype," 91). Abolitionist and former slave Sojourner Truth happily took advantage of the fact that the word referred to both the photographic and the raced subject, selling photographic images of herself complete with the legend "I Sell the Shadow to Support the Substance."

47. Melville, *Billy Budd*, 257.

48. I am grateful to Richard Godden's *Fictions of Labor* for drawing my attention to this passage.

49. As far as I know Spillers was the first critic to focus on the photographic quality of the term "resolve." See *Black, White, and in Color*, 360.

50. According to the definition offered by Kimberly W. Benston in "Facing Tradition," "[The] African American literary tradition . . . is what rhetorical theorists such as Paul de Man and Cynthia Chase would call a prosopopeia, a giving of face to an absent power, a translation into the visible of an endless procession of virtual selves" (99). Benston argues that the paradigmatic moment in this tradition is "the face catching its reflection in some version of the other (be

it racial, familial, or even psychical). This primary speculation of an alternative configuration of the self comprises several scenarios: the shock of one's reflection in the father's or mother's face, the glance of self-discovery or dissociation in the mirror, the confrontation with the face of mastery, the encounter with some emblem of communal visage" (99).

51. The moment anticipates Richard Wright's description in his autobiography of meeting his father for the first time and seeing "a shadow of my face in his face" (*Black Boy*, 34).

52. In *Light in August*, for example, Joanne Burden wants a baby—and not just any baby, but "a bastard negro child"—because she "would like to see father's face" (266).

53. Faulkner, *Essays*, 12.

54. Brooks, *Reading for the Plot*, 299.

55. Parker, "What Quentin Saw 'Out There,'" 326.

56. Godden, *Fictions of Labor*, 81.

57. Kazin, "Stillness of *Light in August*," 525.

58. See Ginzburg's essay "Family Resemblances and Family Trees."

59. Brown, *Material Unconscious*, 224.

60. Sander, "Photography as a Universal Language," 677, 678.

61. Appropriately enough, Galton's method of underexposing multiple prints to produce composite images resulted, Allan Sekula notes, in "individual distinctive features, features that were shared and idiosyncratic, fad[ing] away into the night of underexposure" ("Body and the Archive," 48).

Chapter Four. "Seeing Myself like Somebody Else"

1. Brown, "Reification," 186.

2. Wiegman, *American Anatomies*, 6.

3. McDowell "Viewing the Remains," 154.

4. Ellison, *Invisible Man*, xv. Wahneema Lubiano makes much the same point in her essay "Don't Talk with Your Eyes Closed." According to Lubiano, what she calls the "hypervisibility" of black identity "works to undermine the possibility of actually seeing black specificity" (187).

5. Willis, *Reflections in Black*, xvii.

6. Douglass, "Pictures and Progress," 455

7. Such is the inescapability of this photographic fixing in place that even in a comic fantasy about the invention of a camera-like machine able to change people's race, George S. Schuyler's 1931 *Black No More*, photography remains

the standard of proof as to whether a person is black or white. In one particularly gruesome episode, a group of white racists are lynched because their photographs are in the paper showing them as black—the result of their having "blackened up" to escape detection while living among African Americans. As one of the lynch mob tells the leader of the group, "[Y]ou're a nigger, accordin' to this here paper, an' a paper wouldn't lie" (174).

8. Gates, "Trope of a New Negro," 150.

9. Ibid., 129, 137.

10. Gates, "Face and Voice of Blackness," xxix.

11. Gates, "Trope of a New Negro," 141. As Daylanne K. English has pointed out, this desire to produce idealized images of African American life dominated W. E. B. Du Bois's publication *Crisis* in the first two decades of the century, its frequent photo-essays on ideal black men, women and children lending the magazine something of the character of a "eugenic family album" (*Unnatural Selections*, 47).

12. Gates, "Trope of a New Negro," 143; Fuss, *Essentially Speaking*, 90.

13. hooks, "In Our Glory," 46, 48.

14. Gates, *Signifying Monkey*, 183.

15. The essays referred to are by Barbara Johnson, Michael Awkward, and Carla Kaplan. As Ann duCille observes, the "extended claims for Hurston's voice . . . reflect a bias in current critical practice for vernacular theories of African American cultural production" (*Coupling Convention*, 81).

16. Clarke, "'The porch couldn't talk for looking,'" 600.

17. Jacobs, "From 'Spy-glass' to 'Horizon,'" 345.

18. Hurston, *Their Eyes Were Watching God*, 79. Future references in parentheses.

19. Fanon, *Black Skin, White Masks*, 109.

20. Hurston, *Dust Tracks on a Road*, 34.

21. In *Fiction in the Age of Photography* Nancy Armstrong draws a comparison between the proliferation of photographs and the notion of self-identity very similar to Hurston's model of subjectivity: "[d]riven to close the gap between themselves and some original state of full being, modern individuals layer variant reproductions between themselves as they are at a given moment and the foundational image they imagine themselves once to have been" (23).

22. Johnson, *World of Difference*, 163.

23. Hurston, *Mules and Men*, 125.

24. Hurston, "Characteristics of Negro Expression," 175, 178. Hurston's

observation about "the walls of the average Negro" is echoed by Jacob Riis in *How the Other Half Lives*: "The poorest negro housekeeper's room in New York is bright with gaily-colored prints" (117).

25. Kawash, *Dislocating the Color Line*, 202.

26. As Awkward points out, eleven years separate the moment Johnson identifies as Janie's empowering self-division (when she begins to hide her true feelings from Joe) and Janie's eventual exhibition of a powerful voice (when she actually tells Joe what she thinks of him).

27. Du Bois, *Souls of Black Folk*, 7.

28. Hurston, *Mules and Men*, 1.

29. Hurston, *Dust Tracks on a Road*, 61.

30. That the camera functioned as a kind of mirror has been remarked on ever since Oliver Wendell Holmes defined the photograph in 1861 as a "*mirror with a memory*" (*Soundings from the Atlantic*, 129).

31. Boyd, *Wrapped in Rainbows*, 114.

32. Kaplan, *Hurston*, 82, 283.

33. Gould, *Mismeasure of Man*, 140.

34. Hurston, "What White Publishers Won't Print," 171, 170, 173.

35. Wright, "Between Laughter and Tears," 23.

36. Carby, "Politics of Fiction," 82.

37. Wall, "Zora Neale Hurston"; Gilroy, *Black Atlantic*; Willis, *Specifying*.

38. Hurston's sensitivity to stereotypical representations of African American life is demonstrated by a story told by her first biographer, Robert Hemenway. While on a group research trip in Eatonville in 1935, Hurston objected to NYU Professor Mary Elizabeth Barnicle taking a photograph of a child eating watermelon, an image the novelist found so demeaning that she immediately abandoned the trip and returned home to New York. See *Zora Neale Hurston: A Literary Biography*.

39. Boyd, *Wrapped in Rainbows*, 379.

40. Hurston, *Dust Tracks on a Road*, 237.

41. Ibid., 304. It is hard, needless to say, to ignore the metaphorical connotations of Hurston's use of the term shadow here.

42. Hurston, "How It Feels to Be Colored Me," 152, 153.

43. See Wald, "Becoming 'Colored.'" In this context it is worth recalling that Hurston's autobiography traces the birth of her self-consciousness to the photographic vision of her future she experienced as a young girl: "Like clear-cut stereopticon slides, I saw twelve scenes flash before me, each one held until

I had seen it well in every detail, and then be replaced by another. There was no continuity as in an average dream. Just disconnected scene after scene with blank spaces in between. I knew that they were all true, a preview of things to come, and my soul writhed in agony and shrunk away. But I knew that there was no shrinking. These things had to be" (*Dust Tracks*, 57). Hurston sees her life as a series of images that, though disconnected from one another, eventually form a composite whole in the by-now familiar manner of an image seen in a stereopticon viewer.

44. Hawthorne, *House of the Seven Gables*, 1; Bersani quoted in Seltzer, *Henry James and the Art of Power*, 53.

45. Bérubé, "Max, Media, and Mimesis," 113.

46. Wright, *Native Son*, 380. Future references in parentheses.

47. Bérubé, "Max, Media, and Mimesis," 112.

48. Bigger's sense of awe at the terrifying immediacy of information in the media age is not unlike Clifford's horror in *The House of the Seven Gables* at the telegraph's ability to spread the news of a murder faster than the murderer could distance himself from the scene of the crime.

49. James, *Bostonians*, 82.

50. Ellison, *Shadow and Act*, 91.

51. Seltzer, *Henry James and the Art of Power*, 27.

52. Elmer, "Spectacle and Event," 787–88.

53. Ibid., 787.

54. Ibid., 790, 791.

55. Hence, at the moment the press discovers the remains of Mary's burnt body, Bigger is overcome with "the old feeling, the feeling that he had had all his life: he was black and had done wrong" (219).

56. Jurca, *White Diaspora: The Suburb and the Twentieth Century American Novel*, chapter four.

57. Luhmann, *Reality of the Mass Media*, 2.

58. Seltzer, *True Crime*, 74.

59. Luhmann, 12.

60. Ibid., 1.

61. Seltzer, *Bodies and Machines*, 106.

62. Stowe, *Uncle Tom's Cabin*, 34, 510. The notion that accurate representation demands conflating several different subjects rather than forcing one to be representative of his or her race can be traced back to James Weldon Johnson's preface to the 1912 edition of *The Autobiography of an Ex-Colored Man*:

"[W]riters, in nearly every instance, have treated the colored American as a *whole*; each has taken some one group of the race to prove his case. Not before has a composite and proportionate presentation of the entire race, embracing all of its various groups and elements . . . been made" (xxxiii).

63. Cadava, *Words of Light*, 137.

64. Bazin, *What Is Cinema?*, 12. Indeed, as we saw in chapter one, early photography was castigated for producing masklike images—most notably by Ralph Waldo Emerson, who complained that the daguerreotype reproduced "the portrait of a mask instead of a man" (Gilman and Parsons, *Journals and Miscellaneous Notebooks of Ralph Waldo Emerson*, 117). Heidegger's image also, needless to say, anticipates the relationship between the corpse and resemblance noted by Maurice Blanchot in his essay "Two Versions of the Imaginary." As I outlined in chapter one, Blanchot argues that the dead body, in exposing the "nothing" that the subject has become, can be said to open up a gap within resemblance itself—between the subject and his or her own body. The corpse, that is, presents us with an image of a "resemblance that has nothing to resemble" (*Gaze of Orpheus*, 85) and thus can be said to resemble resemblance itself.

65. Brown, *Material Unconscious*, 218. This is not to slight Brown's wonderfully inventive reading, which explores the links between Henry's loss of his face and the composite images of Francis Galton. Brown observes that "*The Monster* produces what Galton feared in a 'generic portrait' composed from 'heterogeneous elements'—the 'mere smudge,' a result that is 'monstrous and meaningless'" (224).

66. Michael Warner reads the story in somewhat analogous terms, suggesting that Crane's text makes it "hard to imagine face and person as separate" ("Value, Agency, and Stephen Crane's 'The Monster,'" 82).

67. This is what Gilles Deleuze and Felix Guattari mean when they proclaim in *A Thousand Plateaus* that "[t]he face is not a universal. It is not even that of the white man; it is White Man himself" (176). Deleuze and Guattari criticize the "faciality machine," by which they mean the extension of the surface logic of physiognomy to all aspects of the modern world, from identity to landscapes—what they call "the social production of face" (181).

68. Wright, *12 Million Black Voices*, 10–11. Wright's metaphor takes on a disturbing literal life in David Bradley's recent introduction to the text, which somewhat blithely reflects that "[e]ach of the faces in the FSA photographs could easily have been his [Wright's] face, perhaps had been. The face of the black boy at the end of section one could have been the face of Wright himself before he

made his Exodus to the North. The face of the lynched man could have been his had he not left in time. The face of the sharecropper could have been his had he not left but managed to avoid the rope. The face of the black youth in his fancy clothes could have been his had he not been a serious person, a man with a dream" (xviii).

69. Ibid., 102, 146.

70. Stott, *Documentary Expression*, 235; Wright, *12 Million Black Voices*, 18.

71. Baldwin, *Notes of a Native Son*, 25–26.

72. Ibid., 45.

73. Conrad, *Nigger of the Narcissus*, 12.

74. Kawash, *Dislocating the Color Line*, 130. Kawash offers the example of John Walden's insistence in Charles Chesnutt's *The House Behind the Cedars* that "a Negro is black; I am white, and not black." Because Walden's black ancestry trumps his white appearance, this opens up a gap "between what the body says and what the body means" (131).

75. As Ellison notes in "Change the Joke and Slip the Yoke," the mask reduces African Americans "to a negative sign" (*Shadow and Act*, 48). Yet as much as the mask fixes the meaning of race, it also unsettles it. Ellison contends that "out of the counterfeiting of the black American's identity there arises a profound doubt in the white man's mind as to the authenticity of his own image of himself" (49), a doubt exacerbated by the fact that the black subject sometimes wears the mask in order to baffle those who presume to know his identity. Baldwin's account of the black face can be read as an allegory of this process, in which, ironically enough, African American features are formed precisely as a result of the white desire to hide these features behind a mask.

76. Kawash, *Dislocating the Color Line*, 131.

77. Wright, "Between Laughter and Tears," 23.

78. Boyd, *Wrapped in Rainbows*, 144.

79. Hurston, "How It Feels to Be Colored Me," 152.

80. Wald, "Becoming 'Colored,'" 79.

81. Douglass's notion of the photograph as public property is exemplified by the ironic fate of Hurston's own photographic image. Boyd recounts that "[a]s enthusiasm for Hurston swelled during the 1980s, one particular photograph became especially popular. It is an image of a young black woman wearing a loose dress, a wide-brimmed hat, and a big smile . . . Printed in T-shirts, postcards, and even on the covers of some books, this image, ironically, is *not* Zora

Neale Hurston. The photograph was taken by Alan Lomax during the summer of 1935, when he, Hurston, and Mary Elizabeth Barnacle traveled the South together collecting folk songs for the Library of Congress. The picture apparently became mixed up with the library's collection of Hurston photographs, causing archivists to assume that it was a shot of Zora" (*Wrapped in Rainbows*, 437).

82. Jacobs, *Incidents in the Life of a Slave Girl*, 184.

83. As one of the black veterans in *Invisible Man* observes to another about the school founder Norton: "Look at those features. Exactly like yours—from the identical mold" (78). The similarities uncovered in the Golden Day resurface in Ellison's account of the political activist Todd Clifton, who possesses "the chiseled, black-marble features sometimes found on statues in northern museums and alive in southern towns in which the white offspring of house children and the black offspring of yard children bear names, features, and character traits as identical as the rifling of bullets fired from a common barrel" (363).

84. Hurston had already examined the question of physical resemblance in her story "The Gilded Six-Bits," in which the exact likeness between a child and his father ends up saving a marriage. The story recounts Missie May's affair with a traveling salesman, a man she is attracted to because of his gold stickpin—an ornament that turns out, on close inspection, to be fake. The moral of the story, then, would seem to be not to trust appearances. The problem with this reading, however, is that Missie May is reunited with her husband, Joe, precisely *because* of appearances: Missie May only finds out that the child she is carrying is her husband's when she sees Joe's features reproduced in the child's face. Physical resemblance also plays a crucial role in both *Jonah's Gourd Vine*, the hero of which so closely resembles his mother that his grandmother recognizes him at first sight, even though she has not seen him in almost twenty years, and *Seraph on the Suwanee*, whose hero, Jim, finds himself unable to love his handicapped son Earl partly because Earl looks nothing like him. Jim determines that his next boy will resemble himself, and his hopes are justified after his wife Arvay gives birth to a boy who, as she puts it, "[c]ouldn't have been more like Jim if Jim had spit him out of his mouth" (106).

85. That Janie's predicament was a common one can be seen from a moment from Frances Harper's 1892 novel *Iola Leroy*, in which an old man attempts to persuade a young slave not to flee to the oncoming Yankee army: "Who looked arter you when you war sole from your farder and mudder, an' neber seed dem any more, and wouldn't know dem to-day ef you met dem?" (19).

86. Hurston, *Dust Tracks on a Road*, 34.

87. Jacobs, "From 'Spy-glass' to 'Horizon,'" 343.

88. According to Jacobs, the fact that "the first men Janie and Joe encounter in Eatonville instantly recognize Janie's high status suggests that her appearance is decisive, since Joe has yet to prove himself as an economic and political force" ("From 'Spy-glass' to 'Horizon,'" 343).

89. Wald, "Becoming 'Colored,'" 84. The moment is doubly ironic, since in repeating the metonymical violence of the porch sitters Janie identifies herself by two items that could be said not even to belong to her. As she tells Pheoby, "Mis' Washburn useter dress me up in all de clothes her gran'chillun didn't need no mo' which still wuz better'n whut de rest uh de colored chillun had. And then she useter put hair ribbon on mah head fuh me tuh wear" (9).

90. It seems worth noting here that one of the examples of the "verbal nouns" Hurston claims are peculiar to black expression is the phrase "[s]he features somebody I know" ("Characteristics of Negro Expression," 177).

91. Thanks to Hollis Robbins for this suggestion.

92. Barthes, *Roland Barthes*, 36.

93. I am grateful to Avak Hasratian for pointing this out.

94. Wald, "Becoming 'Colored,'" 84.

95. Stepto, *From Behind the Veil*, 165. Awkward offers the most persuasive refutation of Stepto's position, arguing that Janie's "achievement of identity is signaled by her narrative *silence*" (*Inspiring Influences*, 45) in the short chapter detailing her trial for Tea Cake's murder.

96. Du Bois, *Souls of Black Folk*, 7–8.

97. Fascinatingly, this is precisely the example Roger Caillois uses to understand psychasthenia, which he understands as the condition of "*reciprocal topography*" ("Mimicry and Legendary Psychasthenia," 23), in which the organism becomes indistinguishable from its surroundings by reproducing it with perfect fidelity. Caillois calls this process "an actual photography, but of the form and the relief, a photography on the level of the object and not on that of the image, a reproduction in three-dimensional space with solids and voids."

98. Hurston, "Characteristics of Negro Expression," 182. See in this regard Michael Taussig's *Mimesis and Alterity*, 33.

Conclusion. Likeness Has Ceased to Be of Any Help

1. Isherwood, Goodbye to Berlin, 1; Anderson, Sherwood Anderson's Notebook, 71; Orvell, Real Thing, 124–25, 313.

2. Rabb, *Literature and Photography*, 151.

3. Ibid., 154.

4. Barthes, *Camera Lucida*, 103.

5. Holmes, *Soundings from the Atlantic*, 260.

6. Barthes, *Camera Lucida*, 107, 109.

7. Benjamin, *Reflections*, 8, 230.

8. Kracauer, *Mass Ornament*, 48.

9. Ibid., 48.

10. Barthes, *Camera Lucida*, 12.

11. Kracauer, *Mass Ornament*, 48, 58.

12. Ibid., 58, 59.

13. Stein, *Writings 1932–1946*, 357. Future references in parentheses.

14. Ashton, "Gertrude Stein for Anyone," 311.

15. Stein, *Everybody's Autobiography*, 60.

16. Stein, *Making of Americans*, 340.

17. Stein, *Three Lives*, 251.

18. Steven Meyer, "Introduction," Stein, *Making of Americans*, xv; Stein, *Making of Americans*, 81.

19. Stein, *Making of Americans*, 803.

20. Stein, *Selected Writings*, 221.

21. As the poet notes in his essay "History," "Nature is a mutable cloud, which is always and never the same" (Emerson, *Essays and Poems*, 242).

22. Steiner, *Exact Resemblance*, 45.

23. DeKoven, "'Why James Joyce Was Accepted and I was Not,'" 26.

24. Ibid., 27.

25. Stein's comparison of her work to film has been resisted by a number of critics. DeKoven, for example, argues persuasively that Stein's technique should be understood according to the model not of film but of the film strip, "in which each frame largely repeats but slightly shifts the frame before it. Each frame is a new picture shot in the present moment, and therefore it is different from the one before because each present moment is different from the one before, but, when the camera has remained focused on the same thing, each frame largely repeats the one before. So, repetition, which seems to presuppose memory, can in fact negate it. In the Steinian continuous present, the shifting repetition of insistence is inevitable because you rediscover and reinvent in each moment what you know. If you knew you'd already known it you wouldn't have to say it again" ("'Why James Joyce Was Accepted and I was Not,'" 28). Stein's "con-

tinuous present" can, in this model, be understood as exactly anticipating William Faulkner's fascination with what Michael North identifies as "the stillness within motion of the motion pictures" (*Camera Works*, 26) I discuss in chapter three.

26. Seltzer, *True Crime*, 143.

27. Fisher, *Hard Facts*, 145, 147.

28. Dreiser, *American Tragedy*, 511. Future references in parentheses.

29. Fisher, *Hard Facts*, 145, 141.

30. Seltzer, *Bodies and Machines*, 95.

31. Fitzgerald, *Love of the Last Tycoon*, 22. Future references in parentheses.

32. Dreiser, *Sister Carrie*, 636.

33. Adorno and Horkheimer, *Dialectic of Enlightenment*, 117.

34. This face is also shared by the hero of another cinematic Fitzgerald novel, Dick Diver, who is described as possessing an "unaging American face" (*Tender Is the Night*, 119).

35. Fitzgerald, *Great Gatsby*, 136. Future references in parentheses.

Bibliography

Adorno, Theodor, and Max Horkheimer. *Dialectic of Enlightenment: Philosophical Fragments*. Trans. Edmund Jephcott. Palo Alto, Calif.: Stanford University Press, 2002.

Anderson, Sherwood. *Sherwood Anderson's Notebook*. New York: Boni and Liveright, 1926.

Andrew, Dudley, ed. *The Image in Dispute: Art and Cinema in the Age of Photography*. Austin: University of Texas Press, 1997.

Anonymous. "Are We a Good-Looking People?" *Putnam's Monthly Magazine of American Literature, Science and Art*, 1, no. 3 (March 1853): 308–16.

———. "Daguerreotypes." *Littell's Living Age* 9, no. 110 (June 20, 1846): 551–52.

———. "Photography: Its History and Applications." *Littell's Living Age* 92, no. 1182 (January 26, 1867): 208–15.

———. "Photography in the United States: History of the Invention." *New-York Weekly Tribune* 12, no. 606 (April 23, 1853): 7.

Armstrong, Carol. *Scenes in a Library: Reading the Photograph in the Book, 1843–1875*. Cambridge, Mass.: MIT Press, 1998.

Armstrong, Nancy. "City Things: Photography and the Urbanization Process." In *Human, All Too Human*, ed. Diana Fuss, 93–130. New York: Routledge, 1996.

———. *Fiction in the Age of Photography: The Legacy of British Realism.* Cambridge: Harvard University Press, 1999.

Arnheim, Rudolf. "Film and Radio." In *Film Essays and Criticism*, trans. Brenda Benthien, 14–18. Madison: University of Wisconsin Press, 1997.

Ashton, Jennifer. "Gertrude Stein for Anyone." *English Literary History* 64, no. 1 (1997): 289–331.

Awkward, Michael. *Inspiring Influences: Tradition, Revision, and Afro-American Women Writers.* New York: Columbia University Press, 1989.

Babbage, Charles. *The Ninth Bridgewater Treatise.* London: 2nd ed., 1838.

Balázs, Béla. *Theory of the Film: Character and Growth of a New Art.* Trans. Edith Bone. New York: Arno, 1972.

Baldwin, Doug. "Putting Images into Words: Elements of the 'Cinematic' in William Faulkner's Prose." *Faulkner Journal* 16, nos. 1–2 (Fall 2000–Spring 2001): 35–64.

Baldwin, James. *Notes of a Native Son.* Boston: The Beacon Press, 1955.

Banta, Martha. "Artists, Models, Real Things, and Recognizable Types." *Studies in the Literary Imagination* 16, no. 2 (1983): 7–34.

Barthes, *Camera Lucida: Reflections on Photography.* Trans. Richard Howard. New York: Hill and Wang, 1981.

———. *Image Music Text.* Trans. Stephen Heath. New York: Hill & Wang, 1978.

———. *Roland Barthes by Roland Barthes.* Trans. Richard Howard. New York: Hill & Wang, 1977.

———. *S/Z.* Trans. Richard Miller. New York: Hill and Wang, 1974.

———. *The Rustle of Language.* Trans. Richard Howard. Berkeley: University of California Press, 1989.

Batchen, Geoffrey. *Burning with Desire: The Conception of Photography.* Cambridge, Mass.: MIT Press, 1999.

Baudelaire, Charles. "The Painter of Modern Life." In *Selected Writings on Art and Artists.* Trans. P. E. Charvet, 390–436. London: Penguin Books, 1972.

Baudrillard, Jean. *The Transparency of Evil: Essays on Extreme Phenomena.* Trans. James Benedict. New York: Verso, 1993.

Baym, Nina. *The Shape of Hawthorne's Career.* Ithaca, N.Y.: Cornell University Press, 1976.

Bazin, André. *What Is Cinema?* Berkeley: University of California Press, 1967.

Bellamy, Edward. *Miss Ludington's Sister: A Romance of Immortality.* Boston: James R. Osgood, 1884.

Bellis, Peter J. "Mauling Governor Pyncheon." *Studies in the Novel* 26, no. 3 (Fall 1994): 199–217.

Benjamin, Walter. *Illuminations.* Ed. Hannah Arendt. Trans. Harry Zohn. New York: Schocken Books, 1968.

———. *Reflections: Essays, Aphorisms, Autobiographical Writings.* Trans. Edmund Jephcott. New York: Schocken Books, 1978.

———. "Little History of Photography." In *Selected Writings.* Vol. 2. Trans. and ed. Marcus Bullock and Michael Jennings, 507–30. Cambridge: Harvard University Press, 1999.

Benston, Kimberly W. "Facing Tradition: Revisionary Scenes in African American Literature" *PMLA* 105 (January 1990): 98–109.

Bergson, Henri. *Creative Evolution.* Trans. Arthur Mitchell. New York: Dover Publications, 1998.

Bersani, Leo. *A Future for Astyanax.* New York: Columbia University Press, 1984.

Bérubé, Michael. "Max, Media, and Mimesis: Bigger's Representation in *Native Son.*" In *MLA Approaches to Teaching Wright's "Native Son,"* ed. James A. Miller, 112–19. New York: Modern Language Association, 1997.

Blair, Sara. *Henry James and the Writing of Race and Nation.* New York: Cambridge University Press, 1996.

Blanchot, Maurice. *The Gaze of Orpheus, and Other Literary Essays.* Trans. Lydia Davis. New York: Station Hill Press, 1981.

Blotner, Joseph. *Faulkner: A Biography.* New York: Vintage, 1991.

Bogardus, Abraham. "The Lost Art of the Daguerreotype." *The Century Magazine* 48, no. 1 (May 1904): 83–91.

Bogardus, Ralph. *Pictures and Texts: Henry James, A. L. Coburn, and New Ways of Seeing in Literary Culture.* Ann Arbor: University of Michigan Press, 1984.

Bohlke, L. Brent, ed. *Willa Cather in Person: Interviews, Speeches, and Letters.* Lincoln: University of Nebraska Press, 1986.

Bourdieu, Pierre. *Photography: A Middle-Brow Art.* Trans. S. Whiteside. Palo Alto: Stanford University Press, 1990.

Boyd, Valerie. *Wrapped in Rainbows: The Life of Zora Neale Hurston.* New York: Scribner's, 2003.

Bradbury, Malcolm, and James McFarlane, eds. *Modernism: A Guide to European Literature, 1890–1930.* London: Penguin Books, 1976.

Brooks, Peter. *Reading for the Plot.* New York: Alfred A. Knopf, 1984.

Brown, Bill. *The Material Unconscious: American Amusement, Stephen Crane, and the Economies of Play.* Cambridge, Mass.: Harvard University Press, 1996.

———. "Reification, Reanimation, and the American Uncanny." *Critical Inquiry* 32 (Winter 2006): 175–207.

———. *A Sense of Things: The Object Matter of American Literature.* Chicago: The University of Chicago Press, 2003.

Brown, Gillian. *Domestic Individualism: Imagining Self in Nineteenth Century America.* Berkeley: The University of California Press, 1990.

Burgess, N. G. "Amusing Incidents in the Life of a Daguerrean Artist." *The Photographic and Fine Art Journal* 8, no. 6 (June 1855): 190.

Cadava, Eduardo. *Words of Light: Theses on the Photography of History.* Princeton: Princeton University Press, 1997.

Caillois, Roger. "Mimicry and Legendary Psychasthenia." Trans. John Shepley. *October* 31 (Winter 1984): 16–32.

Callahan, John. *In the African-American Grain: The Pursuit of Voice in Twentieth-Century Black Fiction.* Urbana: The University of Illinois Press, 1988.

Cameron, Sharon. *The Corporeal Self: Allegories of the Body in Melville and Hawthorne.* Baltimore: The Johns Hopkins University Press, 1981.

———. *Thinking in Henry James.* Chicago: The University of Chicago Press, 1989.

Carby, Hazel V. "The Politics of Fiction, Anthropology, and the Folk." *New Essays on "Their Eyes Were Watching God,"* ed. Michael Awkward, 71–93. Cambridge: Cambridge University Press, 1990.

Cash, W. J. *The Mind of the South.* New York: Vintage Books, 1991.

Cather, Willa. *On Writing: Critical Studies on Writing as an Art.* Lincoln: University of Nebraska Press, 1988.

———. *O Pioneers!* London: Virago Press, 1983.

———. *Stories, Poems, and Other Writings*. New York: The Library of America, 1992.

Cavell, Stanley. *The World Viewed: Reflections on the Ontology of Film*. New York: The Viking Press, 1971.

Clarke, Deborah. "'The Porch Couldn't Talk for Looking': Voice and Vision in *Their Eyes Were Watching God*." *African-American Review* 35, no. 4 (2001): 599–613.

Cobb, Michael. "Cursing Time: Race and Religious Rhetoric in *Light in August*." *boundary* 2 32, no. 3 (2005): 139–68.

Cofield, J. R. "Many Faces, Many Moods." In *William Faulkner of Oxford*, ed. James W. Webb and A. Wigfall Green, 107–13. Baton Rouge: Louisiana State University Press, 1965.

Cohen, Lara Langer. "What's Wrong with This Picture? Daguerreotype and Magic in *The House of the Seven Gables*." *Arizona Quarterly* 60, no. 1 (Spring 2004): 39–69.

Conrad, Joseph, *The Nigger of the Narcissus*. London: Penguin Books, 1990.

Cowling, Mary. *The Artist as Anthropologist: The Representation of Type and Character in Victorian Art*. New York: Cambridge University Press, 1989.

Crane, Stephen. *Prose and Poetry*. New York: Library of America, 1984.

———. *The Red Badge of Courage: An Episode of the American Civil War*. New York: Modern Library, 1993.

Crary, Jonathan. *Techniques of the Observer*. Cambridge: MIT Press, 1992.

Culver, Stuart. "How Photographs Mean: Literature and the Camera in American Studies." *American Literary History* 1, no. 1 (Spring 1989): 190–205.

Daguerre, Louis. "Daguerreotype." In *Classic Essays on Photography*, ed. Alan Trachtenberg, 11–14. New Haven: Leete's Island Books, 1980.

Daston, Lorraine, and Peter Galison. "The Image of Objectivity." *Representations* 40 (Autumn 1992): 81–128.

Davidson, Cathy N. "Photographs of the Dead: Sherman, Daguerre, Hawthorne." *South Atlantic Quarterly* 89, no. 4 (Fall 1990): 667–701.

Davis, Thadious. "The Signifying Abstraction: Reading 'the Negro' in *Absalom, Absalom!*" In *William Faulkner's "Absalom, Absalom!": A Casebook*, ed. Fred Hobson, 69–106.

Davis, Theo. "'Out of the Medium in Which Books Breathe': The Contours of Formalism in *The Golden Bowl*." *NOVEL* 34, no. 3 (Summer 2001): 411–33.

DeKoven, Marianne. "'Why James Joyce Was Accepted and I Was Not': Modernist Fiction and Gertrude Stein's Narrative." *Studies in the Literary Imagination* 25, no. 2 (Fall 1992): 23–30.

Deleuze, Gilles. *Essays: Critical and Clinical.* Trans. Daniel W. Smith and Michael A. Greco. Minneapolis: University of Minnesota Press, 1997.

Deleuze, Gilles, and Felix Guattari. *A Thousand Plateaus: Capitalism and Schizophrenia.* Trans. Brian Massumi. Minneapolis: The University of Minnesota Press, 1987.

De Man, Paul. *Allegories of Reading: Figural Language in Rousseau, Nietzsche, Rilke, and Proust.* New Haven: Yale University Press, 1979.

de Tocqueville, Alexis. *Democracy in America.* Vol. 2. Ed. Phillips Bradley. New York: Vintage, 1990.

Dickens, Charles. *Martin Chuzzlewit.* London: Penguin Books, 1996.

Dijikstra, Bram. *Cubism, Stieglitz, and the Early Poetry of William Carlos Williams.* Princeton: Princeton University Press, 1969.

Dimock, Wai Chee. *Empire for Liberty: Melville and the Poetics of Individualism.* Princeton: Princeton University Press, 1989.

Doane, Mary Ann. *The Emergence of Cinematic Time.* Cambridge, Mass.: Harvard University Press, 2002.

Dolis, John. *The Style of Hawthorne's Gaze: Regarding Subjectivity.* Tuscaloosa: The University of Alabama Press, 1993.

Douglass, Frederick. "Pictures and Progress." In *The Frederick Douglass Papers, Series One: Speeches, Debates and Interviews.* Ed. John W. Blassingame. Vol. 3, *1855–63*, 452–73. New Haven: Yale University Press, 1985.

Douglass, Paul. *Bergson, Eliot, and American Literature.* Lexington: University Press of Kentucky, 1985.

Doyle, Laura. "The Body against Itself in Faulkner's Phenomenology of Race." *American Literature* 73, no. 2 (June 2001): 339–64.

Dreiser, Theodore. *An American Tragedy.* Cleveland: Meridian, 1962.

———. *Sister Carrie.* New York: Modern Library, 1999.

Dryden, Edgar. *The Form of American Romance.* Baltimore: The Johns Hopkins University Press, 1988.

———. "Hawthorne's Castle in the Air: Form and Theme in *The House of the Seven Gables.*" *English Literary History* 38, no. 2 (June 1971): 294–317.

Du Bois, W. E. B. *The Souls of Black Folk.* London: Penguin Books, 1996.

duCille, Ann. *The Coupling Convention: Sex, Text, and Tradition in Black Women's Fiction.* New York: Oxford University Press, 1993.

Duyckinck, Evert Augustus. "Review in *The Literary World*." In *Critical Essays on "The House of the Seven Gables,"* ed. Bernard Rosenthal, 26–30. New York: G. K. Hall & Co., 1995.

Edel, Leon. *Henry James*. Vol. 4, *The Treacherous Years: 1895–1901*. Philadelphia: J. B. Lippincott, 1969.

———. *Henry James Letters*. Vol. 4. Cambridge: Harvard University Press, 1980.

Edel, Leon, and Lyall H. Powers, eds. *The Complete Notebooks of Henry James*. New York: Oxford University Press, 1987.

Eisinger, Joel. *Trace and Transformation: Americanist Criticism of Photography in the Modernist Period*. Albuquerque: University of New Mexico Press, 1995.

Elliott, Michael. *The Culture Concept: Writing and Difference in the Age of Realism*. Minneapolis: The University of Minnesota Press, 2002.

Ellison, Ralph. *Invisible Man*. New York: Vintage, 1995.

———. *Shadow and Act*. New York: Vintage, 1995.

Elmer, Jonathan. "Spectacle and Event in *Native Son*." *American Literature* 70, no. 4 (December 1998): 767–98.

Emerson, Ralph Waldo. *English Traits*. New York: E. P. Dutton & Co., 1908.

———. *Essays and Poems*. New York: Library of America, 1996.

English, Daylanne K. *Unnatural Selections: Eugenics in American Modernism and the Harlem Renaissance*. Chapel Hill: The University of North Carolina Press, 2004.

Entin, Joseph. "'Unhuman Humanity': Bodies of the Urban Poor and the Collapse of Realistic Legibility." *NOVEL* 34, no. 3 (Summer 2001): 313–37.

Epstein, Jean. "Magnification and Other Writings." Trans. Stuart Liebman. *October* 3 (Spring 1977): 9–25.

Fanon, Frantz. *Black Skin, White Masks*. Trans. Charles Lam Markmann. New York: Grove Press, 1967.

Faulkner, William. *Absalom, Absalom!* New York: Vintage, 1990.

———. "An Introduction for *The Sound and the Fury*." Ed. James B. Meriwether. *Southern Review* 8 (October 1972): 705–10.

———. *Collected Stories*. New York: Vintage Books, 1995.

———. *Essays, Speeches, and Public Letters*. Ed. James B. Meriwether. London: Chatto & Windus, 1967.

———. *Go Down, Moses*. New York: Vintage, 1990.

———. *Light in August*. New York: Vintage, 1991.

———. *Sanctuary: The Original Text.* Ed. Noel Polk. New York: Random House, 1981.

Fisher, Philip. *Hard Facts: Setting and Form in the American Novel.* Oxford University Press, 1985.

———. *Still the New World.* Cambridge: Harvard University Press, 1999.

Fitzgerald, F. Scott. *The Great Gatsby.* New York: Scribner's, 1995.

———. *Tender Is the Night.* New York: Scribner's, 1995.

———. *The Love of the Last Tycoon: A Western.* New York: Cambridge University Press, 1993.

Fleissner, Jennifer. *Women, Compulsion, Modernity: The Moment of American Naturalism.* Chicago: The University of Chicago Press, 2004.

Folsom, Ed. *Walt Whitman's Native Representations.* New York: Cambridge University Press, 1994.

Fowler, Doreen, and Ann J. Abadie, eds. *Faulkner and Popular Culture.* Jackson: University of Mississippi Press, 1990.

Fox-Talbot, William. "Some Account of the Art of Photogenic Drawing." In *Photography in Print*, ed. Vicki Goldberg, 36–48.

Freedman, Jonathan. "The Poetics of Cultural Decline: Degeneracy, Assimilation, and the Jew in James's *The Golden Bowl.*" *American Literary History* 7, no. 3 (Autumn 1995): 477–99.

Fried, Michael. "Almayer's Face: On 'Impressionism' in Conrad, Crane, and Norris." *Critical Inquiry* 17, no. 1 (Autumn 1990): 193–236.

Fuss, Diana. *Essentially Speaking: Feminism, Nature and Difference.* New York: Routledge, 1989.

Galton, Francis. *Inquiries into Human Faculty and Its Development.* London: Macmillan, 1883.

Gates, Henry Louis Jr. "The Face and Voice of Blackness." In *Facing History: The Black Image in American Art 1710–1940*, ed. Guy C. McElroy, xxix–xliv. San Francisco: Bedford Arts, 1990.

———. *The Signifying Monkey: A Theory of African-American Literary Criticism.* New York: Oxford University Press, 1988.

———. "The Trope of a New Negro and the Reconstruction of the Image of the Black." *Representations* 24 (Fall 1988): 129–55.

Gilman, Sander. *Difference and Pathology: Stereotypes of Sexuality, Race, and Madness.* Ithaca, N.Y.: Cornell University Press, 1985.

Gilman, William H., and J. E. Parsons, eds. *The Journals and Miscellaneous*

Notebooks of Ralph Waldo Emerson. Vol. 8. Cambridge, Mass.: Harvard University Press, 1970.

Gilmore, Paul, *The Genuine Article: Race, Mass Culture, and American Literary Manhood*. Durham, N.C.: Duke University Press, 2001.

Gilroy, Paul. *The Black Atlantic: Modernity and Double Consciousness*. Cambridge, Mass.: Harvard University Press, 1993.

Ginsburg, Michal. *Economies of Change: Form and Transformation in the Nineteenth Century Novel*. Palo Alto, Calif.: Stanford University Press, 1996.

Ginzburg, Carlo. "Family Resemblances and Family Trees: Two Cognitive Metaphors." *Critical Inquiry* 30, no. 3 (Spring 2004): 537–56.

Godden, Richard. *Fictions of Labor: William Faulkner and the South's Long Revolution*. Cambridge: Cambridge University Press, 1997.

Goldberg, Vicki, ed. *Photography in Print: Writings from 1816 to the Present*. Albuquerque: University of New Mexico Press, 1981.

Gould, Stephen Jay. *The Mismeasure of Man*. New York: Norton & Co., 1981.

Graham, Wendy. "Pictures for Texts." *Henry James Review* 24 (2003): 1–26.

Green, David. "Veins of Resemblance: Photography and Eugenics." *Oxford Art Journal* 7, no. 2 (1984): 3–16.

Grossman, Julia. "'It's the Real Thing': Henry James, Photography, and *The Golden Bowl*." *Henry James Review* 15 (1994): 309–28.

Gunning, Tom. "An Aesthetic of Astonishment: Early Film and the (In)Credulous Spectator." In *Viewing Positions: Ways of Seeing Film*, ed. Linda Williams, 113–33. New Brunswick: Rutgers University Press, 1994.

———. "In Your Face: Physiognomy, Photography, and the Gnostic Mission of Early Film." *Modernism/Modernity* 4, no. 1 (1997): 1–30.

Halpern, Richard. *Shakespeare among the Moderns*. Ithaca, N.Y.: Cornell University Press, 1997.

Haltunnen, Karen. *Confidence Men and Painted Women*. New Haven: Yale University Press, 1992.

Harper, Frances E. W. *Iola Leroy; or, Shadows Uplifted*. Boston: Beacon Press, 1987.

Hartshorne, Charles, and Paul Weiss, eds. *C. S. Peirce: Collected Papers*. 8 vols. Cambridge: Harvard University Press, 1931–58.

Haviland, Beverly. *Henry James's Last Romance: Making Sense of the Past and the American Scene*. New York: Cambridge University Press, 1997.

Hawthorne, Nathaniel. *American Notes*. Centenary Edition. Vol. 8. Ed. Richard Harvey Pearce. Columbus: The Ohio State University Press, 1962.

———. *The House of the Seven Gables*. New York: Oxford University Press, 1991.

———. *The Scarlet Letter*. London: Penguin Books, 1993.

———. *Tales and Sketches*. New York: Library of America, 1982.

Hemenway, Richard. *Zora Neale Hurston: A Literary Biography*. Urbana: University of Illinois Press, 1977.

Hendler, Glenn. *Public Sentiments: Structures of Feeling in Nineteenth Century American Literature*. Chapel Hill: University of North Carolina Press, 2001.

Henniger, Katherine. *Ordering the Façade: Photography and Contemporary Southern Women's Writing*. Chapel Hill: The University of North Carolina Press, 2007.

Henriksen, Bruce. "'The Real Thing': Criticism and the Ethical Turn." *Papers on Language and Literature* 27, no. 4 (1991): 473–95.

Hitchcock, Edward. *The Religion of Geology and Its Related Sciences*. Boston: Phillips, Sampson, & Co., 1854.

Hobson, Fred, ed. *William Faulkner's "Absalom, Absalom!" A Casebook*. New York: Oxford University Press, 2003.

Holmes, Oliver Wendell. *Soundings from the Atlantic*. Boston: Ticknor and Fields, 1864.

hooks, bell. "In Our Glory: Photography and Black Life." In *Picturing Us: African-American Identity in Photography*, ed. Deborah Wills, 43–55. New York: The New Press, 1994.

Horwitz, Howard. "*Maggie* and the Sociological Paradigm." *American Literary History* 10, no. 4 (Winter 1998): 606–38.

Howells, William Dean. *London Films*. New York: Harper & Brothers, 1905.

Hurston, Zora Neale. "Characteristics of Negro Expression." In *The Gender of Modernism: A Critical Anthology*, ed. Bonnie Kime Scott, 175–89. Bloomington: Indiana University Press, 1990.

———. *The Complete Stories*. New York: Harper's, 1995.

———. *Dust Tracks on a Road: An Autobiography*. Urbana: University of Illinois Press, 1984.

———. "How It Feels to Be Colored Me." In *"I Love Myself When I Am Laughing,"* ed. Alice Walker, 152–55.

———. *Mules and Men*. New York: HarperCollins, 1990.

———. *Seraph on the Suwanee*. New York: Harper's, 1991.

———. *Their Eyes Were Watching God*. New York: Harper's, 1999.

———. "What White Publishers Won't Print." In *"I Love Myself When I Am Laughing,"* ed. Alice Walker, 169–73.

Hutner, Gordon. *Secrets and Sympathy: Forms of Disclosure in Hawthorne's Novels*. Athens: The University of Georgia Press, 1988.

Infante, Cabrera. *Three Trapped Tigers*. Normal, Ill.: Dalkey Archive Press, 2004.

Isherwood, Christopher. *Goodbye to Berlin*. New York: New Directions, 1963.

Jacobs, Karen. *The Eye's Mind*. Ithaca, N.Y.: Cornell University Press, 2001.

———. "From 'Spy-glass' to 'Horizon': Tracking the Anthropological Gaze in Zora Neale Hurston." *NOVEL: A Forum on Fiction* 30, no. 3 (Spring 1997): 329–60.

Jacobs, Harriet. *Incidents in the Life of a Slave Girl*. New York: Oxford University Press, 1988.

Jakobsen, Roman. "Two Aspects of Language and Two Types of Aphasic Disturbances." In *Language and Literature*, ed. Krystyna Pomorska and Stephen Rudy, 95–114. Cambridge, Mass.: Harvard University Press, 1987.

James, Henry. *The American*. New York: Penguin Books, 1987.

———. *The American Scene*. London: Penguin Books, 1994.

———. *The Art of the Novel: Critical Prefaces*. Ed. R. P. Blackmur. New York: Charles Scribner's Sons, 1962.

———. *The Aspern Papers*. London: Penguin Books, 1986.

———. *Autobiography*. Ed. F. W. Dupee. Princeton: Princeton University Press, 1983.

———. *The Awkward Age*. London: Penguin Books, 1987.

———. *The Bostonians*. London: Penguin Books, 2001.

———. *Complete Stories 1898–1910*. New York: Library of America, 1996.

———. *The Complete Tales of Henry James: Volume 8: 1891–92*. Ed. Leon Edel. Philadelphia: J. B. Lippincott, 1963.

———. *Hawthorne*. Ithaca, N.Y.: Cornell University Press, 1997.

———. *Literary Criticism*. New York: Library of America, 1984.

———. *The Sense of the Past*. New York: Scribner's, 1917.

Jelliffe, Robert A., ed. *Faulkner at Nagano*. Tokyo: Kenkyusha, 1956.

Johnson, Barbara. *The Critical Difference: Essays in the Contemporary Rhetoric of Reading*. Baltimore: The Johns Hopkins University Press, 1980.

———. *A World of Difference.* Baltimore: The Johns Hopkins University Press, 1987.

Johnson, James Weldon. *The Autobiography of an Ex-Colored Man.* London: Penguin Books, 1990.

Jurca, Cathy. *White Diaspora: The Suburb and the Twentieth Century American Novel.* Princeton: Princeton University Press, 2001.

Kaplan, Amy. *The Social Construction of American Realism.* Chicago: The University of Chicago Press, 1988.

Kaplan, Carla, ed. "The Erotics of Talk: 'That Oldest Human Longing' in *Their Eyes Were Watching God.*" *American Literature* 67, no. 1 (March 1995): 115–42.

———. *Hurston: A Life in Letters.* New York: Anchor Books, 2002.

Kawash, Samira. *Dislocating the Color Line: Identity, Hybridity, and Singularity in African-American Narrative.* Palo Alto, Calif.: Stanford University Press, 1997.

Kazin, Alfred. *On Native Grounds.* New York: Doubleday, 1942.

———. "The Stillness of *Light in August.*" *Partisan Review* (Fall 1957): 519–38.

Kermode, Frank. *The Classic.* Cambridge, Mass.: Harvard University Press, 1983.

Kittler, Friedrich. *Discourse Networks 1800/1900.* Trans. Michael Metteer. Palo Alto, Calif.: Stanford University Press, 1990.

———. *Gramophone, Film, Typewriter.* Palo Alto, Calif.: Stanford University Press, 1999.

Kolodny, Annette. *The Lay of the Land: Metaphor as Experience and History in American Life and Letters.* Chapel Hill: The University of North Carolina Press, 1975.

Kracauer, Siegfried. *The Mass Ornament: Weimar Essays.* Trans. Tom Levin. Cambridge, Mass.: Harvard University Press, 1995.

Krauss, Rosalind. "A Note on Photography and the Simulacral" *October* 31 (Winter 1984): 49–68.

———. *The Originality of the Avant-Garde and Other Modernist Myths.* Cambridge, Mass.: MIT Press, 1986.

———. "Tracing Nadar." *October* 5 (Summer 1978): 29–47.

Krieger, Murray. *Ekphrasis: The Illusion of the Natural Sign.* Baltimore: The Johns Hopkins University Press, 1992.

Kurnick, David. "'Horrible Impossible': Henry James's Awkward Stage" *The Henry James Review* 26, no. 2 (2005): 109–29.

Lackey, Kris. "Art and Class in 'The Real Thing.'" *Studies in Short Fiction* 26, no. 2 (1989): 190–92.

Levenson, Michael. *Modernism and the Fate of Individuality: Character and Novelistic Form from Conrad to Woolf.* Cambridge: Cambridge University Press, 1991.

Lewis-Green, Jennifer. *Framing the Victorians: Photography and the Culture of Realism.* Ithaca, N.Y.: Cornell University Press, 1996.

London, Jack. *Martin Eden.* London: Penguin Books, 1993.

Lowe, Lisa. "The International within the National: American Studies and Asian American Critique." In *The Futures of American Studies*, ed. Pease and Wiegman, 76–92.

Lubiano, Wahneema. "Don't Talk with Your Eyes Closed: Caught in the Hollywood Gun Sights." In *Borders, Boundaries, and Frames: Essays in Cultural Criticism and Cultural Studies*, ed. Mae G. Henderson, 185–201. New York: Routledge, 1995.

Luhmann, Niklas. *The Reality of the Mass Media.* Trans. Kathleen Cross. Palo Alto, Calif.: Stanford University Press, 1996.

Madden, David. "Photographs in the 1929 Version of *Sanctuary.*" In *Faulkner and Popular Culture*, ed. Doreen Fowler and Ann J. Abadie, 93–109.

Matthews, John T. *The Play of Faulkner's Language.* Ithaca, N.Y.: Cornell University Press, 1982.

McDowell, Deborah E. "Viewing the Remains: A Polemic in Death, Spectacle, and the [Black] Family." In *The Familial Gaze*, ed. Marianne Hirsch, 153–77. Hanover, N.H.: Dartmouth College, 1999.

McGurl Mark. *The Novel Art: Elevations of American Fiction after Henry James.* Princeton: Princeton University Press, 2001.

McKee, Patricia. *Producing American Races.* Durham: Duke University Press, 1999.

McLaughlin, Kevin. *Paperwork: Fiction and Mass Mediacy in the Paper Age.* Philadelphia: The University of Pennsylvania Press, 2005.

Melville, Herman. *Billy Budd, Sailor, and Other Stories.* London: Penguin Books, 1986.

———. "Letter of Herman Melville to Nathaniel Hawthorne 16? April 1851." In *Critical Essays on "The House of the Seven Gables,"* ed. Bernard Rosenthal, 23–25.

———. *Moby-Dick or, The Whale.* London: Penguin Books, 1992.

———. *Pierre or, The Ambiguities.* Evanston, Ill.: Northwestern University Press, 1995.

Meriwether, James B., and Michael Millgate, eds. *Lion in the Garden: Interview with William Faulkner 1926–1962*. New York: Random House, 1968.

Michaels, Walter Benn. "*Absalom, Absalom!*: The Difference between White Men and White Men." In *William Faulkner's "Absalom, Absalom!": A Casebook*, ed. Fred Hobson, 137–53.

———. "Autobiographies of the Ex-White Men: Why Race Is Not a Social Construction." In *The Futures of American Studies*, ed. Pease and Wiegman, 231–47.

———. *The Gold Standard and the Logic of Naturalism*. Berkeley: The University of California Press, 1987.

Miller, D. A. *The Novel and the Police*. Berkeley: University of California Press, 1988.

Miller, J. Hillis. *The Ethics of Reading: Kant, de Man, Eliot, Trollope, James, and Benjamin*. New York: Columbia University Press, 1987.

———. *Literature as Conduct: Speech Acts in Henry James*. New York: Fordham University Press, 2005.

———. *Topographies*. Palo Alto, Calif.: Stanford University Press, 1995.

Millgate, Michael. *The Achievement of William Faulkner*. London: Constable, 1966.

Moretti, Franco. *Signs Taken for Wonders: Essays in the Sociology of Literary Forms*. London: Verso Books, 1988.

Morris, Wright. *Time Pieces: Photographs, Writing, and Memory*. New York: Aperture, 1989.

Natanson, Nicholas. *The Black Image in the New Deal: The Politics of FSA Photography*. Knoxville: University of Tennessee Press, 1992.

Newhall, Beaumont. *The Daguerreotype in America*. New York: Dover Publications, 1975.

———. *The History of Photography*. New York: MOMA, 1997.

Norris, Frank. *McTeague*. New York: Norton, 1997.

———. *The Pit: A Story of Chicago*. London: Penguin Books, 1994.

North, Michael. *Camera Works: Photography and the Twentieth-Century Word*. New York: Oxford University Press, 2005.

Novak, Daniel. "A Model Jew: 'Literary Photographs' and the Jewish Body in *Daniel Deronda*." *Representations* 85 (Winter 2004): 58–97.

Orvell, Miles. *The Real Thing: Imitation and Authenticity in American Culture, 1880–1840*. Chapel Hill: The University of North Carolina Press, 1989.

Parker, Hershel. "What Quentin Saw 'Out There.'" *Mississippi Quarterly* 27 (Summer 1974): 323–26.

Pearce, Richard Harvey. *Nathaniel Hawthorne: The Letters 1813–43*. Centenary Edition. Vol. 15. Columbus: The Ohio State University Press, 1962.

———. *Nathaniel Hawthorne: The Letters 1843–53*. Centenary Edition. Vol. 16.

———. *Nathaniel Hawthorne: The Letters 1857–64*. Centenary Edition Vol. 18.

———. *The Novel in Motion: An Approach to Modern Fiction*. Columbus: The Ohio State University Press, 1983.

Pease, Donald, and Robyn Wiegman, eds. *The Futures of American Studies*. Durham: Duke University Press, 2001.

Poe, Edgar Allan. "The Daguerreotype." In *Literature and Photography: Interactions 1840–1990*, ed. Jane M. Rabb, 5. Albuquerque: University of New Mexico Press, 1995.

Poirier, Richard. *The Renewal of Literature: Emersonian Reflections*. New York: Random House, 1987.

———. *A World Elsewhere: The Place of Style in American Literature*. New York: Oxford University Press, 1966.

Poole, Deborah. *Vision, Race, and Modernity: A Visual Economy of the Andean Image World*. Princeton: Princeton University Press, 1997.

Posnock, Ross. *The Trial of Curiosity: Henry James, William James, and the Challenge of Modernity*. New York: Oxford University Press, 1991.

Prendergast, Christopher. *The Order of Mimesis: Balzac, Stendhal, Nerval, Flaubert*. New York: Cambridge University Press, 1986.

Ray, Robert. "Snapshots: The Beginnings of Photography." In *The Image in Dispute*, ed. Andrew Dudley, 293–307.

Righter, William. *American Memory in Henry James: Void and Value*. London: Ashgate Books, 2004.

Riis, Jacob. *How the Other Half Lives*. New York: Dover Publications, 1971.

Root, Marcus Aurelius. *The Camera and the Pencil: Or, The Heliographic Art*. Philadelphia: Lippincott, 1864.

Rosenthal, Bernard, ed. *Critical Essays on "The House of the Seven Gables."* New York: G. K. Hall & Co., 1995.

Rudisill, Richard. *Mirror Image: The Influence of the Daguerreotype on American Society*. Albuquerque: University of New Mexico Press, 1971.

Ryder, Artemus Ward. *Voigtlander and I in Pursuit of Shadow Catching: A*

Story of Fifty-Two Years' Companionship with a Camera. Cleveland: The Imperial Press, 1902.

Sala, George. "Since This Old Cap Was New." *All The Year Round* (19 November 1859): 76–80.

Salmon, Richard. *Henry James and the Culture of Publicity*. New York: Cambridge University Press, 1997.

Saltz, Laura. "Henry James's Overexposures." *The Henry James Review* 25 (2004): 254–66.

Sander, August. "Photography as a Universal Language." *Massachusetts Review* 19, no. 4 (1978): 674–79.

Sartre, Jean-Paul. "On *The Sound and the Fury*: Time in the Work of Faulkner." In *Faulkner: A Collection of Critical Essays*, ed. Robert Penn Warren, 87–93. Englewood Cliffs, N.J.: Prentice-Hall, 1966.

Schloss, Carol. *In Visible Light: Photography and the American Writer*. New York: Oxford University Press, 1987.

Schuyler, George S. *Black No More*. New York: Modern Library, 1999.

Sekula Allan. "The Body and the Archive." *October* 39 (Winter 1986): 3–64.

Seltzer, Mark. *Bodies and Machines*. London: Routledge, 1992.

———. *Henry James and the Art of Power*. Ithaca, N.Y.: Cornell University Press, 1984.

———. *Serial Killers: Death and Life in America's Wound Culture*. New York: Routledge, 1998.

———. *True Crime*. New York: Routledge, 2006.

Sensibar, Judith. "Popular Culture Invades Jefferson: Faulkner's Real and Imaginary Photos of Desire." In *Faulkner and Popular Culture*, ed. Doreen Fowler and Ann J. Abadie, 110–41.

Shamir, Milette. "Hawthorne's Romance and the Right to Privacy." *American Quarterly* 49, no. 4 (December 1997): 746–79.

Simms, Joseph. *Physiognomy Illustrated; or, Nature's Revelations of Character*. New York: Murray Hill, 1872.

Smith, Shawn Michelle. *American Archives: Gender, Race, and Class in Visual Culture*. Princeton: Princeton University Press, 1999.

Snyder, Joel. "Picturing Vision." In *The Language of Images*, ed. W. J. T. Mitchell, 219–46. Chicago: The University of Chicago Press, 1980.

Sobieszek, Robert A., and Odette Appeal. *The Spirit of Fact: The Daguerreotypes of Southworth and Hawes, 1843–1862*. Rochester, N.Y.: The University of Rochester Press, 1976.

Sontag, Susan. *On Photography*. New York: Anchor Books, 1989.

Spillers, Hortense. *Black, White, and in Color*. Chicago: The University of Chicago Press, 2003.

Stange, Maren. *Symbols of Ideal Life: Social Documentary Photography in America, 1890–1950*. Cambridge: Cambridge University Press, 1989.

Stein, Gertrude. *Everybody's Autobiography*. Cambridge, Mass.: Exact Change, 1993.

———. *The Making of Americans: Being a History of a Family's Progress*. Normal, Ill.: Dalkey Archive Press, 1995.

———. *Selected Writings of Gertrude Stein*. Ed. Carl Van Vechten. New York: Vintage Books, 1990.

———. *Three Lives*. London: Penguin Books, 1990.

———. *Writings 1932–1946*. New York: Library of America, 1998.

Steiner, Wendy. *Exact Resemblance to Exact Resemblance*. New Haven: Yale University Press, 1978.

Stepto, Robert B. *From Behind the Veil: A Study of Afro-American Narrative*. Urbana: The University of Illinois Press, 1979.

Stott, William. *Documentary Expression and Thirties America*. Chicago: The University of Chicago Press, 1973.

Stowe, Harriet Beecher. *Uncle Tom's Cabin*. New York: Vintage Books, 1991.

Sundquist, Eric. *Faulkner: The House Divided*. Baltimore: The Johns Hopkins University Press, 1983.

———. *Home as Found*. Baltimore: The Johns Hopkins University Press, 1979.

Swann, Charles. "*The House of the Seven Gables*: Hawthorne's Modern Novel of 1848." *Modern Language Review* 86, no. 1 (January 1991): 1–18.

Sweet, Timothy. *Poetry, Photography, and the Crisis of the Union*. Baltimore: The Johns Hopkins University Press, 1990.

Taft, Robert. *Photography and the American Scene: A Social History, 1839–1889*. New York: Dover Publications, 1938.

Taussig, Michael. *Mimesis and Alterity: A Particular History of the Senses*. New York: Routledge, 1993.

Thomas, Alan. *Time in a Frame: Photography and the Nineteenth Century Mind*. New York, Schocken Books, 1977.

Thomas, Ronald R. "Double Exposures: Arresting Images in *Bleak House* and *The House Of The Seven Gables*" *NOVEL* 31, no. 1 (Fall 1997): 87–113.

Todorov, Tzvetan. "The Verbal Age." *Critical Inquiry* 4 (1977): 351–71.

Torgovnick, Marianna. *The Visual Arts, Pictorialism, and the Novel.* Princeton: Princeton University Press, 1985.

Townsend, Geo. Alfred. "Still Taking Pictures: Brady, the Grand Old Man of American Photography" *The New York Post* (12 April 1891): 26.

Trachtenberg, Alan, ed, *Classic Essays on Photography.* New Haven: Leete's Island Books, 1980.

———. "Lincoln's Smile: Ambiguities of the Face in Photography." *Social Research* 67, no. 1 (Spring 2000): 1–23.

———. *Reading American Photographs.* New York: Hill & Wang, 1989.

———. "Seeing and Believing: Hawthorne's Reflections on the Daguerreotype in *The House of the Seven Gables.*" In *National Imaginaries, American Identities*, ed. Larry Reynolds, 31–52. Princeton: Princeton University Press, 2000.

Tucker, Jennifer. *Nature Exposed: Photography as Eyewitness in Victorian Science.* Baltimore: The Johns Hopkins University Press, 2005.

Tuckerman, Bayard, ed. *The Diary of Philip Hone, 1828–1851.* New York: Dodd, Mead and Company, 1889.

Tuckerman, Henry T. "Review in *Southern Literary Messenger.*" In *Critical Essays on "The House of the Seven Gables,"* ed. Bernard Rosenthal, 41–43.

Turner, Frederick Jackson. *History, Frontier, and Section: Three Essays by Frederick Jackson Turner*, ed. Martin Ridge. Albuquerque: University of New Mexico Press, 1993.

Valéry, Paul. "The Centenary of Photography." In *Classic Essays*, ed. Trachtenberg, 191–98.

Vance, Robert H. *Catalogue of Daguerreotype Panoramic Views in California.* San Francisco: California Historical Society, ca. 1970.

Vieilledent, Catherine. "Representation and Reproduction: A Reading of Henry James's 'The Real Thing.'" In *Interface: Essays on History, Myth and Art in American Literature*, ed. D. Royot, 31–49. Montpellier: Université Paul Valéry, 1984.

Von Rautenfeld, Hans. "Thinking for Thousands: Emerson's Theory of Political Representation in the Public Sphere." *American Journal of Political Science* 41, no. 1 (January 2005): 184–97.

Wald, Priscilla. "Becoming 'Colored': The Self-Authorized Language of Difference in Zora Neale Hurston." *American Literary History* 2, no. 1 (Spring 1990): 79–100.

———. *The Rites of Assent: Transformations in the Symbolic Construction of America.* New York: Routledge, 1993.

Walker, Alice, ed. *"I Love Myself When I Am Laughing . . . and Then Again When I Am Looking Mean and Impressive": A Zora Neale Hurston Reader.* Old Westbury, N.Y.: Feminist Press, 1979.

Wall, Cheryl. "Zora Neale Hurston: Changing Her Own Words." In *Zora Neale Hurston: Critical Perspectives Past and Present*, ed. Henry Louis Gates Jr. and A. K. Appiah, 76–97. New Brunswick: Rutgers University Press, 1989.

Warner, Michael. "Value, Agency, and Stephen Crane's 'The Monster.'" *Nineteenth Century Fiction* 40, no. 1 (June 1985): 76–93.

Watson, James. *William Faulkner: Presentation and Performance.* Austin: University of Texas Press, 2000.

Welty, Eudora. *One Writer's Beginnings.* Cambridge, Mass.: Harvard University Press, 1984.

Wexler, Laura. *Tender Violence: Domestic Victims in an Age of U. S. Imperialism.* Chapel Hill: The University of North Carolina Press, 2000.

Wiegman, Robyn. *American Anatomies: Theorizing Race and Gender.* Durham: Duke University Press, 1995.

———. "Whiteness Studies and the Paradox of Particularity." In *The Futures of American Studies*, ed. Pease and Wiegman, 269–304.

Williams, Susan. *Confounding Images: Photography and Portraiture in Antebellum American Fiction.* Philadelphia: The University of Pennsylvania Press, 1997.

Williamson, Joel. *William Faulkner and Southern History.* New York: Oxford University Press, 1993.

Willis, Deborah. *Reflections in Black: A History of Black Photographers 1840 to the Present.* New York, W. W. Norton & Co., 2000.

Willis, N. P. "The Pencil of Nature: A New Discovery." *The Corsair* 1, no. 5 (April 13, 1839), 70–72.

Willis, Susan. *Specifying: Black Women Writing the American Experience.* Madison: The University of Wisconsin Press, 1987.

Wright, Richard. "Between Laughter and Tears." *New Masses* 25 (5 Oct 1937): 22–23.

———. *Black Boy: A Record of Childhood and Youth.* New York: Harper, 2007.

———. *Native Son.* New York: HarperCollins, 1993.

———. *12 Million Black Voices.* New York: Thunder's Mouth Press, 1988.

Index

www.ingramcontent.com/pod-product-compliance
Lightning Source LLC
LaVergne TN
LVHW091029080826
845145LV00002B/407
* 9 7 8 0 8 2 0 3 3 5 2 1 6 *